Dressage in Lightness

Speaking the Horse's Language

Dressage in Lightness

Speaking the Horse's Language

Sylvia Loch

Trafalgar Square Publishing

This edition first published in the United States of America in 2000
by Trafalgar Square Publishing, North Pomfret, Vermont

Color separation by Tenon & Polert Color Scanning Ltd
Printed by Dah Hua International Printing Press Co. Ltd, Hong Kong

ISBN 1-57076-183-3
LOC# 00-107358

Text artwork and illustrations © Sylvia Loch 2000

The author acknowledges the work of Rolfe Becker in his book
Schooling by the Natural Method (J. A. Allen 1963) in using colour to
depict the state of equine muscles in movement. This work has been
developed by the author in consultation with her own veterinary
advisers.

The author has obtained permission to reproduce all photographs that
apppear in this book which are not her own property.

Designed by Nancy Lawrence
Edited by Martin Diggle

Contents

Two Important Caveats to All Readers

1. For aesthetic reasons, my publisher requested that I ride for the front cover of this book without a hat. A few more photographs slipped through the customary disciplines with the author hatless.

    In fact I always school and hack out wearing a BSI approved helmet.

    In all lessons taken at my yard, and on external clinics, all my students and I have to be properly equipped with a safety helmet with the chin strap correctly fastened. So please ensure that in following any of the methods or instructions contained in this book, and indeed in all your riding, you are properly and safely attired.

2. Neither the author nor the publishers can be held responsible for any injury or damages, howsoever arising, caused directly or indirectly as a result of following the text, instructions or methods in this book.

    This book is designed for informed people who already ride with competence and confidence and is basically an instructional book for the schooling of their horses and is therefore not intended for beginner riders.

Dedication

To All My Students Everywhere

My previous book was dedicated to my own special horses and to all horses generally. I can never stop thanking them for allowing me insight. But what else makes a teacher? A huge part of it has to be the continuous confidence of one's students. For that reason, I dedicate *Dressage in Lightness* to all my students past and present wherever they may be. Without your loyalty I might so easily have faded long ago into the shadows.

Teaching is a two-way discipline; teachers can only develop their skills with encouragement, positive feedback and confirmation that methods are working. I have rarely been disappointed by either the attitude or the progress of my pupils. Their generosity of spirit has been truly amazing and many have gone to enormous lengths to follow me through two major moves over the past twenty years.

Even before that, there were people prepared to come to Portugal to be taught the classical way and since returning to the UK, I have greatly enjoyed all the clinics away from home, including those overseas. The kindness and hospitality encountered on the way has been staggering. A big thank-you to all those hardworking clinic organisers, in particular Yvonne Bell in Australia, Pam Howe and Susan Grindell in New Zealand, Christine Scott in Kenya, Sue Tuck in Hong Kong, the Committee of the IALHS and Helen Donnell in the USA, with, closer to home, Brenda Angus in the Channel Islands and Jane Barham in the Isle of Man.

Here in mainland Britain, I would particularly like to thank demo and clinic organisers Susan Atkinson, Penny Baker, Carolyn Briggs, Nicky Brooks, Fiona Bubb, Linda Collins, Gayle Couch, Penny Coutts, Bozena Forde, Sue Giordano, Deborah Ascott-Jones, Sandy Jones, Stephen Holmes, Anne Lewis, Claire Lilley, Noel Lovatt, Molly Lloyd, Liz McCurley, Clare Molyneux, Heather Parsons, Francis and Felicity Peto, Sherene Rahmatallah, Sarah Rutherford, Catherine Smith, Mary Stitson, Roger and Eleanor Taylor, Barbara Torney, Anne Wilson and your supporters, as well as all the Classical Riding Club Regional Liaison Members for their brilliant organisational powers.

Foreword

I first met Sylvia Loch many years ago in Portugal when she was President of Honour at the big Golegã Horse Fair. During that time we enjoyed reminiscing about the Lusitano horses, of which I too am a fan, and some years later I rode Sylvia's own horses when I gave a clinic and demonstration in England.

Like me, Sylvia is a person who always wants to feel the state of the horse under her. The sensation of feel is too easily forgotten and people often tend to treat all horses the same. Of course, nothing could be further from the truth: some horses are highly sensitive while others seem more headstrong, but at the end of the day every horse is a little different and we have to remember that in all our riding.

I really like the fact that, in this book, Sylvia addresses the subject of what the horse is feeling with both the good and the bad rider on his back. It is very helpful to have the classical aids for the movements explained correctly step-by-step, and again seeing things from the horse's point of view.

I thoroughly support Sylvia in everything she is doing to encourage riders to be kinder, more sensitive, and lighter with their aids when they ride their horse. It is doubtful that I would have reached Olympic level if I had not listened to my horse in this way.

Nicole Uphoff

On tour in Newcastle with Allegra Loch, Nicole Uphoff, the author and her assistant groom, Catherine Boyle, in front of the Vista Alegre sponsored horsebox for Sylvia's horses.

Acknowledgements

There are several people who have been kind enough to read carefully parts of this book in the writing. Thank you in particular therefore to Veronica Ward, whose confinement to hospital after a most painful hunting accident allowed her the time to read several chapters and to offer helpful comments. Also visiting pupils, particularly Lesley Sendall from London and Jord-Ann Ramoudt from Texas, who, during courses here, took time to bury their noses in my burgeoning typescript.

Thank you also to those of my students, whose names appear in the captions, who so kindly agreed to act as guinea-pigs or gave permission for photographs to be used. Horses are surprisingly difficult to photograph and one needs to be at the ready with a decent camera all the time. Therefore, my grateful thanks to Edinburgh-based pupil, Elaine Herbert, for her enthusiasm and the most generous loan of her Minolta which remained, loaded, in my tackroom for several months. Many thanks to my grooms Suzanne Bratton and Andrea Thomson for being prepared to drop everything – almost – to dash outside when an unpromising sun decided to peep out from behind the Scottish clouds as we were schooling. In addition, a very big thank-you to Terry Burlace for so many superb photographs taken over many months of my own and my pupils' horses in Suffolk. Finally, to Jim Goff in Kentucky for the stunning pictures of his home-bred foals, and to Barbara Currie in California for her excellent pictures taken with Vaughan during one of my 1995/6 West Coast clinics in the USA.

On the biomechanical side, many thanks to Sara Wyche MRCVS and Tim Davies MRCVS for advice and scrutiny. I was also much encouraged by Grand Prix rider, Tina Layton, sparing time to peruse some of the more complex dressage shots. In this context, I owe much to Suzanne, who has helped me considerably here at home with the choice of all the photographs. Her three-year HND Course at Bishop Burton College has educated her eye for deciphering the more complicated stills. Thank you especially for all the generous time taken out of hours.

On the editorial side, I owe so much to Melanie Wilkes, our Classical Riding Club secretary for general support, digging out lost material in an overflowing office, finding missing pictures, sorting out the computer when it blips, dealing with the post, some last-moment typing, fending off telephone callers when I simply had to get my head down and for generally holding my hand throughout the writing of this book. Without you Mel, I would be in chaos!

There is a tremendous support team here at Eden Hall that allows me to get on with my work, so a special word of thanks to Rob Tait, Steve Dunn, Anne Lawson, Arlene Crawford, Catherine Boyle, et al.

My grateful thanks is owed to my publisher Caroline Burt for believing in this book, to Martin Diggle for his editorial assistance and integrity, to Alistair Murdoch for his computer diagrams of the manège, and to Nancy Lawrence for her great patience and highly imaginative skills in lay-out. It's been a huge pleasure working with you all.

There are other friends and colleagues, too numerous to mention who have also given support, but one name in particular stands out and that is fellow author, Lesley Skipper, who gave me such encouragement at the outset of this project. To her and all our CRC Members worldwide, thank you for sharing in the classical ideal.

Last, but by no means least, my thanks to my family who lived through two years of unsociable hours of writing and illustrating behind closed doors. I thank Richard for his enormous belief in me through thick and thin, as well as his untutored but unfailingly percipient eye, to my marvellous daughter Allegra for her frankness and enthusiasm and to the kindest of mothers for her calm serenity upholding one in times of rush and stress. Their combined love of me and of my horses has upheld me through many a moment of doubt and my gratitude to them is as genuine as it is profound.

Introduction

It is always hard to part with a book once written. There's always more to say and more to explain. It's funny that I should feel this wrench when initially, I had no burning desire to write this book. Teaching commitments were keeping me so occupied that the more my publishers pressed me for an instructional dressage book, the less the incentive, the blanker the screen. Each book should have a raison d'être, a sure knowledge that it is truly needed. There were already many excellent books on the market which approached the same subject from varying viewpoints and I saw no need for another. Besides, the horses called.

The motive to write is generally to create and break new ground. My first book *The Royal Horse of Europe* grew out of a commitment to the Lusitano and Andalusian horse. People were unaware of their origins, often looking down on them as exotically alien but for me, knowing otherwise, this hurt. Few realised that our own Royal Mares – to whom the evolution of the Thoroughbred and all sporthorse breeds owed so much – came mainly from Iberia, so they deserved a proper historical acknowledgement from a British author. For too long, people had an oversimplified perception that the Arab alone was responsible, so it has been exciting to research the subject in other directions – particularly exploring the relationship of the Barb to the Spanish and Portuguese horse.

One book led to another and the horses themselves inspired *The Classical Seat* at a time when at home, it had become unfashionable to teach the use of the seat. The third book,

Dressage, the Art of Classical Riding (now in French and German) drew the reader back to the origins of horsemanship. After all, the implementation of today's FEI dressage rules is only the culmination of many centuries of study and endeavour from the great masters of many different countries. It was important to show that nothing with horses is new and everything we know today is just an evolutionary process from pre-history itself.

The Classical Rider had a difficult start too. My publisher must take great credit for the idea. I was doubtful that something so philosophical would ever sell. Yet in its first year *The Classical Rider* sold over 10,000 copies both here and abroad and became a bestseller for J.A.Allen. Truly surprised, I said at the time it would be my last big horse book – I had too much else to do. My publisher had other views; they generally do.

An idea for a fifth book finally emerged early in 1999. Curiously, it was my daughter's horse who spurred me on. At sixteen, Allegra was studying for GCSE exams, and being at boarding school had been fortunate enough to have her pony, then her horse there with her. Not this particular term however; it was suggested that a horse needing to be groomed and exercised every day would not be conducive to extra study.

And so Milo (his full name is Millennium – how appropriate!), her recently acquired 16.3 Irish cross gelding, was left at home. Here he found himself in exalted foreign company alongside our three advanced Lusitano schoolmasters, plus my own Lusitano Thoroughbred cross competition and display horse. Not unnaturally, my daughter had decreed that no one else but mum was to ride the treasured Milo, but I took this with a slight pinch of salt, later – as I found out – to my detriment.

We had bought Milo straight from a hunting yard, since my daughter's main priority at that time was hacking and jumping. Since mine was her safety and Milo certainly knew his job, who was I to quarrel with the fact that he was happily balanced on the forehand, poke-nosed and always seemed to go everywhere, even in walk, at a hundred miles an hour, leaving his hocks trailing well behind? At eight years old he had been ridden for most of his life by a big man, a hard-to-hounds whipper-in but despite all, he had a lovely relaxed character, was good to handle and my daughter had fallen in love with him.

The scenario of course was not unfamiliar; we live in hunting country and many of my pupils lead an all-round type of life with their horses – of which I am hugely in favour. Often on clinics too, horses of a similar type, new to dressage or simply 'not dressage types' arrive for help and I find these combinations a pleasing challenge. Generally, we can gain enormous improvement over two or three days, but Milo was not here for two or three days; a whole two terms loomed ahead. Indeed, I could not help wondering if I would really enjoy fitting this big, ungainly creature into my already stretched schedule.

Milo's real saving grace was the way he balanced himself over obstacles, which had to show some hidden talent for flatwork – or so we thought. How wrong we were! We soon discovered that the very thought of working in an empty school was not his idea of fun unless there were coloured poles scattered around to distract him. For the first few days therefore, we left a couple of small jumps in evidence. However this was not really conducive to the new system. The only time I had tried previously to bring him into some sort of shape for my daughter, he had actually become quite

cross, making his dislike of schoolwork painfully clear by tilting his head sideways, crossing his jaw and resisting through his back at the very idea.

Since Allegra has seen enough dressage over the years to want to do other things, I had decided not to interfere. The pair of them enjoyed a good rapport and when confidence needs to be built between a couple who are only just getting to know each other, it is often wiser not to try to bring about too many changes too early.

So why the book? The more I persevered, the clearer it became that middle-aged Milo was extremely typical of so many horses out there today. Every day I receive letters from unknown readers of my books, owners of horses like Milo, asking for help. The one factor which always seems to unite them is that they feel dressage books and dressage trainers only really deal with the perfect rider and the perfect horse and that neither are appropriate to their situation. The stories are all too familiar: 'My horse loves hacking out, but when I ask him to do dressage, I do not know where to begin. All the things he is supposed to do just don't happen and we generally end up having a fight. Everyone else on the yard tells me to tough it out and be firm but this seems to make matters worse; the more we insist, the more upset my horse becomes. Clearly he is not built for dressage, but I don't want to sell him, so what do I do?'

Even if they had the choice, many owners simply cannot afford a purpose-built 'dressage type' and with an animal who has become used to one way of going, resistance to change is inevitable. There are further stories bewailing the fact that a trainer has been employed but that each session becomes a battlefield and whilst ground may be gained, the two combatants end up unhappy and exhausted. I feel genuinely sorry for both when I read of heavy-handed tactics which may lead to a previously peaceful character becoming defensive and sometimes dangerous. All things considered, this is hardly surprising when the contest is so one-sided. The horse feels everyone ganging up against him; owner, trainer and onlookers, and since he has a strong sense of fair play as well as an excellent memory, this sort of pressure causes real anxiety and even anger.

The golden rule of both horsemanship and the law has always been: never engage in an argument and push it to the point where someone has to win or lose – unless you are 100 per cent sure you will win. Since horses are stronger than us and their primeval instinct for survival can be unpredictable, it is better never to enter an argument at all. If it does happen that you get your way, you may in the meantime lose friendship and trust. In all senses of the word, such victories can be costly.

I have also noted from these sorry sagas that it is always when things are at their worst that those once-eager advisers have a habit of withdrawing from the scene. 'Get rid of it!' is the usual advice. The gullible may do this and a new horse and a new argument ensues. It may take several spoilt horses for some riders to come to their senses. Not surprisingly, guilt then enters the picture and the owner realises, rather too late, that they have allowed their horse to be put through the mill. Most people have good intentions, but often feel that their knowledge is insufficient to disagree at the time. This book is designed to help them and others new to the scene to avoid these mistakes and read the signs for themselves before it is too late.

As a matter of fact, all of these stories were not so very dissimilar in a small way from what I was about to experience with Milo. Even with years of practical knowledge behind me, I made one stupid mistake early on in his work which destroyed so much of that patient, painstaking ten-week partnership. I allowed another professional rider to ride the horse for about fifteen minutes. I have no idea what it was this person did, but the contact taken up and the way in which the legs and seat were used were obviously much harder than my own. I was also disappointed that Milo was told rather than asked, and all without any niceties of introduction first. Horses have a strong sense of etiquette.

The next time I rode Milo he felt completely different; in fact for the first time in all the months we had owned him, he napped, plunged and bucked quite badly and did not want to work for several weeks. We checked his back; little was amiss there but I quickly understood he had lost his confidence and I had no one to blame other than myself. You could tell from his eye just how upset and betrayed he felt.

From this and from the literally thousands of lessons I have taken over the years I began to feel more strongly than ever that it was time to speak out for the horse himself. A book had to be written, not simply explaining how to ride better but to try to show just what each horse feels when we ask for something in a certain way. Riders needed to be more aware of what sensations can motivate their horse to learn new skills and what sensations he will abhor. They needed to recognise certain cues that involve the use and distribution of their weight, and be reminded that the conventional aids can be given in a way that is clear but also in a way that confuses.

For this reason therefore, it is no good just telling the rider to ride better; instead we need to look at things from the horse's point of view *in order* to ride better. We must study his muscle systems, understand his tickly bits, find out just where he needs more support and where he wants us to let go. By appreciating how he tries to balance under us, it is easier to understand what he *needs* to feel from us if he is to respond willingly and instinctively. It is hoped that this book will interpret those requirements through each and every new transition, exercise or movement. After all, the horse hasn't read the book, but he has a wonderful memory, and if we can tap into that memory with good sensations, it will feel as though he has his own private how-to-do-it manual.

Although it is such an obvious fact, I believe

we all need to remind ourselves again and again that horses have no way of speaking out except through body language and behavioural patterns. It is rare that I come across a horse who actively intends to be difficult or naughty. The word 'no' is generally used by horses only as a small *cri de coeur*. Some, of course, may use that word more than others and the reason could be anything from a badly fitting saddle to sore shins or rider posture. 'No' is a very protective response for horses who find their riders have asked too much too soon, feel their balance threatened, or are genuinely afraid of the unfamiliar. How sad therefore that some riders respond to this language by immediate punishment and the assumption that the horse has 'made up his mind' to disobey. When to ask, and how to ask, has to be the foundation of good schooling, yet too often these factors are overlooked in the rider's hurry to achieve.

When I teach, apparently I have a habit of saying 'He's feeling nice and light today,' or 'I'm not feeling him sufficiently around the inside leg', or 'I can feel his right jaw has not quite relaxed', and so on. This would not be remarkable except for the fact that my student is riding the horse and not me! Yet somehow, I can feel what their horse is feeling and almost by osmosis know when the rider is blocking, needs to let go, or make a change of emphasis.

I believe horses are so sensitive that they absolutely know when, from the ground, you are trying to help them. They throw out a telepathic link through eye contact and body language but they will only do this when one's motives are pure and there is no sense of self. Sometimes this transfer of thought can be so compelling that one wants to interfere in someone else's lesson and it takes great resolve to bite one's lip and keep quiet! It is for this reason that I much dislike watching insensitive or boorish trainers at work. On the other hand, one gets real pleasure from those who have the gift of reading and gauging the situation. A notable example was Dr Reiner Klimke who exuded care and responsibility for the horse

from the first moment of a lesson, as does Chief Rider Arthur Kottas, who can be very strict with riders but only on *behalf* of the horse – and clearly every horse knows that.

Understanding the body language of the horse has developed more intensively for me personally in the last five or six years. I have been teaching and training for the best part of three decades and whilst much of this has to be put down to experience and working closely with many different combinations, the sensitivity one develops has nothing to do with being clever; it is very much a gift from the horse himself. I truly believe that once a horse knows you are there to help, he gives something back. Clearly, the horse is a very generous and unique species but to understand him better we have to be exceedingly quiet and receptive if we are to open ourselves to hear what he has to say. Once we can do this, he feels it and will offer more.

Whilst many modern writers have explored the feelings of horses in the stable, in the field or in their natural environment, few have recaptured like Xenophon, that most ancient of equestrian writers, the passions and emotions of the horse under saddle. Maybe the time has come for us all to re-examine these matters.

Not so long ago, instruction in the art of equitation was considered a science. Tied in to the military and cavalry procedure, the Victorian era discouraged any show of emotion either in people or animals. Whilst respect for the horse was paramount, feelings were cast aside. How could a cavalry commander expect his squadron to charge courageously if there was fear and misgiving? Since bold riding and tactics were all part of duty, that was an end of it. I shall never forget receiving a rather sad letter from an ex-Indian cavalry officer who, after reading my book *The Classical Rider* disagreed that army officers had been encouraged to love their horses. In his troop, this had been firmly discouraged since to love your charger was a luxury one could not afford when he might be shot from under you. Hard as that may seem, one can certainly understand the logic behind such an ethos.

As a Pony Club child in the late nineteen fifties and sixties, much of this attitude still prevailed. Stiff upper lip was the order of the day and any wimpish behaviour displayed by either animal or pupil was not to be tolerated. This disregard for feelings led to a rather brash heartiness in the horse community which infiltrated the riding schools as riding lessons exploded for the masses after the war. Today, there are still vestiges of this attitude in all walks of equestrian life and certainly it is often easier not to question but to conform if points are to be scored and goals to be achieved. The good thing about the former years, however, was that traditional methods finely honed over many centuries were still taught as a matter of course in the better establishments. Everyone learned their ABC of riding which, on the whole, ensured the physical well-being of the horse.

Today, unfortunately, much of that ABC has been forgotten and replaced by the current fad or fashion. Too often respect has been waved aside too. Unfortunately, however, the hearty brashness has remained and often covers a multitude of sins, such as not listening to your horse. In some quarters, life tends to be about winning, selectors and making the team, and to hell with the method used so long as you can get there.

It took an American, Monty Roberts to encourage people back to looking at the horse with new eyes when he first came to Britain in 1985 to demonstrate his methods. By this time, openness with regard to feelings, instinctive behaviour and emotions was being encouraged in almost every other facet of everyday life, and the time was ripe. Today, behaviourists both human and animal abound. There is counselling, open discussion, healers of both body and mind, psychiatrists' couches, and often perhaps too much of it all. Psychiatrists will tell you why you hate flying, your husband, or eating cabbage. Horse whisperers will tell you why your horse chomps his bit, rears, is hard to handle in the box, and here and there a mystic will happily take money off you to tell you about your horse's dreams. So where does one draw the line?

I have always believed that step-by-step guidelines laid down by the traditional classical schools hold the clue. Correctly pursued, they affect the muscular development of each animal as well as the mental side. Horses who are tense, unhappy or in pain give out lots of signals. Grinding teeth and swishing tails are the most obvious, but there are many less noticeable and silent signs which should nevertheless ring alarm bells for anyone who has an eye for correct muscle tone and general conformation. Since a horse can be positively transformed and made much more beautiful with good riding, it is equally true to say that he can be disastrously impaired by bad riding.

Unfortunately, not every trainer takes a holistic view of horse and rider working together when a combination comes before them. Many have an agenda to get the *horse* ready for a certain level of competition and the correction to rider posture and balance, so important for him be a happy, relaxed horse, at ease with his work, is neglected. The amount of *time* required to allow this to come about is also neglected; this is often the rider's fault as much as that of the instructor. Consider the dancer from the royal *corps de ballet*! She will have been training for at least ten years before she is even considered for public appearance. It should be roughly the same for horses destined for Grand Prix and certainly this is recognised by the Spanish Riding School of Vienna. Luckily for riders, we have low levels at which we can test our horses stage by stage, but to see these as an end in themselves or to rush through them is to cheat yourself as well as your horse.

In this book, we aim to focus on an equal relationship as regards the giving of aids. At every phase, we will consider both the rider's bodyweight and balance and the horse's bodyweight and balance. Both are influenced by the other. Preparing for and riding through every movement, we try to explore the sense of feel, human and equine. Over the ensuing chapters, it should become clear, not by sentimental surmise or guesswork, why most people – and certainly all horses – prefer to work in lightness. The scientific evidence should be overwhelming.

Once the feel-good factor enters the physical orbit, the horse becomes mentally happy and relaxed too. It is only when all these facets work together that he will begin to flow and delight in the work that is being requested of him, so that he actually wants to offer more. This has to be the objective of every caring owner, rider or trainer. Until this approach to training filters through into the national consciousness however, we will continue to see too many stressed-out horses treated as sports machines – which seems somehow inappropriate to all that life promises in the twenty-first century. Let us make the new millennium the time to take an all-round view of our riding.

Glossary

Riding Terms

Leg on the girth or at the girth (generally the inside)

This implies that the leg is in position close to the girth area, with the *toe* aligned roughly parallel to the girth; leg on the girth does not necessarily have to be touching the horse, although it may. More often than not it will simply be lined up to the girth, hanging just free of the horse's body if the stirrup leather is to remain vertical (most important) to be applied as and when required. Few riders appreciate sufficiently that when the leg is *hanging in the correct vertical position*, this constitutes an effective weight aid in itself. Applied too strongly, the leg *against* the girth can bring about a sideways effect which may not always be appropriate.

Leg back or behind the girth (generally the outside)

This term indicates that the leg will be placed at least a hand's breadth behind the girth, from which position it may influence the hindquarters.

Waist to hands (usually coupled with 'growing tall')

This term was a favourite of the late master, Nuno Oliveira (as demonstrated opposite in walk on the long rein) and further exemplified by the close-up photographs as shown.

It indicates a firm, open position of the rider's upper body, so that the rider's shoulders are squared and lowered, with the collarbones brought into the horizontal, so that the entire ribcage opens out and appears fuller. This will only take place if the rider's back is sufficiently supple to engage the hips well forward in the saddle. Once this is achieved, the rider will appear to ride the horse forward from the centre with the sensation of the waist moving towards the hands, never the other way round.

Both on the long rein and in collection, the late Maestro Nuno Oliveira insisted that to attain correct balance, we must stretch and open the front of the body and ride 'waist to hands'.

In practice, it is the expansion and toning of the abdominal muscles which will advance the sternum and navel as shown here by the Master. Such action frees the loins and hips forward, whilst protecting and straightening the spine. Once the hips are in the vertical, the crotch points downward and the entire seat deepens so that weight now falls away directly through the centre of the body and the centre of the saddle. (Photograph courtesy of Eleanor Russell)

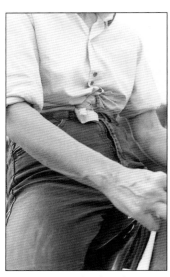

(Left) Standing on the ground, a similar effect is achieved by squaring the shoulders, raising the diaphragm, balancing the head correctly with chin down, and slightly hollowing or bracing the loins forward.

(Right) Now astride, this same action allows the rider's body to stretch up, not only to give the appearance of 'growing tall', but physically achieving greater height. In this way, the rider's seat assumes a three-point contact (seatbones and crotch) with the saddle, which strengthens and deepens the general position.

(Left) This standing position may look easy and relaxed, but the truth is the spine has curved outward incorrectly, the abdominal muscles are collapsed, my unbalanced head is pulling on the muscles at the back of the neck and clearly, I have lost height.

(Right) Astride, this position negates the influences of the seat and upper body since verticality and balance are lost. Collapsed abdominal muscles cause the pelvis to tip backward, directing weight onto the fleshy part of the buttocks (two-point contact) rather than directly through the seatbones.

Riding Movements

Passade

This movement is a partial pirouette, or a very small turn in a half-volte with the hind legs describing a smaller circle than the forehand. The passade is useful to take the horse out of one lateral movement and into another, for example, from shoulder-in into travers.

Volte

A small circle of anything from 6m in diameter up to approximately 10m.

Others

Expert trainer or rider

No rider/teacher/trainer/judge should be thought of or deemed an 'expert' until they have personally schooled and trained at least two or three horses from Novice level through all the movements described in this book to piaffe and passage. This is not to say that lower level teaching cannot be tremendously beneficial and there is no doubt that an eye on the ground is always worthwhile. Nevertheless, it is my belief that there is a danger of incorrect instruction being given when someone has not studied the whole spectrum of training. Without some understanding of the end result, it is unlikely that matters such as correct timing and nuances of feeling in the giving of aids will be truly appreciated.

A Guide to Step-by-Step Schooling and Training

The layout of exercises in this book conforms approximately to the standards required at each level in the FEI dressage tests. The exercises are designed to suit the young horse in his fourth year progressing upward and are highly beneficial for the older horse who has done little or no dressage before.

Each chapter offers the rider a detailed how-to-do-it formula. For those riders who have never schooled their own horse before, the answers as to those 'whys' and 'wherefores' are all here. For more experienced riders, the explanations should offer further insight, particularly as to how the horse reacts to our aids and why it is necessary to ask in a certain way to keep things as natural as possible.

Some riders, depending on their own skills and experience as well as the temperament, type and conformation of their horse, may wish to introduce some of the more advanced exercises earlier. Care should be taken to use these only in an informed and selective way since the general advice contained in the latter chapters is intended for a much higher level overall. For example, an experienced rider (or a less experienced rider under supervision) can use the shoulder-in at walk on a fairly young horse to strengthen the hocks, after the first six months of schooling. However this is strongly discouraged for the unsupervised inexperienced rider since incorrect methods and an inappropriate way of asking can quickly ruin a young horse.

Remember that every horse is different and it is important to keep an open mind about the timespans involved. A very rough guide to the contents of this book with the newly backed horse and the less experienced rider would be:

Work at Basic Level – approximately the first six months of school work.

Work at Novice Level – *after six months* and anything up to eighteen months/two years beyond.

Work at Elementary Level – *after at least one year* and anything up to eighteen months/two years beyond.

Work at Medium Level – *after two to three years* of schooling onward.

Work at Advanced Level – *after three to four years* of schooling onward.

WARNING: *Each horse is different and if, at any time, your horse shows signs of resistance and discomfort, go back to an earlier stage of work to gain his confidence and trust. Also, beware of overfacing a horse who may not be cut out to achieve the degree of athleticism demanded at higher level dressage.*

PART ONE
The Theory Behind The Practice

CHAPTER I
Tuning into a Language – The Horse's Natural Aids

CHAPTER II
Structure and Movement – Aligning the Rider to the Horse

CHAPTER I

Tuning into a Language
The Horse's Natural Aids

Such a joyful athlete!
How can we keep it that way?

However athletic a horse may be in freedom, everything changes once a rider is placed on his back. Good riding promotes God-given beautiful movement; bad riding stymies it. That great Portuguese maestro, Nuno Oliveira once said, 'Whatever you are doing on horseback, remember there is no in-between. You are either doing good when you ride, or bad. And whilst the good should enhance a beautiful horse, the bad can quickly ruin him...'

How true this is! Nevertheless it has to be recognised that some horses are very stoic. In dressage, particularly at lower level tests, there will be those who manage to overcome poor preparation simply because they are inherently very talented with three good, natural gaits. Unfortunately, big bold movement may impress certain judges who award high marks regardless of the quality of execution and of the riding.

But what happens next? Once a combination begins to climb through the levels, the reliance by the horse on proper, methodical suppling exercises and preparation becomes very much greater. Indeed, the need to work correctly at this stage is not so different from that required by the human athlete. Higher level tests make demands for which natural talent is no longer sufficient, and tight corners, tricky turns, precise lateral exercises, and sud-

den transitions all require rather more than beautiful loose, flowing gaits. Suddenly the need for suppleness, balance, engagement and elevation begin to enter the picture and if the basic groundwork has not been laid, with the rider more familiar with the aiding process, it will be the horse who suffers.

It is sad but true to say that there are many horses today who are not only working in tension, but even in pain, simply because someone has failed to lay the foundation stones correctly on the way up. It is at this stage that some riders will resort to punitive methods.

Traditionally, all the riding aids which have been handed down to us from time immemorial have been based on reward and punishment. There are some animal behaviourists who insist that such a method or language of communication consists of nothing more than a trick since, in their opinion, they merely consist of artificial conditioned responses. They are absolutely right, of course, when brute force is employed, with punishment taken to its literal conclusion. Indeed, there is no doubt that, whatever the discipline, some horses are still trained on this basis. They learn to perform through coercion and the fear of punishment, learning each activity or movement as a response to the stimulus of present or remembered pain; a dig with the spur, a jab with the bit, a shove with the seat-

This horse is being ridden between two opposing forces ~ severely restricted in front whilst being driven from behind – a recipe for tension & blocking.

S'L.

COLOUR CODE (for all illustrations)

 = areas of destructive muscular tension

 = areas of constructive/supportive muscular traction

 = energy direction

 = 'gravity' flow (back to earth)

The above code should be referred to again to explain the use of colour and shaded areas in all subsequent pictures throughout the following chapters. The arrows too are of particular significance.

bones and so on.

At higher level dressage, this can be enforced to a high degree of accuracy, and so impressive is the horse, so full of braggadocia, that it takes a real horseman to note the tension within. It is unfortunate that an angry horse may look magnificent, with his blood running high and his muscles straining under taut skin.

So, as the left spur pierces the flesh, and the horse canters right, the people only see the power. Next, a jab right, a violent swagger left, and yet another spectacular flying change! The crowd erupts. 'So expressive!' nod the cognoscenti, and all the time the horse just goes rollercoasting on. Next, a metronome piaffe; was it the tight curb, simultaneous spurring or the memory of a harsh stick on the cannon bones? Who cares as the crowd go 'ooh' and 'aah'? Yes, it can all work like magic – up to a point... and then one day the great horse rebels, breaks down or suffers a fatal attack of colic. It does happen.

Good Sensations

But what if we can transform that language of reward and punishment into a new enlightened language of pleasant feelings where the sensations of security, balance and the well-being that come with praise are remembered? How thrilling when the horse begins to read us like a book and feels the nuance of each request almost as the thought enters our mind! Is it possible to teach the horse to change lead from a moment's invisible nudge of one hip bone or another, or to float from piaffe into passage from the smallest squeeze and release from a hand that is never seen to move? I believe it is; but only when the so-called conventional aids unite themselves into a language where punishment in its deepest sense flies out of the window so that it comprises nothing more than the cessation of reward. This takes horsemanship into the realm of art.

This is the learning process that dwells on liberating sensations and fun-filled memories.

It releases horses from the grinding daily chore of being beasts of burden. It is a process which suits all horses, even the most reticent, since from day one it works with Nature's laws of physics and locomotion and the horse's own brilliant adaptability to balance. It is no accident that riders of the highest quality the world over speak the same language in terms of lightness and the control of weight.

Sometimes, there may be little to distinguish between the body aiding of the best Western rider and that of the professional Spanish Riding School *bereiter* so far as precision work is concerned. Yes, one may ride with a longer stirrup and appear to neck-rein more, but the other too is crotch-deep in the saddle with upright bearing and lowered thighs, and for both it will be subtle and invisible changes in the weight with the outside rein acting on the quarters – it is just a question of nuance.

Correspondingly, for speed riding, the crouched position of the jockey in a modern Derby is not so very different from the position of the Mongolian warrior who used to fly across the tundra. Both perched well clear of the horse's back, found the shifting centre of gravity and encouraged the horse to adopt a posture for lightning speed. Maybe no one taught the Mongolian or even the steerman how to aid the horse. It was something they found for themselves by feeling and working with the horse's own natural impulses and having to depend on his ease of movement for their own lives.

Today, things are different – the majority of riders no longer campaign, fight, claim new territory, herd, depend upon or sleep under the stars with their horse. Few have the time to go outside and really observe their horse throughout the day and halfway into the night. Hours spent in the saddle will be limited. Despite all this, many average sports riders still believe they will somehow 'pick up' the techniques required to teach a green horse what amounts to serious gymnastics.

These horses, although collected for precision work, sudden stops, changes of direction & gait, are both being ridden forward from behind; their riders sit deep, vertical & quiet in the saddle in a 'three point' balance.

For colour code, see page 4

Only when riders are quite advanced in their equestrian scholarship will it enter their heads to turn to the theory of riding. However, as in all things, people then tend towards overkill. An expensive trainer is brought in, complicated concepts are introduced and sometimes the words used are so clichéd or technical that no one dares to question. Soon one cannot see the wood for the trees. Finally, one is left wondering whether the instructor really did want to inform, or whether everything was being kept as a well-guarded secret.

Yet the exercise of studying the horse's way of moving and his natural reactions to stimulii is not complicated. It requires little more than an open mind and wide open eyes. Generally, it is just a matter of using straightforward observational powers to take in certain factors concerning the horse's physical makeup and locomotive powers. So whilst developing technique in both the human and equine body can be complex, if it does not relate back to these factors, it is worthless.

The important point here is that, from the

Studying natural movement and response to stimuli is not complicated

Balanced movement: from his earliest days, the young colt displays the God-given carriage that will serve him for life; note poll the highest point, head flexing from an arched neck, hind legs pushing under and forehand light.

Loss of movement: here, a sudden stop and temporary loss of balance results in disengaged hind legs, hollowing over the topline and a poking nose.

Free, flowing movement: impulsion stems from engaged, supple hindquarters which create spring in the hind limb joints, leading to a raising of the back and forehand.

Disturbed movement: a disturbance leads to momentary fear and tension shows in the young colt's eye and body posture. Note how he draws back with the neck, dips the wither and tenses the gullet (some training gadgets produce a similar effect in the mature horse).

onset, we take these main points or factors on board and gradually assimilate them into the subconscious. Conscientious trainers acknowledge that for everything we do with our horse, there has to be a good reason. If this cannot be explained, then it is back to the drawing board.

Once we understand the ground rules, we should never thereafter forget them in our daily riding. Indeed, our understanding and awareness of how the horse is made up and how he feels us on his back, should influence all our actions in riding for evermore.

Governing Factors

What are the six most important points? To my mind they are these:

- The power and thrust of the horse in movement comes from the ability of the hindquarters to engage and push the hind legs sufficiently under the body to propel the whole length of the horse forward from behind.
- Although balance can shift forward or back, the centre of movement of the horse is situated roughly under the fourteenth vertebra where, well-ribbed up and muscularly supported from underneath, it is most practical to sit.
- The loins are the weakest part of the horse's back and, since the last free rib ends at the thoracolumbar junction, support for the rider's weight at this point is minimal. The vulnerable kidneys lie directly under the loins and depressed loins will hinder the action of the hind legs.
- In all natural forward movement, the back should round and the withers rise as the hind legs engage; this gives freedom to the shoulders and extension to the neck so important for balance. In producing this there should be an arching effect with the poll forming or approximating to the highest point.
- The ability of the horse to bend through the spine is very limited; to achieve an appearance of bend for dressage however, the thorax must be able gently to 'tilt' and rise

True impulsion is about elevation & spring as well as ground-covering ability. Each muscle has a part to play in sending the energy freely forward from hindquarters to forehand giving a vision of roundness.

J.W.

Here, in freedom, the young stallion, Guloso, displays a natural roundness – the result of engagement behind and subsequent lightness of the forehand. A natural position of the horse's neck is an important component of the balancing process. (Photograph courtesy of Marquis of Cadaval Stud, Portugal)

(within the thoracic sling). It is the adduction and abduction of the forelegs that allows the horse to turn and move laterally, with the hind legs supporting the arching of the spine.

- Twisting the horse's neck inwards and sideways away from the wither weakens the muscle structures at the base of the neck, whilst kicking back with the inside leg may cramp the oscillations of the thorax and misalign the connection from the hind end to the forehand.

Looking around the average riding school today, it seems all too obvious that these biomechanical facts are not always understood or taken into account. Riding lessons may be given with a relatively high degree of performance expected from both horse and rider in their flatwork or their jumping, but scant attention is paid to these governing biomechanical factors. Indeed certain rules of Nature seem to be flagrantly broken with the instructor oblivious to the silent suffering of the horse. Frequently, we see riders:

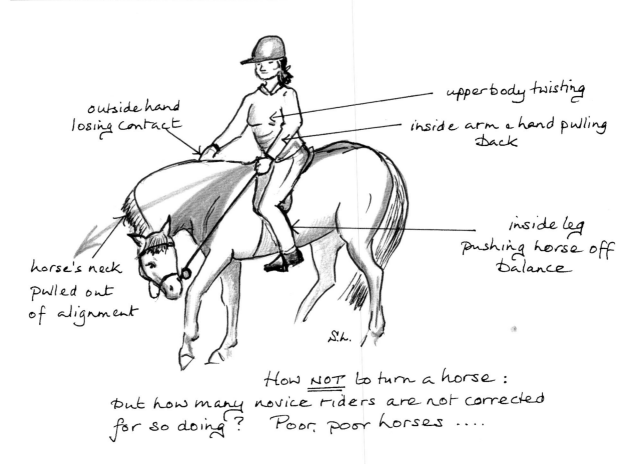

outside hand
losing contact

upper body twisting

inside arm & hand pulling
back

horse's neck
pulled out
of alignment

inside leg
pushing horse off
balance

S.h.

How **NOT** to turn a horse :
but how many novice riders are not corrected
for so doing? Poor, poor horses ....

- Steering the horse from the front end instead of riding forward from behind.
- Failing to sit in the centre of the saddle or over the horse's strongest point.
- Leaning back against the cantle to drive with the seat, thereby cramping the loins.
- Blocking the shoulders and 'shortening' the horse's neck, either with gadgets or by pulling on the reins.
- Failing to support and stimulate the bending/lifting of the thorax with good posture or the leg appropriately placed.
- Mistaking an opening rein for a pulling rein and placing the horse's neck out of alignment to turn, 'bend' (or worse – 'supple' the horse by twisting the neck from side to side).
- Kicking back to push the hindquarters out from under him.

None of which makes much sense.

In those schools where instructors are more educated to the classical principles, it is too often assumed that the student will be too. Nine times out of ten, this is clearly not the case. As for sloppy aiding and a bad position, even top instructors seem reluctant to correct the rider and generally the horse is blamed for an incorrect way of going.

Yet most faults in horses originate from us humans. This becomes self-evident when a better rider is placed on the same horse and an immediate change comes about in his demean-our. When this happens it is clear that the horse is not stupid; he is quite able to tune into the language of the aids provided they are there for him. Domesticated horses look to us as herd leader and strive to mirror every tiny move we make; but if we can't get it right, we can hardly blame the horse when he can't either. In riding it is not so much *what* we do that creates a

Once we make ourselves quiet on horseback, the horse is only too willing to listen, work with us and follow. Here, ex-hunter Milo moves into and around my right leg to turn, simply because it is there for him.

response, but *how* we do it. Unless we tackle the aids from a logical point of view that makes sense to the horse, the most simple request can fail.

Less Becomes More

The funny thing about horses is that generally the less you do, the more they listen. Sensitivity comes not from amplification of the aids but by working with and developing instinctive behaviour. It is important in the first place to ensure that the most simple request is applied with the correct feel to the correct part of the horse's anatomy. Only then can we invoke and expect a correct response.

Building on these natural responses is done with quiet practice and repetition and continual praise so that what feels right is reinforced with words and actions which reassure that it is right. In this way we construct a language. Gradually, as the message gets through, the aids can be made quieter and less obvious until diminution leads to an all-round sharpening of the senses and an eagerness to please. When, eventually, the horse arrives at a point where he not only hears the message but is listening out for our whisper, we can truly say he is in tune and on the aids.

The idea therefore is to work with, heighten and accentuate the horse's own fine senses until such time when the most minute shift of weight or balance achieves a response. This should come like lightning – immediate, brilliant and profound. When the horse's own sense of balance is rendered so fine and fragile in this way, it all becomes wonderful for him too. It is as though he is working without interference and, with his newly developed muscular strength which we have built up through patient and painstaking exercises, our horse feels so expansive and liberated in his own body that he wants to dance for us! All at once the foal in him comes out again and all the beautiful movements which he once made in the meadow will be there for the taking.

Does this sound fanciful? – truly it is not. You may never wish to ride to Grand Prix level, but the most ordinary horse can learn to collect in all three gaits and should certainly learn to offer a few steps of piaffe without tears or stress. While, because of conformational weaknesses, some horses may never achieve multiple flying changes, there is no reason at all why a very passable change cannot be offered. As for the rein-back, dreaded by so many riders and their horses, our own bodies must be tutored to rein-back first; once we put ourselves in the horse's shoes, it all becomes so clear.

Basic lateral work may develop naturally whatever your horse's shape or breed. So really nothing is impossible if you want it enough,

There will come a time when we as riders must replace the mare as herd leader, so our horse naturally wants to follow us.

but remember, without the correct language – the language that horses understand – you will be doomed to frustrating times ahead, risking the goodwill of your horse. It is not what the horse knows, but what he *feels* that counts and in this book we will never depart from that important principle.

Communication Skills

So how do we begin to tune into this unique language? As I have said it is not so much teaching him, but our taking the trouble to teach ourselves. First we must become much more aware of those stimuli which a foal develops from his mother. We must understand about press and release and gentle restraint and freedom so that we can begin to communicate in the same way as he and all his kind have always communicated. And once we are prepared to do this rather than to dominate and control the horse by crude signals which we may not comprehend ourselves, this in itself creates a partnership. Horses have a wonderful way of reading our minds, naturally gravitating towards and working best for those who show positively that they want to help them. In order to do this, I believe we also have to show a humble and open mind.

But first it has to be recognised that in all learning processes there must be some sense of discipline. Nature herself is not without discipline and some lessons have to be hard if only to protect. With the young or even the older horse, discipline is exerted only insomuch as asserting certain boundaries or guidelines. 'You will move over here when I ask you'; or, 'You won't walk all over me when I groom you' ; and 'You will trot at this point when I ask you and you will halt when I stop the movement in my body', etc... 'Please!'

How easily these responses are achieved depends very much on the ability and intelligence of the individual horse but much more so upon that of the owner. No pain or punishment should be involved, but firmness, patience and careful, repetitive lessons will be the likely order of the day. In other words, discipline is established by developing those early natural responses to a point where there can be no misunderstanding and everyone knows what they have to do. Working within unswerving guidelines brings with it security and reassurance, which in turn allows confidence to grow through an expectancy of pleasurable experiences and praise.

Basic Instincts

Let me explain further. Everyone these days is into pressure halters, which clearly work on a system of press and release and in this case teach the horse to move towards the handler rather than away. But far from being localised to the horse's head, this idea is far more all-encompassing. From day one, all horses learn to avoid discomfort. Thus, if we lean on them the feeling of weight against their body makes

Here, Vaidoso is encouraged to raise his back just behind the wither from palpation with the hands around the girth area. The legs can stimulate in the same way.

them want to step sideways. When pressure displaces bodyweight sideways, it becomes uncomfortable not to move that way. This is what a mother will do to her foal if she wants him to move out of the way as she turns.

In the same way, a horse owner teaches their animal to move away in the stable as they walk in the door to groom, feed, muck out and so on. A rider does the same with the leg when asking the horse for a turn on the forehand to open or shut a gate, or with the outside leg brought back to move the horse away from the track in an arena. This pressure should not involve pain, but it does involve a momentary mild feeling of imbalance. As soon as the horse obeys, the pressure is released and that is his reward. It's all quite simple – ask and release! In this way the horse learns very quickly.

In a different way, we can invite the same horse to move into or towards pressure but not just with a halter. Dominique Giniaux, the French equine osteopath explains it thus: 'The equine offers a cutaneous hypersensitivity which allows one to make him easily startle by touching him at spots chosen in accordance with the movement one wants to foster.' This would explain why a quick, light touch on certain areas of the horse's body is generally seen as an invitation. A tiny, inquisitive tap with the fingertips on the horse's body attracts his attention. In the same way that a mare nudges or nuzzles her foal to come and drink, we develop a way of saying 'Hey, come to me!' Most people do this anyway without thinking, but the feeling is always one of swiftness, lightness and attention as opposed to sustained pressure to push or send away.

This aid is developed to stimulate more movement. Horses like to move! Therefore a quicker, more urgent press is soon accepted as a signal for impulsion – provided that, again, we release! On the other hand, sustained squeezing or tightening dulls and inhibits impulsion. That is why it is so important to ask the horse where he is at his most ticklish and where the nerve endings which carry messages to the back, hindquarters and abdomen are most obviously clustered. A light aid applied to this part of the horse's anatomy could not be more different in its nature than that required for the horse to move sideways. Yet, surprisingly, there are still many riders who confuse the two aids. Instead of asking and letting go, they push the horse off balance by squeezing, heaving or displacing weight.

Reflex Spots

In examining the horse's own ticklish spots we soon discover that, as in the human body, there are certain places where palpation results in a reflex action elsewhere. For example, vets know that prodding with the flat of the thumb around the bottom of the horse's ribcage will stimulate the intercostal nerve to bring about a lifting through the back. This may be used by horse chiropractors and in shiatsu, but it also helps the rider to support and liberate the forehand without resorting to more rein. The action is therefore a quick, light touch or 'ask' with the inside leg which can either be done unilaterally or bilaterally. Obviously, both legs asking at the same time bring about a more spectacular result and the drawing up of the ribcage encourages greater freedom in the action of the forelegs. If stimulation is applied too far back however it may cause the back to lift in the wrong place – at least for riding. This could deter the horse from lowering his haunches unless he is already very well engaged.

By contrast, a unilateral leg aid applied behind the girth area will encourage a different response. A pressing action here will allow a very mild rotation of the thoracolumbar column *away* from the source of stimulus. Provided this is done by the outside leg*, this is good. The rider's inside leg then stabilises the horse through downward pressure at the girth, so the horse is then encouraged to encurve to the inside, which enables a fairly uniform 'bend' to take place throughout his body.

However, many riders make the mistake of overdoing things. They use the inside leg with strong sideways pressure and wonder why the horse often stiffens and resists away from it. Inside lateral 'bending' (we will call it this from now on to simplify matters) can only be brought about by subtle *invitation* if it is to be achieved correctly and willingly.

Unfortunately, the average rider tries to make up for lack of success by taking more inside rein and kicking too far back. Here again, this only achieves the opposite of the desired response. The horse may bend the neck inwards, but the quarters fall outward. Only when riders learn the quick 'lightning' touch, beloved of the old masters, will they achieve better bend; this also leads to greater impulsion.

Natural Responses

All these aids are just some of the very natural things we have to bear in mind in our everyday riding and schooling. Invariably a horse comes to me on a clinic and I start to test these natural responses. The first thing people notice, particularly if the horse is normally on his forehand, is that the whole horse looks taller through the frame. Then they see that he has come more together; the freeing up of the back and corresponding raising of the forehand produces an image of roundness. The hind legs may work for all they are worth but if the horse's back is hollow under saddle, they will

---

*The only time the inside leg will need to act in a more backward direction will be in the shoulder-in, see Chapter XI.

remain behind rather than *under* him and he will look very flat. Yes, of course good engagement behind is responsible for rounding the back, but if the horse is not first encouraged by good rider posture and correct leg aids to free his spine, he will be unable to engage in the first place.

At this stage, we collect the walk a little and suddenly the horse is able to offer a little shoulder-in. 'Oh, but he's never learned *that*!' cries the owner. I reply that he did not need to *learn* it. However, he will certainly need to practise it if it is to develop into a worthy textbook shoulder-in, but that is something else. The niceties of the movement such as correct angle, flexion, and correct stepping through on three or four prescribed tracks may have been developed by man, but basically it is Mother Nature that gives every horse the capability for abducting and adducting his limbs to move sideways. In all the basic movements, therefore, it is just a question of first speaking the language that shows the horse this is what we want.

Weight Back in Freedom

The same principle applies for turning. Most riders pull back on the rein, apply the leg halfway down the flank on the same side to shove the quarters round and by turning the horse on the forehand, think they have done a grand job. Yet this is not Nature's way and in the school I find this a rather unkind exercise to give, since the majority of people ride it in such a way that all their weight and that of the horse is borne by the front legs, which were never built to carry such a burden.

Observing our horse playing and turning in the field, we will become aware that he never turns on the forehand but moves around his centre, all four legs shifting at once. When real impulsion or a sense of urgency is present, every change of direction is made with the horse poised and balanced over his hocks. As the horse brings his weight back by tucking his hindquarters under, he is able to turn with great precision exactly as and when he wants.

Indeed an animated and fit horse will often part-pirouette to change direction.

Once weight is balanced over the hind end, the horse immediately becomes upwardly mobile and light through his forehand. This makes it easier for him to move forward with spring and alacrity and his gaits become much freer as the shoulders and withers rise. With the quarters weighted in this way, the horse's balance is preserved ready for the next turn, the next transition or the next surge forward, so he remains in a constant state of readiness for whatever comes his way. Being a flight animal, no horse wants to be grounded on his forehand.

Weight Back under Saddle

Therefore, when teaching turns, I would much prefer to emulate Nature's way and discourage any practice which puts the horse more on the forehand than he is already. For example, once riders learn to use their bodies and the outside leg and rein to turn the horse away from the arena wall, the horse at least has a chance to keep his own balance through the turn and the rider will be well on the way to learning the turn on the haunches, which is far more logical. Performed well, this exercise encourages the hind legs to step under whilst allowing the horse to remain straighter and more balanced after the turn. In a clinic, we generally have every horse on the clinic performing quite passable two-step or quarter turns on the haunches in a couple of days. It is never a case that the horse did not know how to do it, it is always the rider.

Not the Horse's Fault

In circle work, most riders will again use too much inside rein and the horse may fall in with the shoulders or out with the quarters or vice versa. Often, instead of tracking correctly, the horse appears to skid round the circle, which is a bad habit since bending is avoided and stiffness through the ribcage accentuated. Unfortunately, many riders lean or tilt inward, thinking this will help the horse. Instead he becomes more unbalanced, but again bears the brunt of the blame. But is it in fact his fault? Did the horse choose to move like this?

The fact is, a poor circle generally results from inappropriate aiding. With the best will in the world, the loss of balance caused by centrifugal force is hard to resist. Once riders are taught the appropriate body aids however, with the inside leg slotting into and supporting at the correct place for bend, the horse can fan out and stretch himself around the circle so that the circumference is held. Soon riders find they can dispense with so much inside rein and, with the hands remaining level, there is less inclination to steer the horse like a car. The horse relies on the rider only to turn as much as he does and this means almost imperceptibly on each step of the circle. Once the rider is balanced, then the horse can remain in balance and begin to enjoy his work.

Weight Aids

When it comes to straight work on the track or trotting down the centre line in an arena, I like to introduce the subject of weight aids as felt by the horse through the rider's weight in the stirrups. A little more downward pressure here or there applied through the ball of the foot may well draw him to right or left. Again, nobody taught him these responses, he is merely obeying the influence of gravity. This simple aid is developed later in this book as preparation for half-pass, but few riders appreciate its use as a mild correction when the horse is crooked.

Jumpers use weight aids all the time, but too many dressage riders remain blissfully unaware that if the horse is falling in on a left circle, a little downward pressure into the right stirrup will do far more good than grabbing the rein. Gravity is a very strong force and it can be used either to help or hinder. For a human to walk a perfect circle requires miniscule shifts of weight, so why should it be different on horseback?

So far, all the responses we have discussed in this chapter are brought about by logical means. The rules of gravity do not apply simply to the work of the engineer, the technician or the architect. These principles are the oldest in the world and are the horseman's most important tools. You do not have to be very wise or very knowledgeable to work with the physical influences which bind us to our horse. What you do need is a sense of feel to become more aware. For example, the golden rule *what goes up must come down*, is too often forgotten.

In my early equestrian days, I had no confusion over the finer points of the forward seat. The hunting field teaches one all too naturally how to use's one weight to rebalance the horse before, after and over jumps and the knees and stirrups provide a central base of support through which the line of gravity should fall (see figure a, p.26). Sitting into the horse for dressage, however, was altogether something else. If one listened to some instructors, it was all about pushing weight downward, which inevitably caused tension, with the seat slipping back (see figure c, p.26). Only when I went to Portugal in my early twenties, were my eyes opened. In this context, the first clue I received to dressage in lightness and in balance was one simple sentence from Nuno Oliveira. It was this: 'The rider must inflate the torso!'

Whilst still adopting the forward seat on very young or unmuscled horses, I soon found that for sitting work on a mature horse, riding tall and stretching the muscles around the ribcage had a hugely liberating effect. First, one could remain central and deep in the saddle with no real effort other than stretch exercises; second, there was no strain on the back, it felt wonderfully supported; third, the raising of the diaphragm led to better breath control and a release of energy from within.

Even more mind-boggling was the effect on the horse. Raising the rider's centre of gravity encourages the horse to round up and come into balance. Growing tall and riding in the

Riding tall, stretching the abdominal muscles and thinking 'inflate' really does work. Feel that you draw all the horse's energy upward with you. There is truth in the saying that a proud rider creates a proud horse.

Portuguese style of 'waist to hands' can transform a strong horse who wants to lean on the forehand and rush off in trot or canter. It is also the secret weapon of the advanced rider, when teaching the horse passage and piaffe.

Once we ourselves think up and free up, it is much easier to let *weight down* in the correct place for the horse. Tapping into those elusive weight aids, which are barely more than thoughts, then becomes second nature. After all, this is how we ourselves operate from the ground. Remaining upright and moving in balance on our own two feet has nothing to do with pushing down or force; we merely direct our thoughts right or left or forward or backward and our bodyweight takes over naturally.

To *allow* your weight to take your horse right is mind-boggling because it's so simple! By thinking something, then allowing it to happen, we take the horse with us. It is not a question of choice. The horse *has* to move with us and under our weight if he is to remain safe and upright. Fighting the gravitational force within our bodies threatens not only his ease of movement but also his stability. The difficulty for us as riders is to remain centred and balanced and to know which way our weight is moving! Sloppy posture and haphazard movement will throw out conflicting weight aids which can threaten our horse. Only through heightened awareness can we use gravity to work for us, but until this becomes automatic, we need to think, think and think again.

There is no doubt that the influence of the human body over the centre of the horse is far greater that most people will acknowledge. I believe that even experienced riders only utilise around half the capability and half the energy that lies within them. Riding is not about strength. It is about tuning into gravity, toning up, opening energy channels, allowing movement to flow and releasing the horse from his burdensome task.

Once we accept our own responsibility in this way and recognise that the horse can and will move correctly if only we will let him, riding takes on a new depth and a new meaning. This book says nothing different in that each and every aid described here will be the traditional one. What may be revolutionary for some readers is to be asked to think like a horse. However, until we do this, we are only working with half the partnership, and surely our horse is worth more than that?

CHAPTER II

Structure and Movement
Aligning the Rider to the Horse

The horse is a marvellous feat of engineering. Free, natural movement will promote healthy muscles.

In 1869 Francis Dwyer, a respected horseman and saddlemaker, returned to England from Vienna. Having been spellbound by the riding he saw there, particularly in the imperial riding academies, he was moved to write a book, imploring his fellow countrymen to saddle and ride their horses with much greater regard for the horse's back and the simple mechanics of equine movement. He deplored the poor posture of the average British rider, but worse than this was their ignorant attitude. It was as if no one really cared...

The skeleton of the horse is a very wonderful and beautiful piece of mechanism, which no one who takes an interest in such matters can contemplate without experiencing the pleasurable feeling that perfect harmony of proportion always inspires. We were about to add fitness and adaptability to our purposes – but remembered just in time – that this would be after all a very incorrect mode of expression. For in truth, what is highly desirable is, that we should limit and adapt our requirements to the capabilities of this mechanism and not simply to our own convenience, which but too frequently leads to abuse. *Francis Dwyer*

Although much has improved since that time, ignorance still abounds in some sectors. For example, how many present day riding teachers insist that their pupils are familiar with the framework of the horse? While some tackrooms display a chart showing the points of the horse – muzzle, chest, knee, pastern, fetlock and so on – it is rare to find an establishment where details of the equine muscle systems or skeleton are in evidence for all to see.

Yet such visual aids would bring everything into immediate perspective. The stark reality of how the equine backbone is made up, how it virtually hangs in space from the loins backward and how it is supported in front by the ribcage, should not be reserved solely for higher level students. The time has surely arrived where students new to riding should be made more aware of exactly what goes on underneath the saddle, as well as in it.

Unmounted Lessons

Practical understanding can only grow from sound theory. In an ideal scenario, every rider, even the experienced, should receive one

Teaching young riders respect for the horse's back, mouth and mental — as well as physical — welfare is vital to any partnership.

unmounted lesson concerning the biomechanics of the horse. In a calm classroom situation, particular emphasis should be paid to the muscles which affect the horse's back and hind leg action and how rider position affects both. Overheads or projected slides would illustrate in simple terms, how and why every aid can alter the balance of the horse. Misunderstood concepts such as the weight aids would immediately become clearer visually.

Feel, and the importance of touch, should first be introduced on the ground. Long before the reins are taken up, young fingers should be encouraged to probe the fleshy bars of the horse's mouth with the exact position and

effects of the bit noted so that more respect is instilled. Too often the saddle is slapped carelessly into place — the wrong place — so students should be shown how to run their hands from neck to quarters, in order to trace and discover the sensitivity of the various muscle systems. The logic of correct saddle position and weight distribution would thus become meaningful, particularly noting how the rider's seat can either impact and block, or balance harmoniously to liberate the horse's back.

Such instruction would go a long way towards improving matters for horses in top competition yards. Trainers and judges may talk *ad infinitum* about a particular horse swinging through the back, rounding through the back, working through or over the back, but do they know where vulnerable T1 or T2 lies, or how fragile the lumbar region immediately behind the cantle really is?

Once we open ourselves to this knowledge, it becomes immediately evident that the traditional dressage aids are not something dreamed up long ago by some dead maestro who said 'Let's do things this way', rather they comprised a language which, biomechanically, the horse would understand from day one. Admittedly, it takes time and patience to refine these aids and educate to the point where the horse can obey our every whim, but without certain physical conditions being met, his schooling will have little meaning.

Students need therefore to appreciate that:

- it takes time and the correct exercises to build muscle
- flexibility through the joints will only develop with step-by-step practice
- the horse's back is unable to sustain much pressure initially
- it needs to be developed into a state of strength where the horse can move and carry himself with the same degree of ease as he would riderless.

Thus, with greater understanding, a lot of back pain, both human and equine, could be avoided. However, riders too need hands-on help. They need to appreciate the dangers of adopting the chair seat from the point of view of disc damage as well as security. They need to be *shown* how to support their own backs to diffuse the amount of stress and percussion the horse throws up in movement – which in turn will encourage the correct functioning of the horse's back.

Nervous tension – especially in adult riders riding massive, highly athletic horses – leads to human muscle fibres tightening and blocking in all the wrong places. Riders need to be informed as to which muscle groups can be made to tone up and strengthen their position without forcing joints and ligaments to behave in a way for which they were never designed. Once this sort of information becomes available, life for both riders and horses becomes very much easier.

Conflicting Advice

Unfortunately there are still some rogue teachers who ignorantly insist that their pupils tilt their hips behind the vertical with the tail tucked under, in order that they then 'move with the horse'. They certainly will move with the horse, as such a posture places them behind the centre of balance and where the movement is most pronounced. However, the mechanical stress thus placed on the human spine may well lead to lower back pain in later life. How many riders do you know who have bad backs?

Verticality is Nature's way of placing us in balance, whether sitting on a horse or standing on the ground – even in 90 degrees of Californian sun!

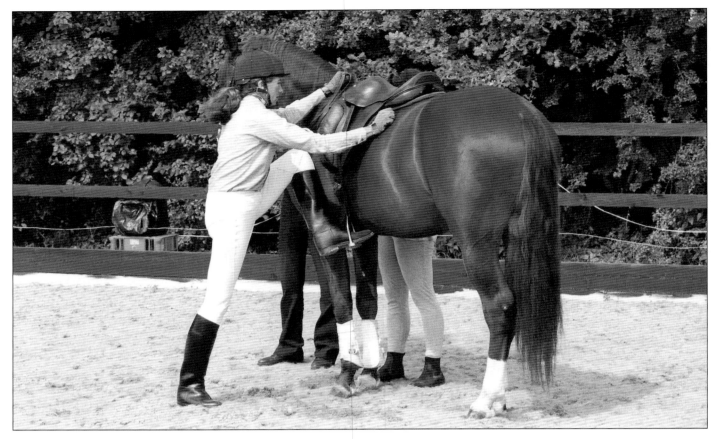

A well-fitting saddle which does not slip is essential for building confidence as well as muscle. Assistance in mounting may be needed as shown here with the recently backed Fabuloso.

To remain in balance Nature's way, we need to keep our torsos upwardly supported whether on horseback or on the ground. Thus in both the forward seat and the vertical dressage seat (see p.26), Xenophon's age-old concept of maintaining a gravity line both in the standing/sitting figure still applies. This helps the rider to maintain an influencing balance over the centre of movement so that horse and rider can merge and absorb movement through the joints or 'springs' of the body in easy harmony.

Equine Back Pain

Ironically, the very fault which causes human back pain may well contribute towards a similar problem developing in the horse's lumbar region. The horse's spine from the withers backward is characterised by being very well supported in one half of its length (termed the thoracic spine) but barely supported at all in the other half (termed the lumbar spine). There is only one part roughly in the middle which is sufficiently flat to bear a saddle without it slipping forward or back.

Depending on the shape and positioning of the saddle and on the shape and position of the person who sits in it, there is all the difference in the world as to the actual point over the equine back at which downward pressure from the seat will be most concentrated. Whether in the light or full seat, the rider can either bring pressure to bear over the strongest available part of the equine back or the most vulnerable. In the early days, even the strongest looking horse may flee away from any pressure on the back at all (opposite) so it is important to be aware of this.

(Above) Some horses may appear strong but are still so tender in the back that they flee away from any real pressure.

(Right) Even the older horse may drop away from the seat unless the back has been warmed up first.

To understand better how rider position affects equine movement, let us now explore further. In Chapter I we discussed the way in which the thorax will very gently 'tilt' to allow the horse to bend, but what about its weight-bearing capabilities?

Referring to Sara Wyche's book *The Horse's Back* we find that this part of the horse is probably the only part structured to support a rider.

> The vertebrae of the thoracic spine are all attached to the ribs which themselves are joined to the breastbone underneath the chest. This forms a solid skeletal cage. There is some movement in the ribs, as the ribcage is expanded by muscles for respiration, but apart from this, movement along the thoracic spine is minimal.

Further back however, things are much more fragile. The same author tells us:

> The lumbar spine begins where the ribcage ends, approximately at the back of the saddle. The vertebrae here have sizeable transverse processes, which provide areas of attachment for the long powerful back muscles... However apart from muscles and ligaments, *there is nothing else between this part of the spine and the*

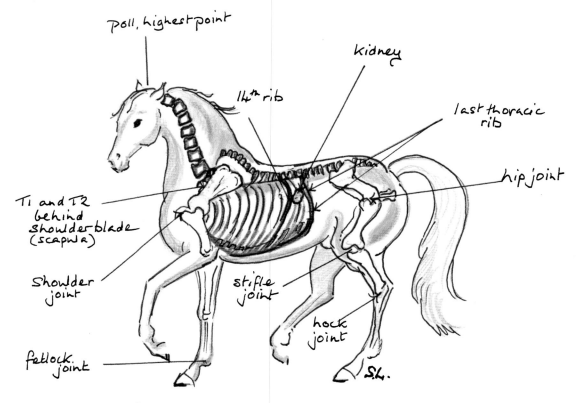

Poll, highest point

kidney

14th rib

last thoracic rib

hip joint

T1 and T2 behind shoulder blade (scapula)

Shoulder joint

stifle joint

hock joint

fetlock joint

S.L.

The fragility of the horse's back becomes very obvious once we familiarise ourselves with the structures therein. It soon becomes all too clear just where we should or should not sit.

(N.B. This drawing is a reasonably accurate artistic impression but is not to scale with many structures omitted.)

ground except for the horse's considerable digestive tract. The lumbar spine is literally suspended between the pelvic girdle at one end and the ribcage at the other.

Since this part of the back is less fixed and almost unsupported, the author acknowledges that pressure here would be highly detrimental for any horse.

Looking again at the diagram above, there is no mistaking the point over which we might comfortably and safely sit, bearing in mind that movement over the supported thoracic spine will be minimal. The problem for most, how-

ever, is how to sustain such a position. Remaining close to the wither and preventing oneself from slipping backward with the acceleration and centrifugal force involved in movement, requires rather more than just a wish and a prayer. Clearly, the rider will need to be as toned and as supple for riding as for any other sport or activity requiring poise and balance. This may well involve exercises on the ground, such as yoga and Alexander Technique to improve general posture, but good carriage can be attained walking round the home and office if you put your mind to it. The main thing is – keep it up!

Supporting Upwards

What many riders fail to appreciate is that the more they tone up through the abdominal muscles and stretch through the thorax and waist, the more they increase the surface area of the seat which acts in a forward-driving way without any necessity to push and shove. At the same time 'growing tall' straightens, supports and cushions the human spine from the jarring of the horse's movement underneath.

By contrast, riders must relax the muscles of the bottom and legs so that they can become more adhesive to the saddle, whilst allowing the joints of the ankles, knees, hips, shoulders and elbows to absorb and go *with* the movement rather than fight it.

Unfortunately, many people are taught to squeeze, push and think downwards when they ride, which contracts muscles, collapses the ribcage and destroys much of the natural spring and support which a toned 'open' body can provide. Softening or folding forward from the waist is only appropriate when we wish to use little or no seat, for example, on a newly backed horse, but once the horse can accept our full seat in the saddle, we can make ourselves easier to carry by riding proud and erect.

Likewise, the horse is cushioned and protected by the development and expansion of his own thoracic muscles around the ribcage, sometimes referred to as the 'ring of muscles'. To quote again from Sara Wyche, 'The muscles surrounding the thoracolumbar spine work co-operatively. They are responsible for supporting the [equine] spine as well as for moving the horse forwards. They provide both suspension and propulsion'. As she goes on to explain, they also have the ability to *lift* the forehand if activated by the rider's leg on the girth, but more of this later.

Centres of Balance

Dressage books abound in lengthy explanations concerning centres of motion, centres of balance and centres of gravity. The idea of coinciding or aligning human and equine centres of motion or gravity as we all hurtle through space can be daunting. For all that, most experienced riders know the joy of feeling in absolute balance with their mount at one time or another, even if the moment is fleeting and cannot always be recaptured.

Like it or not, however, this dual balancing act is very important if we are to become successful riders with a happy and confident horse under us, but if it seems pedantic to pursue perfect balance, perhaps we should remember that no sailor would attempt to sail a ship where the cargo was not secure in the hold, nor would any pilot wish to fly a half-empty plane if all the passengers sat to one end. There is therefore a direct correlation between the positioning and centralising of weight in a vessel and its successful locomotion.

In the case of riding, weight must be constantly readjusted for each new task, but these displacements, intentional or otherwise, must be kept to an absolute minimum so that the stability of the partnership and the smooth flowing operation of the equine muscle systems are not unduly disturbed. Whilst we have discussed the deep muscles of the thoracolumbar spine supporting from beneath, we must now become aware of the long back muscles which pass under the saddle to connect the pushing power of the hindquarters to the carrying forward action of the forehand.

Saddles and Weight-bearing

Again, just a simple look at a diagram showing these muscles should be enough to tell us that we must try to interfere with their mechanical functioning as little as possible if we are not to hamper good movement. For this reason, we have to be careful with our choice of saddle, finding one that is balanced in such a way that we are able to sit quietly and centrally without blocking.

Different ways of applying weight

a)

b)

c)

d)

e)

SL.

Each riding style or seat creates a different
weight effect on the horse's back whether we
are conscious of it or not

There are many further aspects to consider:

- The size of panel should be generous enough to spread or diffuse weight rather than create pressure points on the horse's back.
- Overwide saddles that move about will cause friction and bruise the vulnerable back muscles.
- An over-exaggerated depth of seat will impair freedom of movement in the rider's position and may again create pressure points.
- Pinching of the shoulders may occur if the front strap of the girth is placed too far forward.

Always use your eyes and watch the saddle under the rider; things that look all right in the stable can change dramatically with the rider on top and in movement.

While it is all too easy to block the horse through a tight, unyielding seat, just as bad is the sloppy seat which causes him to proceed in a wandering fashion rather than moving through and straight ahead. The rider must strive always to return to a stable but neutral position after an aid has been applied.

Aids with the seat should be shortlived:

- Driving should occur only for those moments when we wish the horse to push on, lengthen or extend.
- Slowing or stopping the horse through a momentary downward pressure of the weight for halt should cease the moment the horse obeys.
- In the higher work, the idea of lightening the seat to the rear and balancing more on the thighs to free the horse's back for piaffe, should only occur for those moments of the movement.
- In the rein-back a similar aid will be used, but the rider must immediately return to a more forward-thinking position the moment the horse has obeyed.

Since all the aids constitute a change of weight or pressure, we must become more aware of how each and every one of them brings about a certain effect and response in the horse. *In between the giving of the aids there must always be a moment of calm or release.* Think quiet, think neutral between each request. To overload the horse with several signals at once is merely asking for confusion to reign.

Freeing the Topline

To the rear of the horse is a group of muscles known as the psoas. These help to transfer most of the energy from the quarters forward to the longissimus. However, if the horse's back is squashed downward too early by riders immediately going to sitting trot, or sitting too far back on the cantle, these muscles will lock and stiffen, creating tension behind the saddle. It is thus very important for riders to start their work off the horse's back carefully in rising trot to allow these muscles to warm up, stretch and yield.

It is often imagined that the balance of horse and rider will change radically when a light or half-seat is adopted as opposed to a full or deep seat. The light seat is generally associated with jumping or cross-country riding, but it is equally important in dressage if we want our horse to develop a good topline. The main difference for dressage is that we may lighten our weight in the saddle by taking more support in the stirrup, knee and thigh whilst remaining seated (see p.28). In the half-seat, we do not generally fold or incline the upper body as much as we would for going over obstacles, since this places the horse on the forehand (although again with newly backed horses this may be necessary for the first few weeks).

Taking a more vertical balance, with braced loins and a well supported diaphragm, will allow us to lighten the seat with the horse virtually in the same balance as with the full seat, provided the hip-to-heel base of support is retained.

Of course, a feel for balance is vital at this point and it is the hallmark of a good rider

Lightening the seat

(Above) Working the horse in the half-seat, taking more weight in the thighs and stirrups, allows the horse to stretch and round his topline in canter duing the warm-up. Gently steadying the hands on the wither is quite acceptable here.

(Right) In rising trot, a more vertical, nicely toned posture from Andrea helps the novice Milo to come off the forehand.

when he or she can balance over the stirrups and lighten a deep seat at will and at any given moment, with no appearance of disturbing the equilibrium of the horse. Such a rider will know when such a change becomes appropriate and it is helpful to practise moving gently on and off the horse's back in this way during the warm-up exercises. Your horse will soon tell you what he likes best and whether or not you are getting it right. There should basically be no interruption to his forward-going ability whether you are on or off his back once he has warmed up.

Centring

Since subtlety should be the norm for *all* schooling prior to jumping, hacking and cross-country as well as dressage, the early discipline of acquiring a good seat is vital. Not only does a centred seat give the rider real stability, it also

affords the luxury of changing the balance in preparation for the various exercises. There is no reason on earth why a horse should wish to move faster, slower, forward, backward or sideways, or more 'together', if our own balance does not invite him to *want* to make a change. Harmonious dressage is about offering our horse the most logical and comfortable option, so the initial stability or starting point of balance must begin with us. To this end a firm central seat is the core.

It is not the purpose of this book to reiterate too much past work. *The Classical Seat* (1986) gives a precise explanation of how to find that central balance on the basis of Xenophon's concept of the standing/sitting figure and, now in its sixth edition, is still helping riders worldwide. Meanwhile, a glance at our photographs will show that the idea of a 'three point' balance is nothing new. Nevertheless, until the rider has mastered this all-embracing vertical seat it will be very difficult to influence the horse for dressage without overaiding. Regular lunge lessons are highly beneficial and gridwork and cross-country do wonders for balance. However, if still in doubt about the correctness and sensitivity of your position, a one-off lesson on a highly trained schoolmaster will prove an eye-opener, and any inconsistency can be pinpointed and worked upon.

From the horse's point of view, instability of seat, sloppy posture and overaiding blur the parameters between what is wanted and what is not. Too many messages clog the wires, bung up the energy channels and often lead to confusion, stress, discomfort and even pain for both the human and equine body. The horse possesses a hypersensitivity second to none, so there should be nothing overt or forceful about educating the horse for dressage. Those trainers who insist that both horse and rider should be dripping with sweat when they leave the arena must have a very sadistic streak indeed!

What should concern us is our ability to adjust from a light, supportive seat to a full supportive seat and vice versa at will. In both cases we must be supple enough to direct our weight over or as close as possible to the horse's centre of motion. Both seats have their own particular uses.

- In addition to the warm-up, the light seat is invaluable to help free the horse's back to encourage greater forward movement in a young or sensitive horse, or one who has a tendency to hollow or to rush onto the forehand.
- With the more mature, muscular horse, the full seat may be more effective in building impulsion.
- The full seat is also invaluable to steady or contain the horse, develop collection and achieve split-second transitions.
- In the higher airs, the rider may have to slightly lighten the seat again to achieve greater elevation and lend real quality to the movement.

Remember, every horse is different and each requires an assessment in feel, throughout each training session.

The Weight Aids of the Seat

Once the horse accepts the full seat easily and happily, imperceptible changes can be made to achieve different effects. For example, when asking for extension, the rider may draw the shoulders behind the vertical. Provided that the rider's back is supple, this action will cause the seatbones to engage deeper into the saddle, which should drive the horse into a more impressive extension. We must be careful to recognise that this change in the seat is only effective as a weight aid during the actual time-frame of the shoulders moving back. Once that movement is finished, a neutral position should be assumed again immediately if the horse is not to hollow and lose balance before the next request.

Unfortunately, many riders find it difficult to keep the hips forward when using 'more seat'. This is a consequence of stiffness in the loins and it is all too easy to come behind the movement (see p.32). A good test for balance is when the rider can immediately stand in the stirrups from both a full seated position or a light seat without collapsing downward or pushing off from the cantle. This is done by keeping the loins braced forward while the rider takes responsibility for his or her own weight by allowing the balls of the feet, remaining vertically beneath the body, to act as upward springs in the same way as they do in skipping or jogging.

People often argue that the light seat will be no easier for the horse than a full seat, since the saddle remains in the same place. However, the application of pressure is what counts here, so by placing more weight in the thighs and stirrups, we may relieve the muscles under the back of the saddle of much of their load. Subtle changes of this nature depend very much upon the feel and the suppleness of the rider.

Here, out hacking, I can steady and support this older horse over difficult terrain in the full seat by growing tall and squaring the shoulders.

Whatever the seat, a stiff, unfeeling rider may give inadvertent stopping aids.

- An unbalanced rider adopting the half- or light seat may stymie forward movement by tipping downward on the front of the pelvis so the crotch acts almost as a brake.
- A tight or tense rider adopting the full seat may also stop the horse by gripping up with the thighs and calves and blocking forward flow.
- Leaning back with hips behind the vertical, allows the seatbones to dig in; this may create overdrive, but it can also produce tension and cause the horse to hollow away from painful pressure points under the saddle.

Only through feel can we learn to ease or deepen our weight to advantage. There are times when we will want to stop or check the horse, and a seat aid is far more effective than a hand aid. At other times, we will wish to free the horse from all constraint and again the weight aids of the seat can be developed very specifically.

Bringing the legs too far back and collapsing at the waist places the rider onto the crotch which, as shown here, virtually acts as a brake to forward impulsion.

With the young horse however, we must be as gentle and undemanding with the seat as we can. In some cases, too much seat can cause a rear, or make a horse rush backwards. It is far better to play it safe initially and keep the seat soft and light. There are many advantages to be gained. General Decarpentry writes how 'the lighter seat frees the loins and facilitates the flexions of the spine'.

In the same vein, Sara Wyche writes: 'The reason for allowing the horse sufficient time to warm up during ridden exercise and not attempting to sit to the trot until the horse is ready, is to encourage the psoas muscles to relax, which enables to horse to work "through" and then "over" his back as a whole.'

Some horses take years to accept the sitting trot happily – at least with any sensation of swing and real roundness – and even then we must never allow our seat to be seriously heavy. Paradoxically, a major element of sitting deep is to carry the upper body as tall and proud as you can! If you think of the horse coming up to meet you rather than pushing down to meet him, you will be far more adhesive, yet elegant.

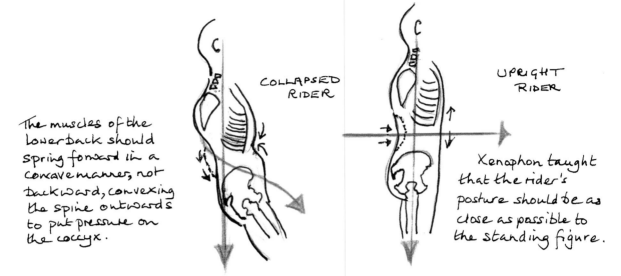

COLLAPSED RIDER

UPRIGHT RIDER

The muscles of the lower back should spring forward in a concave manner, not backward, convexing the spine outwards to put pressure on the coccyx.

Xenophon taught that the rider's posture should be as close as possible to the standing figure.

Hans Handler wrote: "A faulty seat with the buttocks turned under, verging on the so-called 'chair seat' allows the back to be rounded so that a springlike action of the lumbar vertebrae is scarcely possible or at best in the wrong direction . . . . "

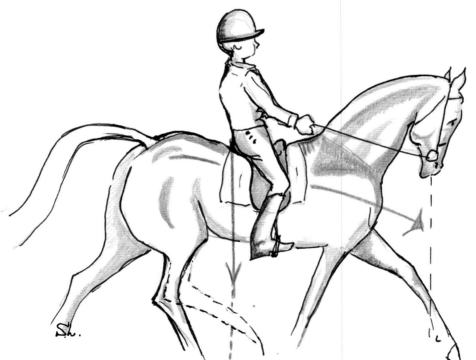

By its very nature a backward-tilted position of the pelvis will put the rider behind the movement to block the potential reach of the hind legs

Unfortunately, there are those who make themselves so heavy they never give the horse a chance to develop his topline. These are the horses who tend to leave the hind legs out behind them since they have never developed sufficient strength through the psoas to engage properly. However, even with horses who are accepting the full seat and have no difficulty in the sitting trot, it is important that in all schooling exercises, and particularly for tackling new and difficult movements, riders return to a light seat to give the back 'a breather'. Once you become more conscious of what your horse is feeling under the saddle, your riding will improve immeasurably. So listen!

For riders who have never found the centre of their own balance, who have always sat in the wrong part of the saddle, on the wrong part of their anatomy, and with the wrong balance in their upper body posture, such nuances of position will forever remain a mystery – until they determine to do something about their position. For position is everything when it comes to the schooling of horses, big and small, novice or advanced.

The Good, the Bad and the Ugly

With so much good riding to emulate nowadays, it is sad when, at times, the crude and incorrect is upheld as the norm. Prejudice against the old English hunting seat, once so prevalent in Britain and parts of the USA, opened the door for the Germanic school of riding to influence global dressage which took off in the 1960s and 1970s. Until that point, most British-based aficionados (such as Henry Wynmalen) had favoured the French and Portuguese style, which depended upon a quiet, vertical seat and a light-handed contact on the reins. Gradually this approach found less favour in competitive dressage; instead a stronger contact attained through a harsh backward-driving seat (often coupled with a nodding head) became fashionable. While some of

the visiting German trainers were very good, there were others less so who merely jumped on the bandwagon.

Too much strong riding did little for sensitive Thoroughbred horses or their riders. Even today, in the supposedly enlightened new millennium, there are many horses worldwide who suffer from a heavy, dictatorial style which was totally foreign to the traditionalist German classic riders, such as Harry Boldt, Josef Neckermann, the late, much missed Dr Reiner Klimke, his son Michael, Nicole Uphoff and Klaus Balkenhol.

It is therefore sad that in this day and age, with all the advantages of knowledge at our fingertips, many horses still have to put up with misguided overdisciplining. However much a rider may love his or her horse, genuine riding with kindness will be hard to achieve without first understanding the theory, and then mastering a correct, balanced seat which works on subtle, invisible weight aids, rather than overt movement and tightened reins.

In *Principles of Dressage*, Brigadier Albrecht, former director of the Spanish Riding School and dedicated advocate of the three point seat explains:

> Neither the effects of legs or hands can compensate for the inadequacy of the seat. The potency of the seat – that is of the weight effect – as an aid – is due to the fact that it evokes from the horses instinctive reactions to physical laws; reins and legs can do no more than reinforce the weight effect and co-ordinate the working of the different parts of the mechanism of movement. The smoothness of the movement depends on proper co-ordination of all the aids.

Therefore, by being balanced ourselves, we can dictate the speed, balance and direction of the horse through the application of our natural body aids, thus negating the need for restrictive gadgetry. Once we have refined these aids to the point where aiding is more about allowing than doing, not only will the horse understand us better, but we in turn will understand

Here, in trot, Vaidoso accepts Suzanne's full-seated position without any loss of engagement. This is helped by the rider's supple back, vertical balance and supportive leg aids.

him. In this way, he will lead us to a gentler, more subtle way of riding.

Discovering the techniques of riding in lightness is again very little to do with self, but nearly all to do with listening to him. There will come a time when every movement made by the horse will look as though it was all his idea, where there is no visible sign from the rider that this or that aid has been applied and where rider and horse seem to become part of each other – joined together through the waist like the centaur.

PART TWO

Theory into Practice

CHAPTER III
Focusing Forward – Relaxation and Use of the School through Walk

CHAPTER IV
To the Aids and Forward in Trot – Aligning the Horse to the Rider

CHAPTER III

Focusing Forward

Relaxation and Use of the School through Walk

Straightness and staying out to the track will benefit from a slight flexion to the inside.

Relatively few people nowadays have the time or facilities to breed their own horse. For those who do, there are many excellent books on the shelves which start with foalhood and proceed to early backing as well as work on the long rein and lungeing. The cornerstone of all training is to teach the young horse to go forward – so if problems arise under saddle, it is often better to return to the unmounted work to re-establish certain basics.

Many owners like to start the work without side reins and only apply them later to create more balance. This is largely a matter of personal taste but there is no merit in sending the horse round and round if he falls onto the forehand or snakes this way and that. Habitual unevenness can cause damage to the musculo-skeletal system, so the owner must make an informed decision as to whether some assistance is needed.

Forward, Forward, Forward!

Appropriate lungeing with side reins not only gives the horse a sense of rhythm and balance in every gait, it also teaches him to reach out, work his length forward and accept the bit within a guiding framework. There should be no question of pulling him into a restricted outline; on the contrary, the reins must be adjusted to allow the neck to stretch fully forward so that he is *encouraged* to seek the bit. Providing sensible parameters within which to work leads to controlled impulsion, longitudinal and lateral flexion and helps develop a good posture.

Like lungeing, hacking is a vital preparation for all school work and is psychologically most important for all horses. It is a mistake to separate dressage from cross-country work. Both are complementary to each other and, quite apart from the interest and pleasure introduced to our partnership, riding out will test the horse's natural skills over undulating terrain, and develop instincts for sure-footedness, self-preservation and overall awareness.

Gridwork and jumping small natural obstacles can only improve the skills required of the future dressage horse. Not only does this build up communication and trust, but again it develops timing, rhythm and balance. Gradually the horse discovers it is more comfortable to bascule and round through the back in a way that may be more difficult to achieve with flatwork alone. It too helps stimulate a desire for forwardness, as well as introducing the sensation of elevation.

While this book is designed to make dres-

Trotting over poles encourages forward thinking. Here, Fabuloso really begins to stretch through the neck, back and shoulders – an important part of the strengthening process.

sage easier, clearer and more natural, it is hoped that the reader will not neglect those other disciplines which make life so much more fun for the horse they wish to educate. Schooling can be done outside the ring as well as inside, as you will note from many of our photographs. By looking at things from the horse's perspective, tuning into what he feels and how he responds to outside stimuli, we can begin to refine and align our aids in a way which complements his own natural movement.

Different Types of Horse

Whether our pupil is a recently backed youngster, or ideally has reached at least four years of age and gained confidence and forward-going ability in all three gaits outside the school, the first lesson in the manège needs to be kept as low-key as possible. Big or small, flighty or phlegmatic, willing or wilful, breed or type will have little bearing on the actual tenets of training pursued within its boundaries. Broken down into step-by-step guidelines, the classical principles are designed to help *all* horses and all riders understand and achieve their future potential.

The *approach* to these tenets will, however, differ from horse to horse. For example, the rider's position on the newly backed mare or stallion will differ initially from that of the rider on, say, the experienced hack or hunter – even though both are new to schoolwork. Both are green in their way, but one will be physically much stronger than the other.

The greatest mistake made by many riders is to overface the horse from day one. This only leads to a permanent dislike of schoolwork because it is made onerous, difficult and uncomfortable. Generally, people expect far

Don't run before you can walk!

(Above) *Until ex-hunter Milo can be persuaded to accept the contact he will only hollow and rush onto the forehand...*

(Left)...*so one must take time in walk to develop trust in the contact and the willingness to lift the back, balance out and push from behind.*

too much too early. We often seen unmuscled horses, young and old, hauled together in front on a demanding contact, kicked hard in the ribs to push from behind, and somewhere in the middle the two ends unhappily meet. Since the horse is stronger than the rider, a struggle evolves, leading to harsher methods of control. After that, the problems can only get worse.

Clearly, this is not the classical way forward. There is a pleasanter way to train the horse, but it must be done in stages and without coercion or unrealistic expectation. In the next few chapters we shall discover a path which will bring our horse correctly to the aids, provided we accept that every horse is an individual and that every horse has the right to approach his work at his own pace. It is important to understand that each stage of training is progressive.

Nothing will be taught, that has later to be changed or undone. Thus a living, growing partnership can be built upon solid foundations.

What may vary slightly from horse to horse is the order in which one does certain things. The degree of emphasis or approach may also alter according to each horse's age or personality. What will not change are the actual principles employed. However, the lazy horse may require rather less schoolwork initially, since the idea is not to overcook the cake, but to make it temptingly short and sweet for him to want to savour more. As regards the more excitable or sensitive horse, it may be advisable to spend longer, especially in walk to settle and relax him and allow plenty of time to assimilate new lessons.

Frequent rests and praise during a schooling session improves performance at every stage – but remember to keep a good posture out of respect for your horse's back.

Rewards

In all cases, the important thing to retain is the horse's willing participation and enjoyment of the work. For this reason, rewards should be given at timely intervals. Mints are popular and give great encouragement after a difficult exercise, but you may not want to stop at that particular moment, so use the voice – but with real expression. 'Good boy!' should really *sound* pleased; your horse will respond by pricking his ears and really bursting with pride when high praise is given and deserved. Also reward through rests, caresses, and giving the rein. Do not, however, do this in the middle of some feat and risk throwing him out of balance – that would be seen as a punishment and not reward!

A horse who seems very stiff from the outset will require a shorter lesson than one who is naturally supple and athletic. Muscles will ache when asked to do new things, and an overlong lesson may result in damage. Discomfort in the body often shows up as resistance through the mouth, but once this becomes a habit, things can snowball and lead to new resistances. A horse who has become rigid through the body and hardened himself to the aids, cannot move freely forward because the energy channels are blocked. When the rider demands impulsion, he may appear to move faster, but without suppleness there is no real forward flow *through* the body.

It is often better to school such a horse one day on, one day off, with rest days or hacking or some jumping in between. All this is mostly a question of common sense. There is no point in 'going for the burn' if you wish to retain your horse's goodwill. Once a horse has truly 'burned', he will remember it and may thereafter make it very clear that he has no wish to repeat the experience.

As a general rule of thumb therefore, my advice to newcomers to dressage is hack or lunge first for about twenty minutes and start the schoolwork with no more than another twenty minutes initially, with much of the work in walk. In this way, you should secure the interest of your horse. Gradually you can build up the schooling, although it is rare that I work even my advanced horses for as much as an hour – but they do go out in the field every day. We have to remember that it is not just a matter of muscles getting tired; we need to work with the horse's mind too, and for this he wants to keep fresh and mentally positive.

Visualisation and Working to Markers

Assuming therefore that this is our first proper lesson in the school – whatever that school may be – marked out in a field or on a prepared surface, do make yourself familiar with the letters.

For the sake of clarity, many of the instructions contained in this book will involve their use and it becomes easier for everyone if you know your way around them. If you can't remember the King Edward rhyme, try this one: A Kind Easy Hand Creates Many Beautiful Feelings. It really helps... in several ways.

The discipline of working to markers is not so much to emulate that of a dressage test, but to bring about positive action. The influence of visualisation over everything we do is now recognised scientifically as being one of Nature's many miracles. The problem is we do not use this power enough!

Feel that your gaze takes the horse to the markers, and never your hands. It is important that you know exactly where you are heading in order to ride the various movements and exercises with easy confidence. There is nothing less encouraging for the horse than to be ridden aimlessly here and there. On the other hand, when you are focused, minute changes occur in your body language, which influence the horse long before you apply the conventional aids. Decide what you want, visualise it and you may be surprised how your horse learns to feel your wishes.

If your school is an unconventional size, remember you will have to make adjustments if and when you compete. When I first imported my present schoolmasters from Portugal, we had to make do with a rough grass area that was only 14 m across and about 30 m long; however, we managed. A lack of size is unlikely to worry your horse; he just needs to feel that you are absolutely decided about doing a certain thing in a certain place.

Try to enter the school with a meaningful plan of campaign already laid down. First, you should relax the horse by walking round the perimeter on a long rein, but it is still important to decide how many times you will do this, and where. On straight lines, do this on each rein at least two or three times in a 20 x 60 m school and rather more in a smaller arena. When you change rein, try to keep the diago-

nal line as unwavering and accurate as you would in a dressage test. In this way the horse intuitively feels a positive force at work, bringing a discipline to even the simplest exercises. The time will come when your horse will seem to read your mind in everything you do.

Walk

The walk is a gait of four beats with a regular marching rhythm always present, the steps even and forward-going.

Whether ridden on a long rein, or more together in medium, and finally at a higher stage of training in collection and extension, the walk must always show those four even beats. Forwardness is the key, but hurrying it will destroy rhythm and ruin the gait; so will over-restriction with the hands. François Baucher called the walk 'the mother of the gaits' and the classic French and Portuguese schools insist that all the higher exercises should be developed first in walk. Take time therefore in your walk work and return to it again and again.

Walk on a Long Rein

This should be introduced at the beginning of every schooling session and at regular intervals throughout to freshen up the other gaits and to free up the various muscle systems. It is not the same as the walk on a loose rein, which should be done as complete reward. Riding round with washing line loops will neither encourage the horse to become 'soft in the hand' nor develop self-carriage. Instead, ask the horse to move forwards off the leg, and allow him to take your hands forward and down as he lowers and extends his neck. To start with he may drop onto the forehand, but he will soon learn to balance better if you encourage him with a light seat and 'asking' legs. As he responds to the forward aids by seeking the bit, do not be afraid to softly *feel* his mouth.

The walk on the long rein stretches the horse and teaches him to push his whole length

Walk on a long rein

(Above) This six-year old gelding stretches nicely into the long rein. The rider sits up and uses a more positive feel from a lower hand position than is the case with the youngster (right). In this way Thomas is able to retain a good balance. This work may be ridden on the track, across the diagonal or on the circle.

(Right) With the young horse (in second week of schooling) the support of the rail will be important. Initially, you may need to use a little more pressure against the horse from your inside leg to keep him out to the track. Encourage the horse to stretch into a soft, inviting rein. Here, Fabuloso already shows an understanding of what is required although he is naturally still on the forehand.

forward without restriction. The most important reason for starting with this exercise is that it allows the muscles which clothe the joints to shorten and lengthen fluidly and easily. This allows the blood which feeds the entire musculo-skeletal system to pump round in an unconstricted way.

So often we observe quite the opposite in the warm-up arenas at shows. A new horse arrives; it's straight off the lorry and into the school! Immediately, the rider gathers up the reins, kicks on and the horse runs energetically away in a spanking trot! Surely, I hear you say, this is the best way of warming up, particularly if it is a cold day? After all, those equine muscles must be made to work!

Strangely enough, that is not the best way. Equine joints are as vulnerable as human ones, and after standing in the stable or on a journey in the box, everything, even in the fittest horse, tends to stiffen and tighten. It is the slow, stretch work which gives the joints and tendons the chance to soften, yield, flex and bend. Put on an exercise rug if the weather is cold. With a tense, 'hyper' horse, charging round and round in trot can make a horse tighter rather than looser. Muscles take time to work correctly; too much activity too soon denies them of oxygen and consequently blood sugar. From this, injury can develop.

As you work through, remember that the horse must participate actively in the whole process as much as you. Contact is a two-way thing. Forwardness must remain at the forefront of your mind, but this does not mean rushing. There is all the difference in the world between a horse who drops the contact and a horse who seeks it. Stretching involves both partners being proactive so, while you have allowed your horse to take the contact forward, be aware that your seat and legs keep him up to the bit in balance. In this way a sensation of roundness is retained, which is a very different feeling from the horse merely dropping onto the forehand with a disconnected back.

The more we ask the horse to stretch, the more we need to improve our own upper body posture. We may need to lean forward to lighten the seat, but try to keep the tummy muscles toned. I always say to my students – even in the forward seat, still think tall. Remember, you are the balancing pole for the horse.

Reluctance to Stretch

While some horses are quick to respond and take advantage of the long rein work, it is not unusual to find a horse – often an older animal – who carries his head artificially high, from tight, tense gullet muscles, who simply seems not to understand. To show him the way, try the following:

- Set your hands as low as possible on either side of the neck; they should remain still and quiet.
- If your hands tend to jiggle about, turn them slightly in so that your knuckles rest against the horse's skin; this gives an extra feeling of support to both you and your horse.
- Now allow your fingers to actively 'ask' or 'sponge' on the rein.
- Be prepared to sacrifice the 'classic' vertical posture by bringing your shoulders forward initially, but try not to collapse; instead take more weight into your knees, thighs and stirrups.
- Send your horse onward from legs which alternately press and release to encourage forward movement.
- The moment he moves actively forward and mouths on the bit, allow more rein out.
- In this way, gradually feed the rein out to him step-by-step, encouraging him to take it forward and down.

Remember, all this may take time. Be content with lowering his head and neck a few inches the first day, then gradually build it up, with encouragement and praise. Within a month he should be able to stretch down so that his nose reaches around the level of his knees. Later you can develop this work into long and low work (see Appendix). Do *not*, however, try deep work in trot or canter until the horse has achieved a modicum of self-carriage. Attempted too early it may well encourage the horse onto the forehand.

Going back to our very novice horse, if he feels earthbound or 'sticky' in the walk, try not to use tight, forceful legs, which may block him. The leg should be light, but insistent. Soften the seat, allow more forward with the shoulders and elbows, supple the lower back and really concentrate on free, forward movement. Visualise your horse stretching through his back and try to feel that you have made this possible by opening up as many channels as possible.

Some riders find it helpful to 'walk' through the seatbones with alternate leg aids to encourage forwardness. The legs stretch further back to activate the hind legs, but be careful not to tip the pelvis too much forward and create

Improving the basic walk – young horse in second week of schooling

Too much seat may initially hollow the horse's back. Here, two weeks into schooling, Fabuloso appears to drag his hind legs and stiffens through the gullet.

By sitting in a slightly perched position and supporting myself on the thighs and stirrups, I lighten the weight in the saddle to 'walk' with the horse. Now, Fabuloso begins to stretch his topline and push from behind.

inadvertent weight aids which stop rather than encourage. The feeling should be that as the hocks engage, the horse carries each of the rider's seatbones forward alternately, so it is simply a matter of synchronising the hips with the action behind. However, in practising this, take care to keep your waist vertical, your shoulders square and support the loins.

Basic Walk – Clarifying the Aids

Having therefore stretched your horse on both reins on more or less straight lines, progress now to a basic (later to become medium) walk for some circuits, always remembering to change the rein in between. Again, maintain a feel of marching, but be careful not to hurry the horse out of his natural four-beat rhythm. Now is the time to build up his acceptance to your leg aids, while all is peaceful and calm.

As you take up the contact, try to keep the feeling through your fingers, wrist and arms as elastic and light as possible, but do not drop the bit. Your hands must yield a moment *before* you apply the leg. In concentrating on for-

wardness, we must not confuse the young horse by using any resistance through the rein until he learns to move forward and 'off' the leg. However, at this stage there must be sufficient 'feel' for the horse to know we are there. Our first task therefore is to teach the horse to recognise:

- that the yielding of the rein means forward
- that the action of the leg applied once and then relaxed – also means forward
- that the horse should remain forward-going although the aid of the leg will be much reduced – gradually it will become little more than a breathing action.

The young horse will normally carry his nose forward of the vertical, but so long as he is reaching towards and into our hand, this is good and must not be discouraged. All this is a very different feeling from putting the horse on the bit, which will involve the restraining use of both leg and hand, and which we shall explore later.

At this early stage, the young horse needs to be able to *stretch his neck*, which should rise

Clarifying the aids

(*Above*) *Ten weeks into schooling, Fabuloso remains out to the track from a much more discreet inside leg position. The inside rein is soft to encourage flexion to the inside.*

(*Left*) *Now the young horse is able to accept a more upright upper body posture, pushing off from behind in the turns, which allows the forehand to lighten naturally.*

gently upwards from the wither and act *as a balancer*. If there is too much constriction through the rein, we will make it very hard for the horse to stabilise behind. Whilst a connection is made from the impulse of the hind legs to the hand, there must be no attempt made yet to dictate an outline. Instead, we merely provide our horse with simple guidelines in order to indicate to him where he should be in space.

Some big half figures-of-eight work, interspersed with straight work both in medium walk and in walk on the long rein, is a good way to test balance and to get the horse listening to the body aids, rather than the hand alone for direction. At first, the untutored horse and rider may find this hard, but once you focus on exactly where and how you are going to do this, the horse soon gets the idea. It is now that the weight aids of seat and leg start to become more relevant.

Basically, the rider should always sit *fractionally* deeper into the inside seatbone on a bend. However, we must be careful not to overdo this. If the horse falls in, for example, as you commence a 20 m half-circle to the right, it may be that you are sitting too much to the right. If this happens, simply sit up and think a little more downward into your outside (left) stirrup. A momentary shift of pressure and the

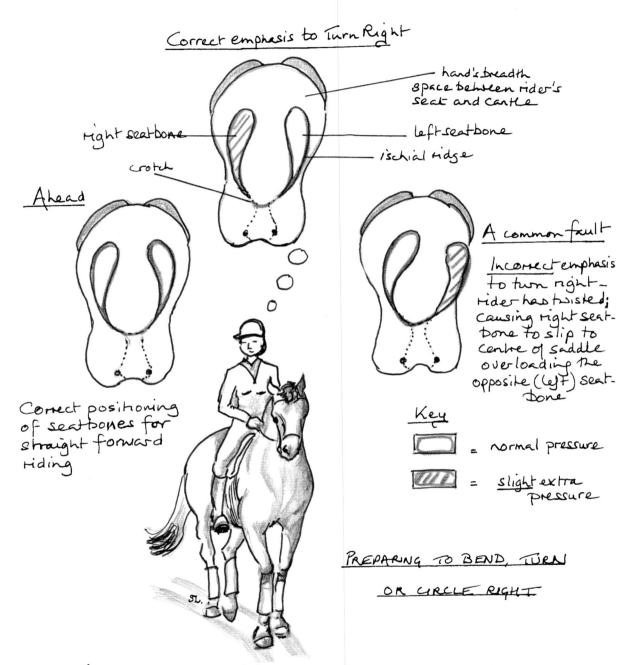

Correct emphasis to Turn Right

hand's breadth space between rider's seat and cantle

right seatbone

left seatbone

ischial ridge

crotch

Ahead

A common fault

Incorrect emphasis to turn right — rider has twisted; causing right seatbone to slip to centre of saddle overloading the opposite (left) seatbone

Correct positioning of seatbones for straight forward riding

Key

☐ = normal pressure

▨ = slight extra pressure

PREPARING TO BEND, TURN OR CIRCLE RIGHT

Visualise your seat in the saddle from an aerial perspective and be aware of what pressures your horse is feeling through his back in order to aid correctly and to avoid common mistakes horse should move out again. De la Guérinière wrote: 'The aid of putting weight onto the stirrups is the subtlest of all the aids... by the mere act of putting more weight on one stirrup than the other, a horse is brought to respond to this movement.'

Out to the Track – the First Weight Aid of the Inside Leg

When you return to the track, whether in medium walk or on the long rein, the concept of riding large and straight forward is similar. Many horses meander on and off the track because the rider tilts this way and that; others refuse to leave the track at all because the rider collapses to the inside (see p.79). To stay out and straighten, try the following:

- Sit up quietly *vertical* and erect and imagine both sides of your waist have grown an inch taller than before.
- Feel that you ride with square, level shoulders, open hip joints and relaxed buttock muscles.
- Visualise your seat from an aerial point of view (opposite). Make sure that both seatbones remain on their respective sides; it is all too easy to allow the inside seatbone to slip towards the saddle twist, and lose position.
- Keep the hip-to-heel alignment and stretch your inside leg downward to support the horse at or just behind the girth.
- Improve the tone of the inside thigh by stretching down through the knee; this allows the whole leg to fall snugly into place by its weight (not grip).
- Feel that your inside leg is now a pillar around which the horse is encouraged to 'bend' without falling in – it may press inward or more downward as required.
- Use your outside leg lightly behind the girth to keep the quarters active.

In this way we support the horse, so the gentle pressure of our inside leg acting on the forehand keeps him out to the track.

Remember, straightness can only develop from suppleness.

Inside Leg to Outside Hand

The popular concept 'inside leg to outside hand' to stay out definitely has its merit, but overdone, it can be counter-productive. As discussed, most people use the leg too far back; also, if the outside rein is too strong, the horse will end up bending the wrong way. Staying out to the track is mainly to do with bodyweight, but the outside rein may provide the finishing touch. Think of having a fine thread attached to your outside hand, which slides along the rail of the arena as you and the horse progress forward – this will help you not to block with the outside hand; equally important, it will prevent it from being ineffectual and limp.

Turning – Opening Direct Rein

When it comes to turning off the track or riding part of a circle, it will be the inside hand which softens forward and invites. This is a very different feeling from pulling back. By *allowing* with the hand, the horse is encouraged to look into the arena and to move off the track. To encourage more, we need to introduce a gentle feeling of 'ask' on the inside rein. This is known in equestrian terms as the *opening rein* – which then yields for the horse to move into it as the inside foreleg is in the air.

Too many riders are taught to pull on the inside rein. This is counter-productive since it twists the neck, blocks the shoulders, and encourages crookedness behind. The action of the opening rein should be in a forward direction, never backward. In the early days we may have to show the horse the way by bringing the hand a few inches away from the wither, while the fingers gently ask. Soon the horse will get the idea, and the mere softening of the rein with the hand remaining at the wither will be enough to indicate the opening rein which is also the *rein of direction*.

As we turn, it is important that the outside

Turning off the track

Too much inside leg applied in a backward and sideways-pressing direction may push both horse and rider off balance in the turn. Here, Milo falls out onto his right shoulder.

Downward pressure into the inside stirrup invites the horse off the track and more around the inside leg in a correct turn to the left.

rein does not restrain the horse. For this reason the outside rein must yield enough to allow the outside shoulder to come round, but not so much as to create too much neck bend or allow the horse to fall onto his forehand.

Turning – the Second Weight Aid of the Inside Leg

By now, the young horse has learned to move forward and 'off the leg'. He has also learned to stay out to the track. To turn more correctly, he must be attuned to a new weight aid in the legs (and seat).

- Imagine that your waist – to the inside – has grown an additional half inch: in this way your inside seatbone should feel *fractionally* more weighted.
- Think now of 'allowing' with the inside leg to release the horse from the track.
- Stretch the muscles of the inside thigh and calf and deepen the stirrup a little outward or away from the girth.
- Now slide your outside leg behind the girth

to encourage your horse to move away from the pressure, to send him into and around the inviting inside leg.

- As your horse turns, help him by putting more downward pressure into the ball of your foot as though stepping off the track yourself.

Pressure exerted *downward* in this way is a very different sensation for the horse than pressure against his side (as with the outside leg). Most people tense the inside leg, which may discourage the horse from moving into it. By becoming more aware, you will soon learn to use both the pressing and the allowing or stepping down aids of the inside leg, particularly on corners, in all you do (see photographs).

Of course, the turning of our upper body is another very important natural weight aid when moving off the track but, again, we must only turn as much as is necessary for the horse to come with us. Allowing the inside hip and shoulder to slip back may push the horse sideways through the outside shoulder instead of

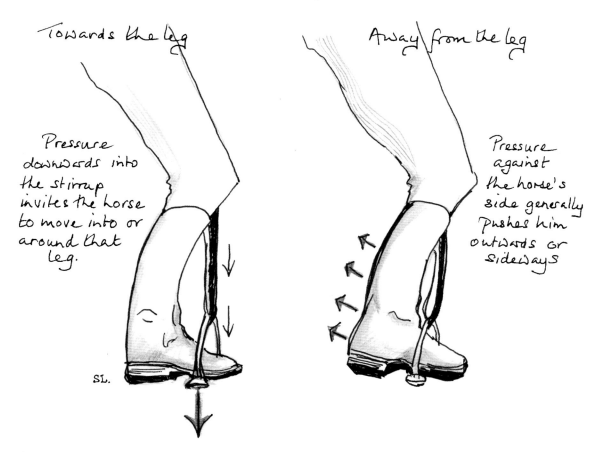

THE WEIGHT AIDS OF THE LEG CAN DIFFER ENORMOUSLY

Towards the leg

Pressure downwards into the stirrup invites the horse to move into or around that leg.

SL.

Away from the leg

Pressure against the horse's side generally pushes him outwards or sideways

A combination of both leg aids used in the correct spot with lightness but sufficient tone will encourage impulsion and lend support simultaneously.

turning him. Top trainers generally advise riders to concentrate on advancing the inside hip to avoid this mistake. Your shoulders should take care of themselves.

What Happens Next – Connection!

Whilst we are nowhere near looking for any form of collection, we should, after a couple of weeks, start to look for some connection from the hind legs to the hand. The elastic contact with the rein remains vital so that the horse can still use his head and neck for balance, but we want to encourage the hind legs to step a little more under. Camped out hind legs are very common in the young horse, but the sooner we can help them to support the back, the better. Now is the time to take a more positive rein contact to *connect the hind end to the forehand*.

Provided no difficulties have been encountered to date, gradually we can begin to *frame* our horse a little more. The horse must understand that, as well as saying forward, our legs can also be used to slow or to halt; and that

A well balanced walk. This picture shows a good understanding of the inside leg aids. Not only does Thomas move off the track in response to the weight aid on the inside stirrup, he also bends and stays out to the circumference of the circle, influenced by the tone and slight sideways pressure of Jodie's inside leg.

when we feel more on the rein, it does not necessarily mean stop. These are matters which are built up slowly. Forwardness and straightness remains our main objective, but at a later stage the horse must also learn the paradox of the hand appearing to ask and yield at the same time – generally known as the 'give and take'. For now however, it is enough to recognise the difference between:

- leg-on and rein-yield to go forward
- leg-on and rein-ask to stop
- leg-on, then relaxing again to stay forward.

He must also recognise that, having stopped, yielding on the rein does not mean to go forward again, unless he feels the legs act as well! It is quite daunting when we look at it from the horse's point of view.

For this reason, these aids will obviously be much clearer if we can think through a moment of 'neutral' in the early stages. As the horse becomes more attuned, the time lapse between each aid will diminish, but even in the most advanced stage of training, it never totally vanishes.

Straightness through Bend

At this stage, crookedness will nearly always be apparent, with the majority of young horses being naturally bent to the left. In addition, the equine shoulders *en masse* are narrower than the quarters, so in a manège, the latter will give the appearance of falling in, particularly on the horse's convex (generally the right) side.

We are not yet ready to ask our horse to

work deep into the corners, but at the same time it would be counter-productive to allow him to cut corners. Remaining out however requires suppleness, which involves the merging and synchronisation of all the aids and a constant feel for the balance of the horse.

If natural stiffness is not corrected in the walk it will become an ever-spiralling fault in the faster gaits. We have all seen the horse who canters madly round the arena bending the wrong way as the rider pulls on the outside rein and kicks in vain with the inside leg drawn back towards the quarters. How, therefore, may we straighten and ask for more impulsion without the same thing happening to us?

The secret to restoring balance to the horse is first to know which aids will help the problem and which may exacerbate it. The old masters taught that to *straighten the horse we must act on his forehand, not on his hindquarters.* Thus, by asking for mild bend at the girth, we combat natural crookedness by bringing the forelegs onto the same track as the hind legs.

Again, it will be the action of the outside leg and the two weight aids of the inside leg which place the forehand correctly. In all straightening and bending work, it is therefore counter-productive to draw the inside leg too far back. Finding nothing around which to bend, the horse in passing through a corner would inevitably drop out of balance either onto the inside or outside shoulder, depending on the rein. As a consequence, the hind legs then misalign so that effective thrust from behind is lost. Things are unlikely to improve until the rider has regained that soft lateral bend which enables the horse to push the forehand ahead of him and track up correctly.

Whilst it is the rider's legs that mainly encourage forward activity and bend, it is the refined but positive seat, assisted by the rein

which maintains the flow.

With a very young horse, the seat and hand should remain as passive as possible. Later, when he is totally familiar with the forward and straightening aids, we may ask in a more active way (see Chapter VIII), encouraging him to chew on the bit and relax his poll and jaw. We look ahead to a time when the horse works with us as though he were part of us. His desire to move forward never being that he wishes to get away from us; instead he wants to join up to us – through his back and through the reins.

Now, as our bodies, legs and the reins sketch out the rough parameters, we can begin to see how counter-productive it would be if the horse felt trapped by our aids. As with lungeing, there is all the difference between helpful support and restriction. *True impulsion, straightness, balance and outline all come as a result of suppleness and strength behind.* They take time to develop, so await these offerings with patience.

In these first days of schooling we are merely setting the tone for the future. If we have observed the guidelines, it is nonetheless perfectly possible for the horse to offer good quality steps in the walk from correct pushing behind by the end of the first month. A rider who sits quietly centred should have complemented the horse's natural-born movement from the beginning. Therefore, there is no reason on earth why any horse should want to, or be encouraged or allowed to fall onto the forehand in the first few months. Many people enter the school on a young horse and just ride around, asking for nothing and expecting nothing. This does no good at all and is almost as bad as expecting too much. Riders who think they are being kind by adopting an attitude of non-interference should think again. Be positive, visualise, support and ride forward!

CHAPTER IV

To the Aids and Forward in Trot

Aligning the Horse to the Rider

In trot, the diagonals should be perfectly matched. Flexible hind limb joints give spring and propelling power.

We have already discussed the importance of teaching the horse to stay out to the track when he first enters the school. We have also discussed the importance of initial stretch work to relax him physically and mentally. This should have led to a calmer, straighter and more supple horse – although it has to be recognised that so far, only the bare rudiments of the straightening work have been tackled. This will need to be constantly renewed and reiterated through progressive exercises.

As well as lengthening his frame, the horse will have experienced being gathered more together in the medium walk. This has involved listening to our seat and body as well as responding to the forward impulse from our legs and the asking of our fingers on the rein.

By allowing us to support him on turns and through changes of rein, he will gradually come to regard the inside leg like an old friend. It must always be there for him, reconfirming the direction of the rein, asking for bend, stimulating forward flow and giving support to the forehand. Once we can show him how to carry us more easily by being *around* our leg, he will begin to trust us simply because he can trust himself. It must be hateful to feel yourself rushed and hastened out of balance by a haphazard, thoughtless rider. The horse loves an established pattern of behaviour; as herd leader

we therefore owe it to him to develop a consistency of actions which will give him security in his work.

For our part, we need to understand the *logic* of the aiding process. It is not enough that we know to do this or that; we must understand why and for what reason each aid is designed, if we are to develop feel. We should also become more aware of how each conscious (or unconscious) displacement of our own weight may have a different effect on our horse's balance.

Now, as we consider the trot and the start of the work proper, we should be aware that the walk must be used to intersperse the more demanding exercises that lie ahead if our horse is really to enjoy his work. There is no merit to be gained in circuits and circuits of trot if the horse is rushing or stiff. Thus walk is returned to again and again to reinforce a particular lesson or intermittently to rebalance, calm or freshen up the other gaits.

However, slopping about on a long rein and neglecting to maintain impulsion merely invites the horse to drop his back, or trip. Periods of stretch must therefore be highly controlled, with the rider assisting the horse forward through good deportment and an encouraging use of the leg. Periods of medium walk should involve asking the horse to accept our contact

Young horse – second week of schooling

Until Fabuloso settles into the bridle, I neither sit nor rise to the trot. Instead, I take more weight into the thighs and stirrups; this takes pressure off his sensitive back for the first few circuits to encourage forwardness and diminish tension.

Once Fabuloso accepts my weight in the sitting phase of the rising trot, I can close the leg a little more to encourage him into a more positive contact.

and walk actively, but not hurrying, with nice smooth steps in a good four-beat rhythm.

Occasionally we may ask for halt. Until the horse is on the bit, halts should not be practised too often and the transition must be progressive. Perfect squareness will not be attained with confusing leg aids; it is much more to do with evenness in the reins and good rider posture. Out hacking, we can ask for halt to pause and admire the view or to give the horse a short break. The horse should also learn to stand straight and still when we mount and dismount and if we always pat him and dismount immediately he stands square at the end of a lesson, he will soon associate this as a reward.

The Trot

The trot is a gait of two-time with rhythmical, forward and regular steps taken on alternate diagonal legs.

- There is a split second of suspension between the grounding of each diagonal pair.
- Rising trot encourages the build up of rhythm in the trot by freeing the horse's back, particularly during the moment of suspension.
- In an arena, the rider should sit as the outside fore and inside hind strike the ground; and rise as they move forward and are in the air.

Proceeding to work in trot will be our first real test of both balance and the horse's understanding of the work to date. The trot lends itself to the idea of building up a rhythm which will help the horse develop his back muscles as we determine to ride him forward. Although some riders expect a young horse automatically to lean on the hand and feel 'downhill', there is no reason why this should be the case and it is better, sometimes, to give with the hand so the horse has to take responsibility for his own actions. This removes the incentive to lean from the very beginning. Trotting comes easily to all horses, and some types, including cobs and carriage breeds, have a pronounced inbuilt rhythm and sense of balance.

Although, at this stage, we are still mainly working the horse on straight lines, we must recognise that a soft bend should be more or less uniform throughout the horse's body if the trot is to remain regular and rhythmic within the confines of an arena. We must be aware that every time a corner comes up, the horse needs to yield his body and deepen the inside hind commensurate to the bend if he is to remain in balance. Later, we will ride deeper corners, but for now we should be content with just a soft, flowing feeling of conforming to the track without falling in. The rhythm should remain constant.

Around the Leg

To achieve this however, the young, stiff or old horse will need rather more support now that we are moving at some speed. In addition to producing impulsion, our aids must help our horse through the short sides as well as the long sides of the school. Without resorting to more rein, we must learn to feel how much help he requires as he works through the bends. As already explained, we know there is an optimum place to stimulate and support the forehand if the horse is to turn in balance and give the appearance of bend, but these aids must never be obtrusive. A light touch applied at the girth can achieve small miracles, which is why the area around the intercostal nerve is sometimes referred to as 'the magic spot'.

Apart from bend, we have also learned how an encouraging touch of both legs acting together near the girth can free the back and stimulate greater impulsion. This allows the ring of muscles which support and liberate the dorsal muscles to carry out their function so that the thrust of the hind legs becomes more efficient.

'Off the Leg'

Asking for impulsion therefore should never be about force. This does not mean that we should not, at times, be energetic with the leg. Some horses need to be motivated more than others, but in the end all should learn to respond to a flick of the inner leg rather than a thud. No one wants a horse who hangs onto the leg; I always want to feel my horses move forward and off my leg. Most people say 'in front of the leg' but to my mind this indicates a picture of the horse going away from me, which is the last thing I want. The feeling is much more subtle than that; it would probably be more accurate to say my leg is on the horse for a moment, then relaxes 'off' again.

The secret to achieving this is to know when and how to ask. In the beginning, we must encourage a swift reaction to the aid, so when we say go, the horse really does understand to go! An understanding of the horse's most ticklish spots and an instinct for the right moment to ask is very important. The rule of thumb on a circle is that whether sitting or rising, we close the legs as the inside hind engages, which involves a softening of the outside rein to allow the impulsion to be carried through. The last thing we ever want to do is to push and pull at the same time – that is the quickest away to deaden impulsion.

Generating Energy

To produce a more impulsive reaction, the sequence is approximately as follows:

- The rider sits up with vertical hips, straightens the spine and stretches both legs away from the body so they hang, long and toned, just free of the girth area.
- The rider thinks 'project and forward!', softens the outside rein as the outside shoulder moves forward and closes both legs in a swift but firm motion against the girth – the action is forward rather than backward.
- The moment the horse responds, the legs relax; the hand resumes the normal contact.

As Jodie's legs act in a nutcracker action, so the 'nut' pops out. Here, six-year-old Thomas gives Jodie a lovely uphill feeling in his working trot in response to her encouraging 'waist to hands' posture and effective leg position.

- If the horse does not move forward, the legs must 'ask' or close again with greater urgency.
- Once the horse goes forward, don't go on asking and asking with the same intensity; the idea is not for the horse to chase the contact but to work into it.
- The legs should simply resume their 'breathing' action and the hands remain allowing but steady.

The feeling of asking with the legs is somewhat akin to a nutcracker action. The only difference is that, as the legs close inward, the 'nut' pops outward and forward rather than breaking! It is important that the flatter, bonier surface of the lower inside leg and ankle acts since the horse feels this aid immediately and, as he becomes more responsive, it can be diminished. This aid will only work if the rider has learned to open the hip joints in order to keep the knee turned in. Rolling the knee outward and squeezing with the fleshier muscular calf merely dampens down energy rather than electrifying it. At this stage we want action, not absorption!

Once the horse is trotting obediently forward, the rider should continue to think tall and rise in rhythm with the horse. It is important to be aligned at this stage so that everything is forward-facing. This involves head, eyes, upper body, hips, knees and feet. Everything must look the same way as the horse. In particular the rider should note that one knee or the other has not gaped open, a common fault. Inconsistencies in the upper leg can create mild twisting in the saddle, which creates crookedness in the horse.

Check that both legs fall away from the hips, so the feet drop naturally into the stirrups with an even, downward pressure in each iron. If the horse is to move freely forward and in balance, the stirrup leather must hang *vertically*. Once the rider's hips and legs are positioned correctly in this way, the trot should feel regular, free and forward-going and the rider should be able to maintain impulsion with just a gentle closing or breathing action of the inner lower leg in each stride.

Even on the laziest mount, it is counter-productive to clamp on or draw the leg back; however, the odd sudden sharp kick to wake up the horse may, on occasions, be acceptable – but keep these to a minimum! At this stage, it is better not to ride with spurs. A dressage whip giving a swift tap behind the leg should back up the aids from time to time, but again be careful never to overdo such action. Forwardness generally benefits from less of the same, not more.

The Rider's Role

To sum up, therefore, the rider enhances the trot by:

- Adopting a quiet, central and balanced seat which can support and allow as required.
- Providing a positive but elastic contact with the hand.
- Learning which leg aids are required for impulsion, which for bend and which for turning.
- Thinking up and forward in every movement, thereby encouraging the horse to think likewise.
- Using the school exercises appropriate to the horse's level of training to help him come to the aids.

As a result the horse needs to feel:

- SUPPORT from my rider's seat – it's like a balancing pole; if it topples, I topple – but I don't want to feel weighed down or blocked by it.
- CONTACT AND GUIDANCE from my rider's hand – I need to know where to place my head; my head is heavy, it helps to feel a light tension on the rein to understand where and how I should balance my head and neck so I can reach into the bit.
- DIRECTION – I can only feel my rider use her weight if she is correctly aligned; then her seat and leg can support me through the corners and short side of the school and show me where and how to go.

- FREEDOM – there has to be sufficient space, or an opening into which I can move easily. If any part of my rider is tight or heavy, my task will be so much harder. I need my rider to sit up and free herself up in order to project me forward through her whole body.
- INCENTIVE – I find it hard to follow the exercises unless my rider constantly shows me the way with her legs and body in every stride. Far from my rider following me, I want to follow her. Then I can really start to use myself from behind.

On the Aids

Having made a good beginning, we must now recognise that no young horse can remain on the aids for very long. For any horse to be able to sustain the correct correlation of responses to our requests for any length of time, he will need to develop sufficient muscular strength throughout his body as well as flexibility in every joint. This takes time to achieve and depends at any given moment, on two things:

- the rider's position, understanding and application of the aids
- the mental and physical state of the horse.

Horses may collect up naturally when excited, a young horse may even piaffe on the spot for a moment when he sees other horses at a show, *but to maintain these states of balance for more than a few steps as and when required is quite beyond him.* Obedience to the aids is therefore not only a question of whether the horse understands or wants to comply or not; but also very much a question of – is he fit and supple enough to do so?

The Physical Reality

Unfortunately, this is not always understood by riders who think horses can immediately offer them what they want at any given time. For example, 'I want you to canter now!' only becomes possible when the horse is helped into

ON THE FOREHAND

DIFFERENT CAUSES~
SAME EFFECT

This horse lumbers along with most of his weight in his shoulders since his rider blocks him at every level with a heavy seat and tight, clasping legs.

Key

⊠⊠⊠ = 'disconnected'
muscle fibres
indicating lack of tone &
freedom to flex & extend

This horse has a naturally high head carriage but since there is no connection from the rein to the hind end & he is incorrectly aided, he hollows onto the forehand.

a state of balance for this to happen easily. When it comes to 'I want to canter on a given leg and make a small circle at the same time!', far more factors concerning preparation and suppleness come into play, and it is not unheard of for a very novice horse to fall over whilst circling simply because he is too stiff to cope with the bend required in such a feat. This loss of balance has nothing to do with cussedness, stupidity or disobedience, it is simply a matter of equine biomechanics, which require certain physical conditions to be met – for which clearly not all horses will be ready.

For the many who have been used to hacking out with a particular horse and who later turn to dressage, it is sometimes difficult to understand why their normally willing and easy-going mount suddenly becomes awkward. Is there really such a difference between a forward-going trot down a grassy track and a similar one down the long side of an arena? The answer, unfortunately, is yes! The grassy track generally peters out naturally so the horse does the same; in the dressage arena or manège, a corner looms and the horse, not used to having to bend suddenly and turn sharply in the same gait feels threatened by it.

The truth, is the whole discipline of dressage could not be more different and difficult for a horse who has previously been ridden largely on the forehand all his life. To be required constantly to turn and to maintain impulsion, rhythm and balance within the unyielding confines of the arena in all three gaits can only become possible when some of the weight of the combination is transferred to the hindquarters. If this is not done, the rider will risk losing the mental as well as the physical equilibrium of the horse.

On the Forehand

There are many riders who are not always aware that their horse is on the forehand. If the horse does not bore on the hand but goes along, light on the rein from a naturally high head and neck carriage, it is not always recognised that the horse is in fact on the forehand but is simply evading the contact by hollowing. By the same token, there will be those riders who enjoy what they term to be 'a good positive feeling in the hand' which is their proof that the horse is using himself behind. Too often however, one look at the horse in question illustrates that, far from activating his hocks, he is merely leaning on the rider's hand with the weight in his shoulders. In both cases, it has to be tactfully explained that the horse is still on the forehand and that changes will have to be made.

In order to correct matters, an important lesson can be learned on how not do things. Observe the rider (we see many about) who finds it difficult to stop the horse from breaking into a jog from the walk, into a canter from the trot, or into a gallop from the canter. The weight or balance of the horse falls forward because the rider's body is doing the same, so the whole thing spirals out of control.

Balancing a weight which is top-heavy or unsupported threatens the horse in every stride. Since the horse will always try to retrieve our weight if we ourselves are out of balance, dropping onto the forehand is his way of catching up. Unfortunately, the forelegs cannot always cope with the strong propelling effects of the hind legs, so the horse feels as though he is falling downhill. This makes him want to run on even more – it is a no-win situation.

Even at walk I see horses who are allowed to 'run' in the gait. Often riders mistakenly believe that this shows good impulsion, but the truth is that hurrying allows the energy to escape or fall away through the shoulders long before it is harnessed and put to any effect. Real impulsion indicates energy that is partially *retained* in order that it might be converted to power. Then the power remains at our disposition – it would be a mistake if the horse thought it was all his!

In order for this to happen we must learn to be proactive – not by pulling back but by joining forces and framing our horse through the

Balancing the older horse

(Above) Shadow, the eleven-year-old part-bred Arab is naturally a little croup-high, but assuming a supportive posture in rising trot improves rhythm and balance. In general, sit as the outside fore strikes the ground...

(Left) ...and rise as the outside fore moves forward. In both sitting and rising trot, try to keep your weight centred.

aiding process. Strengthening our position in the saddle, thinking 'support', and understanding the channelling effect of rein will achieve this.

A horse on the forehand with a weak, ineffectual rider could well be likened to a sailing vessel that spirals out of control, spinning this way and that, with a slack mast and flapping sails. There is plenty of movement, but no direction to the movement. However, once the mast is made firm and the ropes are secured, the wind can get behind the vessel and bowl it along straight and efficiently, with real contained power. As control is restored to the pilot of the sailing vessel, so it is with horses.

Rebalancing

To help the horse come into a better balance, we must therefore have a vision of our posture and aids supporting the horse in every stride, rather than allowing energy to drift away. Sitting centrally and maintaining the shoulder-hip-heel alignment, generally removes the incentive for the horse to lean on his shoulders. Indeed, it will come as a relief to him when our mental and physical support allows him the time to dwell a little more on his hocks.

But this is not a time of idleness; steadying down the front end may involve a different use of our legs from the one already described. As

Here, my older schoolmaster Vaidoso gives Suzanne a lovely feel of lift in the collected trot in response to a good position; note the flexion of the (right) stifle and hock clearly evident.

well as encouraging the horse to work more from behind, the legs can frame him more positively so that greater energy is produced by the quarters.

There is no doubt therefore that energising the quarters in this way improves life for all horses, whether used for showjumping, cross-country, long distance or hacking out. Riding permanently on the forehand places great strain on the forelegs, which were not designed by Nature to bear the main weight and thrust of the horse, let alone ours as well. A horse who is perpetually ridden on the forehand is unlikely ever to make it into old age as a nimble, fit riding horse. Early arthritis, stiffness in the joints, over-at-the knees, splints, ruptured tendons all take their toll, so how can these difficulties be avoided?

Engagement

Again, an appraisal of the horse's anatomy helps us to appreciate just where the seat of power or locomotive engine is based. Nature has endowed the horse with powerful haunches liberally served by groups of muscles around the lumbo-sacral junction. These are the muscles which will ultimately drive the hindquarters. The hind legs in themselves are more sturdy than the forelegs, but it is the hind limb joints which are so beautifully engineered for their purpose. Not only are they fashioned to bend, flex, extend and push the entire frame of the horse forward; they are also designed to carry weight, as will be seen.

Indeed, a horse is only considered to be in true self-carriage when he fully engages the joints of the hip, stifle, hock and fetlock. With a very athletic horse in a highly collected movement, the bending of the joints allows the hind feet to step almost under the rider's heels. Thus the forehand is rendered so light that the role of the forelegs in balancing the frame is reduced to an absolute minimum.

When we ride, it is therefore up to us to learn how to give our horse back this natural mobility despite our weight on his back. We may not want him as weighted behind as in the High School horse (see p.227) but we owe it to his future well-being and health to at least *relieve the forehand of some of its burden.*

Transferring Weight to the Quarters

So where to begin? While it is not so difficult to return the horse to his natural balance for short periods, it has to be recognised there are no shortcuts for sustained work. Those attempting this work for the first time must prepare themselves for the fact that it takes time and great patience on our part as riders to learn how to correct the balance which we have unwittingly knocked awry.

It probably takes even more time and patience on the horse's part. He has to be *helped* to develop new skills, new points of balance and new strengths and powers within

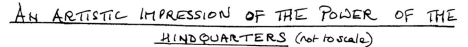

AN ARTISTIC IMPRESSION OF THE POWER OF THE HINDQUARTERS (not to scale)

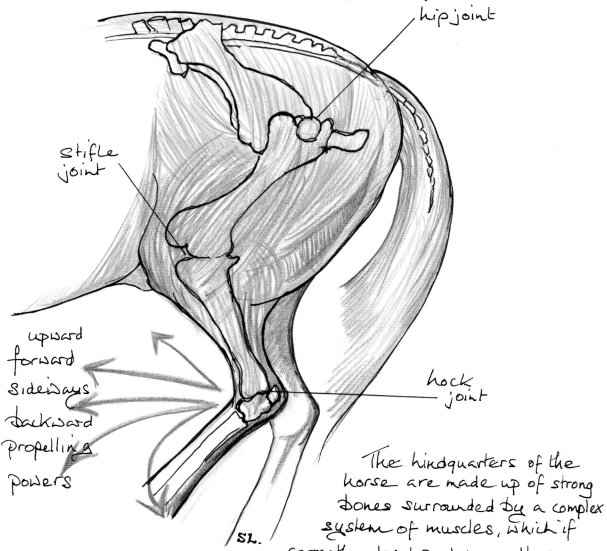

hip joint

stifle joint

hock joint

upward
forward
sideways
backward
Propelling
Powers

52.

The hindquarters of the horse are made up of strong bones surrounded by a complex system of muscles, which if correctly developed, may allow extreme flexion in the joints of the hip, stifle, hock & fetlock. These will act in a propelling & weight-bearing capacity but their full potential will only be reached by correct riding and step-by-step exercises conducted over a long period. Bad riding can destroy mobility & correct muscle growth.

Concentrating mind and energy

(Above) *In the early days, the young, inattentive Espada would rush off into a fast, 'whizzy' trot, with a stiff back, high head carriage and hocks left behind. My first priority was to relieve the weight on his back, to lower the hand and then...*

(Left) *...to work him quietly forward from my leg into a steady contact. Note how a forward but upwardly toned seat allows him to round his back, bend his limbs and soften through his entire body.*

ties when they literally have to think back to front.

However, once we make a little time for the theory of riding and take intelligent steps towards helping our horse to cope with our weight, we will be well on the way to keeping our horses sound, happy and long-lived. In so doing, the first thing that we will discover is how important it is to channel the weight of the horse by helping him to put it back where it belongs – over the haunches.

All the dressage exercises we shall explore in this book are therefore designed to transfer the carrying power of the horse to the haunches and to energise them step-by-step. In order to

himself in the same way as a human athlete exercising with weights for the first time. Suddenly, everything changes and the hardest thing for the horse may be that the rider has previously always done things the wrong way round. It may well come as a shock to both par-

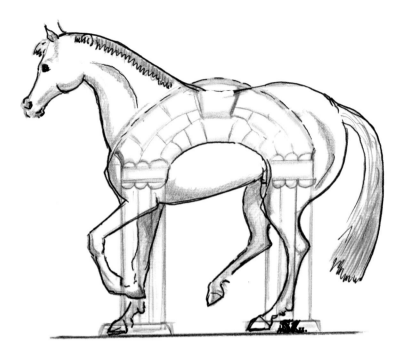

Think of your horse's back as an arched bridge, supported at both ends. Feel that you sit just 'above' the keystone and allow the horse to round & come to you.

do this, we should think of our horse's back as an arched bridge which is supported at one end by the forehand and at the other by the hind legs. There must be no undue stress to the muscles that span and connect one support to the other, so it is important in the early stages that the rider does not push down too harshly, which could partially interrupt this connection.

The Bridge Effect

To keep the back supported, the horse will rely on the unifying effect of the rider's legs, seat, upper body and hands to prevent the forehand taking too much load. In addition to supporting the horse on turns and circles, the rider's legs must stimulate the hind legs and undercarriage to play their part in supporting the bridge.

Once working well underneath the horse's body, active, supple hocks will distribute more weight to the haunches. It is important even in the early stages therefore, that the rider is aware of *making room* for the hind legs by keeping the hips as far forward in the saddle as is comfortably possible.

Stiff, lazy hocks, unable to bend and bear weight, promote a hasty running action in front. When the horse is moving in this fashion and unable to track up, there may be an appearance of 'disconnection' through the back, which is particularly prevalent in very young or old, unfit horses, or when the rider's leg is applied in the wrong place. As already discussed, no young or sensitive horse should be made to sustain long periods of sitting trot.

The part played by the rider's hands at this stage has to be fairly passive, but steady and supportive, if the horse is not to be dropped or pulled more onto the forehand. 'Shortening' the neck will tense the back, which in turn prevents the horse releasing power from the hind legs. The hands must therefore allow sufficient freedom for the back and forehand to come up and bridge naturally, so that roundness will develop from *behind*. Sensitivity for the balance of the horse should show the rider just how positive the feel on the reins will need to be. The idea is to channel the energy, but never to block it.

We have already discussed generating energy and how to teach the horse to be light and impulsive 'off the leg'. Since every forward stride offered by the horse constitutes a complete cycle of energy, the rider's awareness of when to act to rechannel or divert that energy may be attuned to a fraction of a second between each aid. If our horse is very forward-going however, we may need to consider some attempt at recycling or energy conversion – which will later be developed into collection.

Converting Energy

- Stretch the upper body as if to receive the horse's back.
- Increase the contacting surface areas of the seat and legs to absorb energy by stretching the legs more around the horse's barrel, with the buttocks relaxed and open.
- Open and square the shoulders, as though momentarily absorbing the horse's energy more upward.
- Channel the increased energy by feeling more with the fingers from steady hands.
- Believe that, once fused together, you and your horse may become as one – in every movement, every direction; in this way energy can be recycled back to its source.

In this way we ride the horse like a surfer; although in contact we stay *above* the wave, never allowing it to break under us and throw us down. But first we have to catch the wave and this requires real balance. An adept rider, who understands how to stay over the crest of the movement, can help a weak horse. Such a rider gives the horse his or her own balance and the horse, always anxious to align himself with us, follows.

A weak rider is merely a passenger, going along with whatever the horse does. If the horse is on the forehand, the rider encourages this more by also falling on the forehand. The horse can never come off the forehand until the rider decides to support upwards. This requires mental work and body tone. It also requires timing and a real sense of feel. That is why it is helpful for the more novice rider to experience the balance of a schoolmaster horse and thus learn the right sensations.

Only when the seat is quiet and balanced, and all conflicting messages have been removed, can the horse allow himself to be brought into a state of balance where he is ready and willing to listen to the aids. For make no mistake, good riding is about reinstating the horse's independent balance and there is no quick fix. The horse will come gradually to the aids as a result of his own prowess, through the guidelines we lay down and the exercises we introduce.

Every horse will approach this work in a slightly different way and timescale. For some horses, certain exercises will be comparatively easy; others more difficult. With a different horse, the converse may be true. Until we start, we have little idea of what to expect.

What we can expect, however, is that once the groundwork has been laid in an inviting format and the exercises can be achieved without resistance, the appearance of the horse will change and improve. Gradually he will be

(Opposite) A square halt is often easier to achieve out on a hack. Always stop once or twice on a ride and your horse will soon get the idea.

endowed with more muscling over his topline so that the crest, back, loins and quarters will begin to look more rounded. The belly will be well toned and will not sag. The withers, shoulder and chest will seem to flow into each other with an appearance of padding under a rippling skin. The whole horse will look more compact, impressive and generally athletic.

Since all this goes hand in hand with balance and ease of movement, the horse should become happier. He will take pride in his work and every movement will seem fluid and natural. There will be impulsion and rhythm; forwardness and suspension; strength and lightness; energy and calmness; control and freedom. All these qualities denote a horse who is on the aids, but for beauty to emerge, it must all look as though it was the horse's idea in the first place.

But here lies the rub... the use of the aids must be minimal. The horse will need to be educated to hear them, but if they are applied in a crude or obvious way, he is more than likely to resist them. How many riders do we see pushing and pushing with the seat, while the horse gets slower and slower? The truth is, there should be no pushing; it is much more a case of lightening and allowing and receiving – but it takes patience to develop the feel which enables us to know when and how to do this.

PART THREE
The Work Proper – Basic Level

CHAPTER V
Bending and Suppling Exercises – Clarifying the Circle

CHAPTER VI
Confirming the Canter

CHAPTER V

Bending and Supplying Exercises
Clarifying the Circle

This foal has naturally inflexed his head; but to balance under our weight, the adult horse will need to bend through the body.

The time has come to progress to the exercises which will change the shape and ability of our horse under saddle for ever. As we start each new movement, even the simple circle, it is better to use the rising trot. Later, of course, they will be ridden in sitting trot, but only when the horse is able to accept the change without losing rhythm or freedom through the back. Since few people ride the sitting trot well enough to enhance the movement in those early days, it is better to play safe and rise.

Another factor which will benefit from rising trot, will be the control of the rider's weight from one side to the other. Too many riders slide to the outside of the saddle in a circle ridden in sitting trot; this overloads the outside seatbone and pulls the horse out of the bend. As discussed earlier, it is the inside seatbone which requires to be a little more loaded, particularly on smaller circles. Be aware of slightly advancing the inside hipbone as you turn, just as you would if walking a circle on the ground – it's worth practising this to get the feeling.

Eventually, the correct alignment of hips and seatbones should take place naturally, provided you sit up erect and square. To start with, however, it may require some thought and concentration. The advanced position of your seatbone clearly complements the support of the

inside leg at the girth; it also frees pressure from the back of the saddle. Once bodyweight flows down naturally *into* the stirrups, the horse has a better chance of moving into the bend.

At this stage another factor comes into play. It is a well-known fact that only light legs will create light horses. The very nature of rising to the trot stops the rider clamping on too much with the leg and interrupting the flow. By keeping the hip-to-heel alignment, the rider can use gravity to balance and remain light on the horse's back.

In the moment of sitting, the rider should use this first phase to close the leg, and ask for forwardness with roundness. In the second phase, the leg stretches down for the rider to push off from the ball of the foot in the stirrup whilst keeping the heels lowered. It is in the moment of rising that the horse is released, almost as though he is rising up and forward with the rider. In this way, we provide a clear pathway for the horse's energy to stream *through*.

Riding off the correct diagonal is important, although it is a good idea sometimes to change the diagonals without changing the rein, particularly when working the horse's more hollow side. This will help strengthen the weaker

Circling right

(Above) Riding a good circle is all to do with remaining in balance with your horse. Sit up and look between your horse's ears to remain in alignment. Here Jodie demonstrates an exemplary position allowing Thomas to bend naturally around her deepened and supportive inside leg.

(Right) Too many riders try to steer the horse around the circle with their hands. Pulling back on the inside rein generally causes the upper body to twist with the weight sliding outward and away from the direction of the movement. Both horse and rider will lose balance.

hind leg which is less able to step under and engage. In changing diagonals, make sure that your horse remains in the same rhythm.

It should go without saying that it is essential to change the rein several times in periods of trot. You can either sit through the centre line or as the horse approaches the new track. The vast majority of people (myself included) still tend far too much to stick on a favourite rein and thereby the same diagonal. It takes real concentration to work your (and your horse's) less favoured side.

The Value of Circle Work

Most people recognise one-sidedness, but too often seem confused as to how to correct it. In Chapter IX, we will be tackling this issue in greater depth but the simplest way forward in the early stages of training is to combine straight work with big half-circles and circles with *constant* changes of rein. Not only will these simple exercises encourage the horse to push more from the hind legs, but generally they will smooth out any resistances in his body

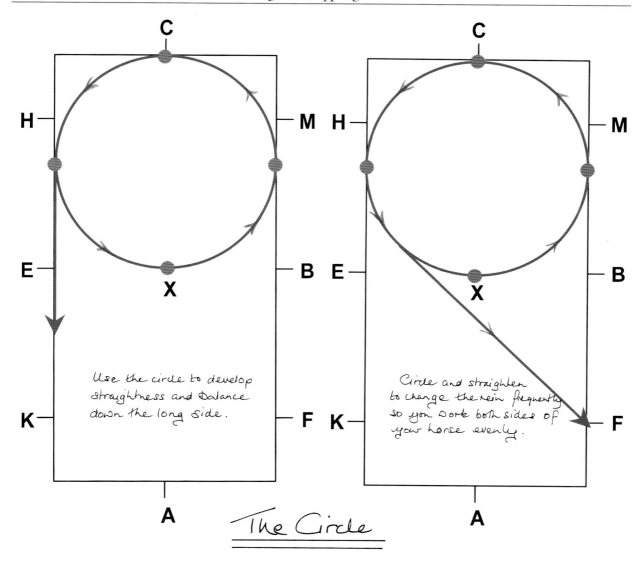

Use the circle to develop straightness and balance down the long side.

Circle and straighten to change the rein frequently so you work both sides of your horse evenly.

The Circle

Unless stated, arenas shown will represent the 20 x 40 metre size. Where movements are only shown on one rein, this is for purposes of clarity; naturally, all movements should be ridden equally on both reins.

as he learns to bend and stretch on both reins. Provided that the rider understands that the entire body of the horse must mirror and comply with the arc of each figure, the horse will learn to accept the influence of each rein in their different roles. For this reason it is important not to ride circle after circle; instead, after just a couple initially, ride straight forward and onto the track again to reaffirm an even contact and to make sure the horse is straight. Should further difficulties occur, the young horse should be brought back to work on the long rein, encouraged to lower his head and stretch through the neck whilst still maintaining impulsion behind.

Time spent consolidating this basic circle and straightening work is time well spent. If these basics are not established correctly, the higher, more complicated work will be fraught with difficulties. We must never forget that from day one in our schooling, the object is not so much to ride beautiful figures, but to allow the figures to make a beautiful horse. In other words, whatever the horse, his gaits, balance,

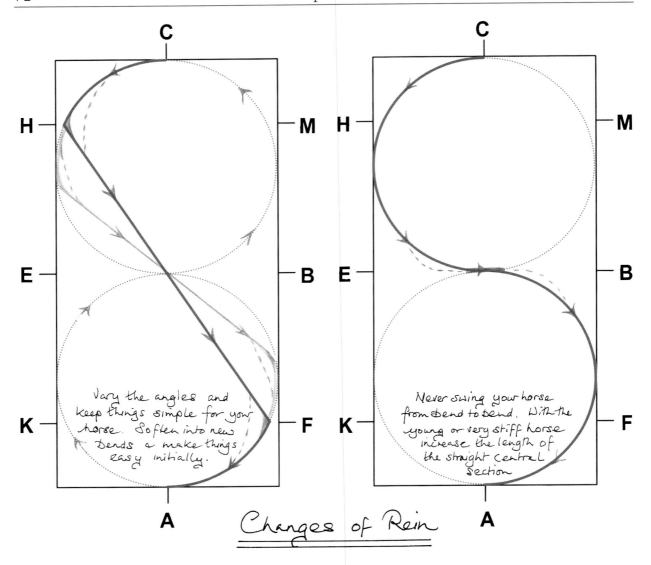

C   C

H — — M   H — — M

E — — B   E — — B

K — — F   K — — F

A   A

Vary the angles and keep things simple for your horse. Soften into new bends & make things easy initially.

Never swing your horse from bend to bend. With the young or very stiff horse increase the length of the straight central section

Changes of Rein

power and fluidity of movement should be purified and enhanced.

Twenty Metre Circles

When one starts this work, it is important to keep the circles big initially. The 20 m circle is ideal for the young or novice horse, the older, stiff horse or simply as a warm-up for the advanced horse before he starts the more demanding athletic work. The generous size of the circle encourages the horse to think forward and outward – once you have moved off the track, never think of riding your circle inward! If working in an enclosed arena, give the horse a sense of security by starting off circles at the A or C end of the school.

Once these are established and the horse feels 'safe' in the circle you can graduate to making your circles at E or at B. Be sure that the circle remains a circle however, and the horse does not hug the walls of the school. The rider should think of just touching the track or centre line at each of the four 'points' of the circle (see diagram).

Changing the Rein

- Initially, changes of rein should be long, simple and straight (see Chapter I).
- Gradually introduce half figures-of-eight joined together through a long diagonal line

The horse must be straight through the diagonal part but encouraged to look into the new bend well before he approaches the corner.

- Later, half figures-of-eight may be ridden more together in the form of two half-circles with a short straight section of 3–5 strides in between. Don't attempt these too early, since the horse will need more balance and time to adjust for the new bend.

- The three-loop serpentine (progressing to five in a larger arena) is also excellent as a suppling exercise and to change the rein throughout.

Balance through the Exercises

At this stage, the novice horse may not yet be sufficiently balanced to take an even contact on the circle. It is therefore up to the rider to allow him to place his head wherever it is most comfortable for him to carry out the work without either creating a resistance or – just as bad – feeling as though there is nothing at all in your hands. Even in the most highly schooled horses you must *feel* the contact – even if is no more than an ounce!

Initially, many green or naturally croup-high horses find it easier to carry their heads a little low. This is in order provided that the neck remains stretched and they do not lean, or drop the contact. When the neck is shortened and the nose tucks back into the horse's chest to avoid contact, the horse is said to be behind the bit. This should be discouraged by sitting up, using more leg and possibly adopting a higher hand position.

Generally, the rider should be looking to keep the horse's nose just in front of the vertical, aided by the inside leg. Once the longissimus dorsi muscles have been well stretched, toning and rounding should follow. Too much insistence on position may tense the gullet muscles under the neck so that the horse supports his head from *below* instead of above, which is most undesirable. If the rider finds the horse unwilling to keep his head in front of the

vertical, it could indicate that forward impulsion and confidence in the bit have been lost and it may be necessary to resume work on the lunge in order to establish a willingness to travel forward towards the contact again.

A Two-way Exercise

It is now time to become more aware of what happens to the horse as we ride our circles. In Chapter I, we discussed how the horse cannot 'bend' without the outside of his body having to stretch laterally, in this case away from the influence of our outside leg. This actually brings about a lateral lengthening to the outside, whilst a corresponding shortening occurs to the inside. To understand this better, we might be wise to consider in simple terms the way in which muscles are made up and how they always work in antagonistic pairs. Therefore in flexing our arm, for example, the biceps shortens as the triceps lengthens. It is a firm rule of Nature, that without stretch, bend simply cannot occur.

Consequently, with the horse, muscles work in the same way. Riders should be aware that when they ask the horse to flex to the inside, *they must lengthen and stretch the outside of the frame to accommodate and make possible the bend to the inside.*

For this reason, the influence of the rider's outside leg aid is as important as the inside, but too few people use it appropriately. They tend to concentrate on the inside leg only for bend, forgetting that without encouragement from the outside, all their efforts could be wasted. No single aid will be of value unless the corresponding aid is also applied. In most cases the two leg aids are applied in quite different ways to cope with two different functions. On the circle:

- think of your inside leg supporting and stimulating the forehand
- use your outside leg to bring the horse round and to activate the haunches.

Bending and stretching

(*Above*) *Riders often forget that correct bending to the inside of a circle involves a subsequent lowering and engagement of the horse's inside hip, stifle, hock and fetlock as he takes more weight behind. This will depend upon...*

(*Right*) *...equal stretching and lengthening to the outside. Thus the rider's outside aids are just as important as the inside aids on a circle.*

Upper Body Position on the Circle

Before we go through the individual aids, try to align the entire trunk with the horse by looking through his ears as he moves into the circle. It's also a good idea to line up the zip of your breeches and jacket with the wither. At no time on the circle, even as it decreases in size, should your zip be looking anywhere other than at those withers! This will ensure that each seatbone remains firmly on the correct side of the saddle.

An accurate circle is not nearly as easy as most people think, since most riders start to turn before the horse has turned and this throws out conflicting aids. It's important to initiate turning through the *horse's* body so that he is brought to you! This is mainly done by:

- opening gently with the inside rein
- advancing the inside hip
- sitting into the inside seatbone and with the outside hip back
- allowing the outside leg to act with sideways pressure a hand's breadth behind the girth.

This brings the horse into the circle and around your inside leg. Once there, you may think of riding a little inside leg to outside hand, keeping the inside rein soft.

Here Andrea's inside leg acts as a pillar for right bend, but by tilting through the waist she has pushed the novice Milo off balance through his hollow side so he bulges out through his left shoulder.

For this reason, the rider must not drop a shoulder or lean in. On the contrary, the correct balance is achieved by sitting erect and merely allowing the inside knee to drop down and remain deep. Again, think of your inside leg as a pillar of support for the horse, but be careful to keep the hip-heel alignment. With the inside stirrup a little more weighted in this way, the horse not only wants to move into that direction but is also encouraged to *bend* around it.

Even Contact

In so doing, we should feel an equal degree of stretch to the outside whether on a right or left circle. However, since most horses have a hollow or stiff side, this is rarely the case. Nevertheless, establishing contact should never involve shortening or pulling on the rein; instead it's about evening up muscle tone in the horse's body. Unevenness can be corrected as follows:

- When the horse's concave side is on the outside of the circle, he avoids taking contact on the outside rein. To encourage greater lateral lengthening to the outside, our *outside leg* should act in a *smoothing forward* way from behind the girth. By creating more stretch therefore, the horse is gradually made to uncoil the shortened muscles on his concave side until he himself fills the rein that he previously avoided.

- The same horse will have found it difficult to bend into the circle, being known as 'stiff to the inside'. Physiologically, this problem is another aspect of the above, but a light, asking inside rein should entice more bend coupled with insistent, but *light taps* from the *inside* leg to the outside hand.

Alternatively:

- When the horse's hollow side is to the inside, the horse generally feels heavier on the outside rein, and somewhat wooden through his body. Stroking the neck and giving a little more with the outside rein will help soften the thoracic and neck muscles

Be very subtle! You will need to check constantly that the hands remain as a pair, since it can be tempting to pull back on the inside rein. This is exacerbated if there is too much turning with the upper body. Although you must remain as part of the horse and allow the shoulders to turn with him, be careful that your seatbones do not lose position. You would be amazed how many people allow their inside hip to slip back in sympathy with the inside shoulder, so the whole seat drifts sideways.

which need to yield; use firm presses with the outside knee and thigh to discourage bulging into the outside shoulder.

- Do not overaid the inside hollow side too much. The active support of the outside leg should encourage a softer contact with the inside rein, but try to maintain a fairly passive inside leg position.

Clearly, the circle works both sides of the horse, but it is all too easy to stick to a favourite rein – which often accounts for the above difficulties. *This is where the serpentine is such a useful exercise since it works both sides of the horse's body.*

More on the Serpentine

Start this exercise more as a zigzag, with diagonal approaches to the loops onto and away from the long sides of the school, but ride at least three strides along the wall with bend to the inside, before zigzagging back onto the new diagonal.

Gradually straighten your serpentine up through the middle and think of each loop as being well rounded at each extremity. Here again, thinking a little inside leg to outside hand is helpful. Straightening through the middle is most important, before moving into the next bend and the next rounded loop.

When you ride onto the track, you may again need a little more encouragement from the inside leg to the outside hand. However, when you ride away from the track, think of more outside leg. This will prepare the horse for pushing off more on his hocks as he leaves the arena wall. In both phases of the serpentine, the inside leg must always support the forehand with the weight well down into the inside seatbone and stirrup.

The serpentine also offers an excellent opportunity to introduce the trot to walk and walk to trot transitions on a more regular basis. Try riding half the middle loop in walk, after crossing the centre line. Later reduce this to just two or three strides down the long side in

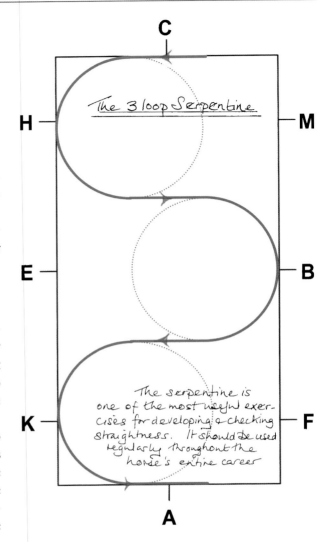

The 3 loop Serpentine

The serpentine is one of the most useful exercises for developing a checking straightness. It should be used regularly throughout the horse's entire career

the middle of the movement (see diagram). Always make sure the horse trots 'off the leg' again after these transitions.

The Combined Effects of the Rein

It should soon become self-evident that greater success is gained when we think of the reins merely framing the horse rather than steering him through these exercises. Imagine bringing the wall to the horse when you turn off it, rather than the horse off the wall. In this way we develop a more skilful use of the legs and body, which should now do the major work when it comes to directional aids – whether going straight, round or making a change of rein.

Here, Milo stretches gratefully into an inviting outside rein encouraged by Andrea's supportive leg aids. Since she now sits erect, we see that her waistcoat buttons line up nicely with the horse's withers!

It is now time to be more aware of the role of the outside rein, always backed up by the outside leg for greater precision. The downward transitions will always require a little more feeling on the outside rein on a bend or circle if the horse is to remain in balance. However, even on straight lines, the contact of the outside rein and aiding of the outside leg are as important as the inside to ensuring forward progression. Too much preoccupation with the inside aids may allow the hind legs to stray out. A wiggly horse is often simply avoiding working through from behind.

As in our own bodies, everything in the horse's biomechanical make-up is connected to something else. What happens in the equine neck has an overriding effect on the rest of the horse's spine and so on and so forth. We have already discussed how too much inside hand will pull the horse's neck out of alignment with the rest of his body. How many riders actually realise that this will discourage the horse from actively engaging? Consider the following scenario, where horse and rider are moving normally up the track, but the rider wants to circle away to the inside:

- rider pulls back on the inside rein
- the outside rein slides correspondingly forward
- the horse obliges by bringing his neck and head more to the inside of the school, but he begins to slide outwards through the outside shoulder
- the outside hind steps out in sympathy
- the horse is no longer 'connected' behind and thus engagement is lost as he moves onto the circle.

However, once the outside rein is maintained with gentle traction and the inside hand allows forward so that the two hands remain as a pair, the horse will straighten up. The rider now has the chance to circle away from the track correctly – with the horse soft to the inside, but engaged and pushing from behind. If the reins are the correct length, it requires little more than a feel with the fingers on the inside, opening rein to lead the horse into the circle. You should just be able to see the glimmer of his eye and the outer edge of the nostril – no more. The inside hand action should still be more *forward* than backward but, at this stage, we should no longer have to bring the hand so much away from the neck if the work discussed in Chapter III has been understood.

'Out' to the Circle – However Small

Once the turn is instigated, the rider should feel that the outside hand maintains the horse on the circle. The horse yields to the weight aid of the inside leg and inside seatbone, by bending, but the idea is for him to stretch to the outside so he fans out and maintains the circumference.

Since it is all too easy for him to fall *in* towards the centre, the outside hand must act by gentle restraint, telling the horse just how much he may bend, and checking that he does not depart from the figure he is making. It is therefore the combined effect of all these aids which is so important in riding circles; the inside hand has less part to play than is generally imagined.

Once the horse is making good 20 m circles, the rider may want to start spiralling-in, gradually attempting 15 m circles and later 12 or 10 m. This spiralling is a very good way of testing the efficacy of the outside leg and hand aids. The horse should move in and away from the influence of the outside rein and outside leg readily and easily.

Whatever the size of the circle, it is important that the channel made by the rider's aids retains the arc of the circle for the horse to remain bending but forward-thinking, so that his energy really continues to travel *through* from quarters to forehand. As with the straight line, there must be no false openings through which his energy can dissipate. The rider will only take charge of the horse's energy when he or she realises that no hand aid should be made in total isolation, since everything has an effect on everything else.

Circling Right – Correct ✓

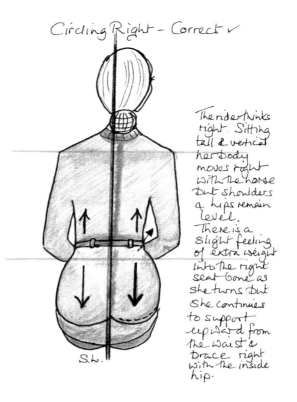

S.h.

The rider thinks right. Sitting tall & vertical her body moves right with the horse but shoulders & hips remain level.
There is a slight feeling of extra weight into the right seat bone as she turns but she continues to support upward from the waist & brace right with the inside hip.

Circling Right – Incorrect ✗

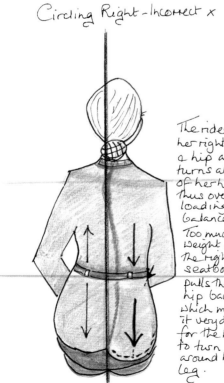

The rider drops her right shoulder & hip as she turns ahead of her horse, thus over-loading the balance right.
Too much weight into the right seat bone pulls the inside hip backward which makes it very difficult for the horse to turn around her leg.

Circling Right – Incorrect ✗

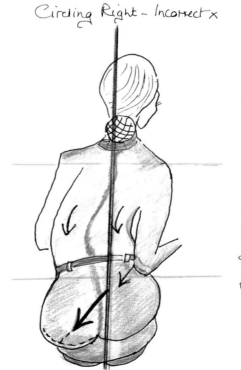

The rider twists right which throws her weight left. With the right side of her waist collapsed, her aids are rendered ineffectual and she loses position with her shoulder and hip alignment. Such a position is damaging to the spine

What We Mean by 'Riding through a Channel'

In our minds we must have a clearly defined route to follow – the channel idea is nothing new, but too often is not sufficiently explained. First think of a channel of energy moving up from the quarters, through the horse's back to your hands. Now think of how you can influence it. This can only be done if you can keep it all flowing forward in one continuous stream. For this you need the framing effect of:

- the thighs, knees and lower legs
- the two seatbones
- the two sides of the rider's upper body
- and finally the two reins.

All these component parts combine to maintain the width and direction of our imaginary channel. Now think of threading your horse through the channel, being careful not to let energy spill out on the way. While the horse is moving straight ahead all should be relatively easy, since it is not too difficult to ride through a channel where everything is forward-facing.

However, even with the best intentions in the world, it is much more difficult to ride a circle, especially a smaller one, without allowing part of the channel to disintegrate. Any opening made to one side must be carefully matched with a corresponding adjustment to the other side if the energy of the horse is not to leach inward or outward.

Many riders find it helpful to keep the hands low and to bridge the reins at this stage. *One should never underestimate the stabilising effect of each rein lying against each side of the horse's neck.* Such a situation not only helps to improve rider position by centralising the hands (which in turn helps to centre the body) it also does much to spare the horse's mouth.

We all know that the horse needs to bend from nose to tail to follow the arc of any circle. The smaller circle requires more bending and more impulsion (not speed); the larger circle less.

Different Effects

Quite apart from the falling outward of the *horse's* body when too much inside rein is used, we should recognise that the *rider's* body tends to do the same. All of us who drive a car cannot have failed to notice how, when moving the steering wheel to right or to left, the body veers in sympathy and all sense of squareness is lost. Through a chain of mechanical reactions throughout the body, hand and arm movements can ultimately change the position of the pelvis from moment to moment.

It is the same on horseback, and when the rider pulls back on the right rein to turn right, the body twists and the horse is pushed left! With all sense of centring lost, the direction of the channel is now changed. Things can become very difficult for the horse when what was intended as an opening right is effectively blocked and closed off.

What normally happens next is that the horse compromises his natural movement to try to comply with both commands. Thus, he turns his head and neck into the right-pulling rein, but allows his body to drift left. In the circle, this tends to result in a bulging out through the left shoulder, which may cause the hind legs to move onto a different arc or track from the forelegs. It results in a twisting of the horse's body which mirrors the twisting in the rider. It is not a comfortable position for the horse. The sad part is that, all too often, when the rider no longer feels the horse connected or tracking up on the circle, this is construed as the horse's fault. To correct the imbalance, the rider then resorts to harsher legs and harsher hands in an attempt to rectify the situation.

However, nothing can be radically corrected until the channel provided by the aids is restored to a semblance of unity. Until the rider improves, problems for the horse tend to multiply. No wonder so many people now employ gadgets and spurs for their 'difficult' horses. Unfortunately, the difficulty lies with them and their inability to understand the theory behind the aiding process.

ON THE CIRCLE
Ride your horse through an imaginary
channel. Feel the outside posts keep
you turning; let the inside posts
support you & allow the
energy to flow through ....

Moving in Without Falling In

So how do we progress to smaller circles and tighter turns without this overuse of the inside rein?

- Stay focused and think of bringing the wall in – this will give your outside leg and body the right sensations.
- Allow your outside rein to guide the circle from the outside inward.
- You may invite – but more importantly – make room for the horse through your inside hand and inside leg.

In this way, the flow will remain.

Since circles are the logical start to all figure work, we have had to be very strict with ourselves to understand the principles involved. In all this time, however, we must never forget that the horse has his balance to keep too, so we need to get it right. Let us now consider what he is feeling in the circle work.

THE HORSES'S THOUGHTS (under the now-educated rider)

- My rider has just invited me to turn off the track, asking on the inside rein and through her weight. There is a sensation of pressure into her inside stirrup, so I begin to yield my body in that direction, assisted by her outside leg.

- To balance, I have to bring my inside hind leg more underneath me, but luckily she keeps her inside seatbone well forward, so there is room to engage! In fact she seems to be sitting nice and tall and light.

- As I turn, I feel the outside rein telling me how far I can go, which is just as well as I might have turned completely around! It seems we are to go on a circle... so I comply.

- Her inside leg remains deep, but now it also gives me small nudges at the girth which keeps me in contact with the outside rein.

- As we progress round, I try my best to give her the bend she requires, but it is comforting to know that my outside rein will tell me just how much that should be!

- To work more easily I know I have to stretch my body to the outside, otherwise I would not be able to bend! Sometimes this is difficult... Ah! now it's easier, as she releases that tight feeling in her outside hip by drawing her thigh back. At last, I feel I can unlock my back and really stretch forward through the outside of my body.

- Excellent! There is more encouragement and support from her lower outside leg too, so I feel motivated to drive forward more and really work through this circle.

- As I make more effort behind, I could do with a little more room to manoeuvre; now she shows she is really listening to me – she has momentarily eased the outside rein too, so we can really make a nice, forward and rounded circle!

Multiple Benefits

As can be seen, it takes time, preparation and mental effort to ride circles correctly, but if the rider can tune into what the horse is feeling at all times, he will soon grow in confidence and suppleness as he works from one circle to another.

The beauty of circle work is that it *enhances the straight work*. No horse can be made straight without plenty of gentle bending work – but don't go for overkill. The rider must take care to keep the horse impulsive and in the same rhythm on and off the circle, neither too fast nor too slow.

The circle is a wonderful movement for developing good tempo and allowing the horse to find the rhythm in which he feels most comfortable. Most riders tend to hurry their horses round and this is a grave mistake, since it leads to the horse rushing, tensing and losing bend.

Once the horse becomes familiar with circle work, he will soon find it *easier to accept the bit on both reins and to carry his head and neck in a better balance*. It is the exercises which will lead to a correct outline through self-carriage becoming established, never, ever the other way round.

Circle exercises, especially those that incorporate transitions, encourage the horse to *use more power behind*, since they require that the inside hind leg steps further under to balance the horse by taking more weight. Decreasing the size of the circle does not require more hand, but simply requires that the rider brings everything round together a little earlier in the turning process. Remember to keep the *whole channel* turning.

If you listen to your horse, he will dictate when he is ready to progress to smaller circles. A rough guide would be 20 m in the first three months of serious schooling (irrespective of the age of the horse), progressing gradually to 15 m in the next three months and later 12 m circles. (10 m circles should not be established at this stage, although 10 m half-circles in walk are a

In the smaller circle, Lesley's right rein encourages a greater degree of left bend from Palomo, as does the close application of her outside knee and thigh which support his forehand.

good exercise).

Obviously, it is better by far to establish regular forward-going large circles in a steady rhythm, than to hurry round smaller ones. The horse should feel equally easy on both reins. If there is the feeling that the horse is falling away from you to the inside, which would indicate 'motorbiking', then clearly the horse is not yet sufficiently supple. In such an event, always return to the bigger circle and wait.

Every horse is different, but no matter how one-sided yours is at first, always intersperse your circles with numerous changes of rein, some transitions and plenty of straight work. In this way, you will be working on *all the muscle systems within your horse's body* and are well on the way to establishing a thorough grounding for your dressage.

CHAPTER VI
Confirming the Canter

Balance in canter requires freedom in the back and neck.

Once the horse is confident in his 20 m and 15 m circles in trot, it is time to think about using part of that circle to improve the canter. Until this point, I generally tell my students to save their canter work for outside the school, to be conducted in open spaces and mainly on straight lines whilst hacking out. There is nothing more detrimental to the horse's confidence and balance than to be cantered round and round an arena before he is able to engage a little behind and to comply with the ground rules of the manège such as:

- staying out to the track
- bending sufficiently through the corners not to fall in
- responding with a degree of understanding to the all-important channelling aids of the rider's legs, bodyweight and reins.

The idea of directing the energy of the horse from back to front and through the horse in canter is both essential and attainable, but it takes time. Unfortunately, most young horses feel threatened by the rider's weight, and if they are not sufficiently strong through the back to elevate as in Nature, they will tend to fall onto the forehand. This leads to loss of lateral balance as well.

It is for this reason that a horse who may look nicely 'together' and harmonious in trot can suddenly deteriorate before one's eyes when his rider puts him into canter. Suddenly, the balance goes awry as horse and rider veer recklessly inward on a corner, with the combination more reminiscent of a motorbike than a nicely controlled horse apportioning weight to all four feet!

But why is the canter so difficult to maintain compared to the trot, and why is it so important to maintain a light seat to help the horse initially? Let us look at the nature of the canter before we consider how best to ride it.

The Canter

The canter is a gait of three-time, which consists of a series of jumps or bounds. Unlike the even, tick-tock rhythm of trot, where both sides of the horse work in a symmetric two-time movement and two legs are always grounded at the same time and lend support, the canter depends much more upon freedom through the back to balance.

The canter is made up of three phases, with two separate footfalls or beats and one co-joined beat. Before the whole sequence starts again, there will be a moment of suspension in the air. In canter right, the sequence of beats should be:

84

Balancing the canter

(Above) With the very young horse, the first canter will generally feel 'downhill' and rushing. Don't fight against the movement or restrict the horse's neck; simply take your own centre of gravity forward to balance, use the stirrups and keep the elbows bent and elastic.

(Left) With the mature horse who is simply rather strong in the hand (Milo after one year out of hunting), a checking influence can be obtained by bridging the reins and firming up rider position. Here, Allegra capitalises on the hip/heel alignment by weighting the stirrups. Leaning back would inevitably cause this headstrong horse to flatten and pull away.

- left hind to push off and commence the gait;
- left fore and right hind touch down together;
- ultimately followed by the right fore, which is known as the leading leg.

The moment of suspension, when all four feet will be in the air, will occur before the first stride of the next sequence, the engaging left hind. It is this phase in particular which can make things quite tricky for the young horse with an unaccustomed weight on his back.

It is often said that cantering is much akin to skipping in the human, in that the horse feels as though he is leading not just with one foreleg, but also with the same side of his body throughout. In other words, there is a slight sideways feel about it. When we ourselves skip to the right for instance, the feel is similar, and whilst our opposite left leg does the pushing off, our right leg and the entire right side of our body leads us into the movement.

Most animals, particularly the family dog, favour one way of travelling; it simply feels easier for them in one particular direction – and we ourselves are no exception. The difficulty for horses is that, despite our own inconsistencies, we expect them to canter with an equal sense of ease and balance in either direction. Such a requirement generally poses problems; particularly if the rider does not have the knowledge to help the horse.

When there is tension or a lack of impulsion, the canter can become irregular and go to four-time. Instead of three clear beats, therefore, the beat of the diagonal pair would be split. This is not generally an insurmountable problem to solve once the horse is better balanced and the rider learns to ride forward with the correct leg and bodyweight aids.

Much more worrying is when the canter starts off correctly and then a change occurs at a particular point and it becomes disunited. This generally happens around corners or on the circle when the horse changes behind. If allowed to become a habit, it can become very difficult to correct but first we must understand why it happens. A disunited canter generally results from:

- An imbalance in the muscle systems, that is a weakness associated with one-sidedness.
- Extreme stiffness over the back or through the ribcage – generally the result of the above.
- Stiffness or weakness in one hock (often the right), preventing sufficient engagement with the required inside hind.
- Incorrect aiding from the rider, which may exacerbate the above.

(We sometimes see a disunited canter in more advanced training when the rider asks for a flying change and the horse changes correctly in front, but does not change behind; rushed or inconsistent training in the early days is often the cause.)

It is therefore important that, if the young or novice horse shows any inclination to go disunited, we take a few steps back in our programme of schooling to improve general suppleness. Further work in bends and circles at walk and trot may be necessary before trying to canter round the whole school. So whilst it is easier to make the upward and downward

transitions correctly on a bend, most of our canter work should be on long, straight lines in the initial stages.

Setting the horse up for canter in a corner will generally ensure a correct strike-off. If this fails in the first corner, we simply ride forward to the next one and ask again. At no time should we allow the horse to rush into the canter strike-off. If the trot becomes faster and faster, it should be slowed down and the process started again.

Once cantering from the corner is accepted and understood, try picking up canter from a trot circle and then go large. A whole circle in a balanced canter if often too much to expect of a very green or stiff horse – although unfortunately people expect this all the time. No wonder so many canter problems become worse rather than better.

Thus on a 20 m circle ridden from A on the right rein:

- Ask for the canter transition only *after* crossing the centre line.
- If all goes well and canter is established, complete the circle, then canter large down the long side of the school.
- Take care not to ride too deep through the next corner.
- With the very novice horse, make a transition to trot before or on reaching C.
- However, if the horse is happy and balanced, continue past C and use another big circle to return to trot.

It is always prudent to ask for the downward transition when things are going well, rather than waiting until balance is lost. Going disunited is most likely to happen on a tight turn where the horse feels threatened, so be aware. It is far better to pre-empt something before it happens rather to have to correct it after it happens.

Every horse knows how to canter, but most faults are undoubtedly caused by rider errors. Hurrying the horse out of the moment of suspension is a common fault. Collapsing the

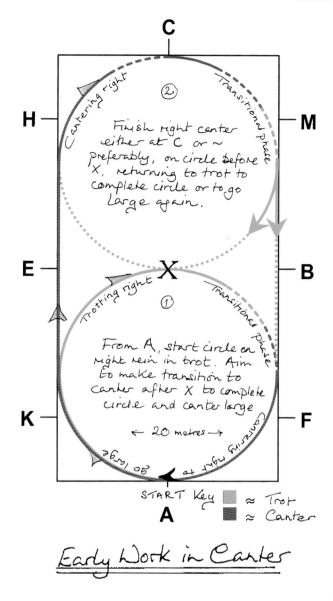

C

H — M

E — X — B

K — F

② Finish right canter either at C or ~ preferably, on circle before X, returning to trot to complete circle or to go large again.

Cantering right

Transitional phase

Trotting right

① From A, start circle on right rein in trot. Aim to make transition to canter after X to complete circle and canter large

Transitional Phase

← 20 metres →

Cantering right at first

START Key ▨ ≈ Trot ▨ ≈ Canter

A

Early Work in Canter

able understanding of where our own weight should be.

When returning to trot, do not be surprised if the horse slightly drops into the transition initially. This is to be expected if the back is weak and the hind legs are not yet sufficiently under the horse to buoy him up in the downward transition. To help this become easier, the rider should never think 'down into trot' but always 'up into trot'. Good upper body posture is generally enough to achieve this; merely jerking on the reins to slow down will do little to encourage the horse to work forward and *through* into his transitions.

Try, therefore, to allow the horse to find his own balance as much as possible. Too much dependence on the rein will put him on the forehand and this will mar the development of strength behind the saddle as well as shortening the strides. Ultimately, we want more engagement of the hind legs to take the horse through his transitions, whether up or down. When the horse makes an obedient transition to canter and back to trot on a softer rein, no matter how 'ragged' it may have felt, praise lavishly and allow him to stretch down on a long rein before trying again. Canter work must be done in a calm atmosphere. If the horse gets over-excited, do something else for a while.

Remember that sustaining the canter within the confines of the school for too long may threaten a young or unfit horse and cause confidence to be lost. It is better by far to build up the work through relatively short bursts of canter or work over poles, realising that the transitions are far more important than the length of time spent in the gait.

As we have seen, every horse can canter, but the canter will not become brilliant until the transitions become easy and effortless. For this reason it is now important to see how we can improve the way in which we ask a horse to make the canter depart.

Why from a Circle?
By now, the rider may be wondering why we

body, so that the horse falls on the forehand, is another. We must remember that the greater the speed of the gait, the more important it is that we riders complement the balance of the horse. At this stage, too much demand on bend and outline can also be counter-productive.

Most people have a tendency to pull back on the inside rein, which may disengage the quarters and this is the very last thing which the horse needs. Therefore, our main priority with the young horse is to allow him to canter freely forward and to interfere as little as possible, other than supporting him with a knowledge-

Encouraging engagement

(Left) *After a few weeks, cantering over poles will help the horse to bascule, engage his hind legs and elevate the shoulders. Do not restrict with the rein, but keep balance by maintaining tone through the upper body as you ride forward into an elastic contact and look between the horse's ears.*

(Above) *The work over poles has brought the canter more together. There are now early signs of future spring and balance. If we are to allow all this to develop and come through (see p.96) it is important still to keep the seat light and the legs asking. Taking time in the early stages always pays off...*

should even consider making the upward transition from a trot circle, having already stated that bending and cantering at the same time can be difficult for the stiff or unbalanced horse. The reason is this. The trot circle prepares the horse for the canter depart by encouraging the inside hind leg to step a little more underneath the horse. This will help the horse to carry himself in a better balance when he goes to canter.

If the inside hind leg is unable to step under in this way, the canter depart will be much more difficult, as the horse will feel unsupported to the inside. He may therefore try to run on in trot and be unwilling even to try to canter. The engagement of the inside hind is there-

fore vital for a confident, balanced canter depart but it may be difficult for the horse to sustain this engagement into the next corner – hence the reason for an early downward transition before things go wrong.

Now let us see how our weight, leg and hand aids can help our horse so that soon he will be able to offer canter easily on both reins, and can sustain the feeling of bend through his body all the way round the school.

Diagonal Aids

The aids for canter in the classical school are generally known as diagonal aids. This involves an asking with the inside rein and leg for bend, whilst the rider's outside leg activates the outside hind leg and causes it to start the first canter stride. The outside leg also helps to align the quarters correctly. Once the horse softens the length of his body to the inside, he can push more from behind.

The slight feeling of advancement with the inside shoulder and inside hind in canter can be checked out if we study the hoofprints of the horse in the sand. In normal canter down the long side of the school, it will be plainly seen that the inside set of prints will be in advance of those made by the outside hooves.

Problem Areas

In riding we try to mirror-image what we wish from the horse in order to complement his balance; clearly it will be counter-productive to pull our own bodies out of alignment with his and yet this happens time and again in canter. Problems are mainly caused by the rider hanging on with the inside rein, which has a snowballing effect on the whole combination. Too much inside hand:

- blocks the horse's advancing inside shoulder and leading leg
- causes the rider's inside shoulder to slide back so that a twist to the inside occurs in the upper body
- as a result, the rider's outside shoulder slips forward taking with it –
- the outside hand – which loses its regulating effect on the degree of bend
- the rider's inside hip turns back and no longer supports the inside leg
- weight transfers to the rider's outside seatbone
- the rider's balance is now in direct opposition to the horse so harmony is lost.

It is therefore not at all surprising that so many horses have difficulties in canter when they first start work in an arena.

For this reason, the giving of the diagonal aids must never, ever, involve a pulling round of the horse's head or a twisting of the rider's body to the inside. The hand merely softens or opens gently with the inside rein so that the horse can move into it; the outside hand plays a more passive, supporting role to regulate the bend.

After that the rider must concentrate on keeping the seat as forward to the pommel as possible to complement the way in which the horse is moving. This will involve sitting with the inside (leading) seatbone a little more forward than the outside, to encourage the horse to engage through the inside hind. If the inside hip were to slip back, as it does with so many riders who are unaware of these matters, it can create a disturbing pressure towards the back of the saddle which may block the oncoming inside hind leg. Deepening the inside seatbone forward by taking more weight into the inside stirrup not only supports the forehand and encourages the correct lead, it also frees the fragile back just where it is needed.

The other important player in the application of diagonal aids is the outside leg. This is placed a few inches behind the girth, but the horse must feel the entire leg stretching back to aid and empower the outside hind. This simple action frees the joint, allowing the rider's outside hip to take a position a little behind that of the opposite, inside, hip. Without the rider giving conscious thought to it, this will automatically facilitate the canter depart. Even if we don't subscribe to the maxim of rider's hips to horse's hips (which to my mind is sound advice) freeing the outside hip joint makes our outside leg aid spectacularly more effective and with far less effort. It also keeps the quarters in check and pushing under, so the canter can be maintained just as long as it is required.

There is a third aid which is very useful to apply just before the outside leg aid is given. The use of this 'extra' aid may be given simultaneously with a verbal command, which may help the youngster through association of ideas. Although the horse should be looking slightly to the inside of the circle with a soft, opening rein, just prior to the canter depart the

The canter depart

(Left) Even when the horse can accept more seat, we must still be careful how we ask for changes of gait. Here, on the corner, Jodie's seat has slipped back as she pushes too much against the inside stirrup and Thomas simply 'runs on' and through her aids, instead of engaging behind.

(Above) By sitting tall and advancing her inside hip and seatbone from correctly braced loins, Jodie can now step down and into the inside stirrup. Correctly supported to the left, Thomas now offers canter left with confidence and push from behind.

rider may gently check or half-halt with the outside hand. On our big trot circle, the moment for this would be as the horse moves from the centre line back towards the track in the second half.

This swift and tiny action helps to free the horse's incoming leading leg by momentarily straightening the horse; it also warns the horse that the new impulsion aid does not mean that he is to trot faster. As the horse responds to the asking influence of the outside leg, the inside rein should gently ease forward a little to allow him to jump into canter. *We must always try to give the horse sufficient room to manoeuvre.*

When I am schooling a young or slightly reticent horse, I often find it helpful to say 'Can-ter!' out loud. Using the voice like a balancer, I separate the two syllables to complement the aids. I therefore set the horse up with the inside leg asking for bend and position, then just prior to making the 'extra' check with the body and outside rein, I draw out the 'C-A-N'... as though alerting the horse that something is about to change. Finally, as the asking outside leg goes on, I finish the '...TER!' on a higher, lighter note and the horse is usually cantering by this stage.

Whilst, eventually, we want to be able to drop the use of the voice, as well as lessen the intensity of all the aids, we should never forget the two stages of preparation. The horse has to organise his body in the canter depart and each minute change of our bodyweight must be recognisable and clear.

Time taken in this will pay off hugely when we come to teach him counter-canter, canter half-pass, part-pirouette and the flying change. If the leg and seat aids have not become totally as familiar as the ABC, then we will have laid up real problems for ourselves. To dispense with the voice is fine; with the leg and weight aids, never.

Handy Hints

Here now are some further tips which will complement all we have discussed to date, and which may shed more light on the situation if difficulties are encountered in the early stages. These are rarely mentioned, but they are important to keep in the back of your mind.

- Whilst the rider's knees and thighs continue to *frame* the horse in the direction of the movement, the feeling through the inside leg is almost one of asking and then freeing up for a second – i.e. press and release.
- The release is done by pressing down with the ball of the inside foot into the inside stirrup which should hang just free of the horse's side and *lead* the horse into canter.
- By consciously weighting the inside stirrup leather so that it hangs *vertically* down, more weight is brought to bear on the rider's inside seatbone – this helps free the back when the horse springs off his outside hind.
- The action of the outside leg is one of opening back and then acting in a forward manner (against the hair) as if to lift the horse

into canter.

- The checking action of the outside rein not only straightens the horse's neck but guards the quarters and encourages them to work under the horse's body (indirect rein of opposition – see Chapter XII).
- Your seat and upper body should make a momentary check too; if you are too slack or 'allowing' in the trot, the horse will feel inclined to go faster in the trot and fail to realise that you wish to move up a gear into canter. Try to let him feel the difference.

And now back to some more obvious reminders. In the canter, remember the horse:

- must push off with the outside hind – so should we
- must feel sufficiently forward-facing to want to move forward – so should we
- must feel he is jumping into the inside leg – so should we; the feeling is like skipping.

More Seat or Less?

There are differing schools of thought concerning how much push should come from our seat in the saddle. To my mind, the legs should take care of almost all of the push in the early stages, so pushing with the seat is better saved for special occasions such as introducing medium or extended canter. It should also be used if the horse is really naughty and refusing to go past or over an obstacle. In other words, I advise using a pushing seat very rarely at this stage. We hear a great deal about pushing or driving with the seat but often those same people who talk about it appear to do very little! Those who push in an obtrusive way generally hollow their horses.

With the sensitive or novice horse, it will be more helpful to *ease* our weight slightly forward into our knees and thighs for the transition so that we take *more weight off the back of the saddle*. This will make room for the horse to lift his frame for the first jump into canter, particularly if he is not very muscled over the back.

Since cantering is made up of a long series of jumps, we should be careful not to change our position too drastically after the first jump.

The young horse may require that we free his back in this way just as long as the canter lasts. Provided we do this with a toned upper body posture with well-supported loins and a straight back as opposed to a rounded one, there will be no loss of balance and every chance of a bolder, more confident canter.

With the older or lazier horse who may want more seat to send him more onward and forward-bound, the rider may stay on the three points of the seat but, again, should be careful never to round the back and block the movement of the hind legs.

Clear Leg Aids

As regards the leg aids, these must be *textbook* plain to the horse – although they should be scarcely noticeable to an onlooker:

- the rider's 'canter position' means inside leg at the girth; outside leg a hand's breadth behind the girth
- so long as the canter is to continue, the rider must maintain the 'canter position'
- the legs need not always be *asking*, but should remain *at the ready* to freshen up the canter as and when required.

Every time we move our legs out of this position whilst still cantering, we should be aware that this constitutes quite a considerable change of weight and direction to the horse. In such a case, we should not be at all surprised if the horse goes disunited, changes leg or breaks to trot. *Try not to remove his mainstay of support, if you want him to be confident in canter.*

The way to attain a smooth, forward and efficient canter is, therefore, to interfere as little as possible and, once in the gait, let the horse get on with it. No horse should be expected to continue in canter if the rider changes these important aids halfway through. Every tiny movement will mean something to

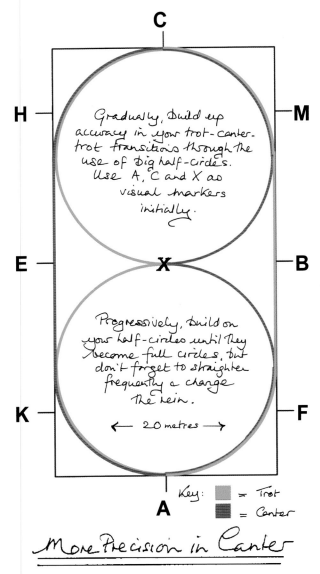

Gradually, build up accuracy in your trot-canter-trot transitions through the use of big half-circles. Use A, C and X as visual markers initially.

Progressively, build on your half-circles until they become full circles, but don't forget to straighten frequently & change the rein.

← 20 metres →

Key: = Trot   = Canter

More Precision in Canter

the horse if he is really listening to us. For this reason we must be very aware of exactly where and how we place our aids, and having applied them, we must remain very consistent if we are not to upset the balance. Of all the gaits, canter relies on a very fine balance indeed.

Striking-off Correctly

So many riders worry about the correct lead in the strike-off. First, remember that the horse does not know what is the 'correct leg', since he can canter on either lead. Second, be aware that, despite being on the right rein, he can only canter right if he feels our balance take him right.

Often, riders are so engrossed with making a good circle that they fail to give clear aids to ensure a correct transition. It is often better to forget the circle for a moment in order to concentrate on what the horse is feeling, since often the rider's perception of the circle aids are in conflict with what the horse needs to feel to strike-off on the required leading leg. Let us therefore look at things from the horse's point of view to see just what can go wrong.

THE HORSES'S THOUGHTS (under an uneducated rider)

- I'm happily trotting on a 20 m circle left; then I feel my rider sitting back, pushing and urging me on. I respond by going faster...
- Speeding up in trot, I then receive a big check through the mouth on both reins, so I guess this is wrong.
- Ah! now she is bringing my head more to the inside with the left rein. At the same time she has twisted her body to the inside, and there is no support from the outside rein. With my neck twisting left, I feel trapped through the left shoulder.
- Now she pushes again with her seat, checks with both hands and kicks! Although her inside leg is on the girth, most of my rider's weight seems to be on the right of the saddle, so I bound into canter right to pick her up! It feels all wrong but it's my only option...
- Oh dear – clearly it was wrong – again! I receive a real pull through the mouth and we are brought back to trot. Just as well really as it is so difficult to canter on the outside leg on a circle at my stage of schooling.

However, once the rider has a better understanding of the correct aids, all should be relatively easy for the horse. Let us look at the same horse under a better rider.

THE HORSES'S THOUGHTS (under an educated rider)

- My rider has helped me to bend on the trot circle by supporting me through the girth with a supportive feeling of the inside leg.
- There is plenty of impulsion because she carries herself in a good balance and her outside leg helps me to push from behind and to move around the circle.
- Her hands are more or less together, but there is a gentle 'opening' feel on the inside rein. Nevertheless, I feel supported by the outside rein and in this way I can keep my neck forward and unconstricted in front of me.
- As I approach the track, I suddenly feel her draw up a little taller as though preparing for something different; she then checks me gently through the outside rein and I feel as though I am more together.
- Then I feel a definite order! She pushes her inside seatbone more forward, deepens her weight into the inside stirrup and gives a distinctive and firm tap with the outside leg clearly behind the girth. This motivates me to want to jump off my outside hind into canter.
- As I finish circling back to A, the downward pressure into her inside stirrup allows me to feel I am bending around a pillar of support.
- On reaching A, the inside leg presses rather more *against* me and the outside rein gently leads me back onto the track.
- I still feel my rider is cantering with me and provided she does not remove this sensation of lead and support from her inside leg and nothing changes behind, I am happy to continue in canter down the long side.
- I pass through the corner and past C, still feeling supported to the inside and motivated behind, and I would be happy to keep going, only now my rider's inside leg moves back and her outside leg has resumed its normal place. Clearly the balance has

changed as she asks more on the rein, so I resume my trot. I hope this is what she meant!

- Yes! I guessed right. She sits up; the rein eases a little and we come back to walk. I am allowed to stretch my neck and am rewarded. I'm glad to report it was all very clear.

If only more riders would look at things from the horse's point of view in this way, we would see many more successful partnerships in the very early stages of training. Good walk, trot and canter circles are an absolute prerequisite to suppleness and bending. Try it yourself; walk a circle and discover how your inside leg has to engage more forward and under you particularly in the smaller circles – so do this when you ride.

Once the horse becomes more established in his canter depart, the rider can continue the canter right round the school. Every time the rider feels the balance waver a little this way or that, it is helpful to bring the horse again onto a big circle. When things go wrong, it is very much harder to correct a problem such as pulling or leaning in on straight lines.

At no time should the horse be punished for striking off on the wrong leg. So far as he is concerned, it was probably the correct leg for him at that moment. Simply allow the canter to continue for a few strides (we must never discourage the canter) then bring him quietly back to walk or trot and try again. If working in an enclosed place, there is a psychological advantage in asking for canter just before a wall comes up. A natural sense of self-preservation should prevent the horse from taking the (wrong) outside lead in such a case.

Refining the Transitions

As the horse strengthens behind, the rider should find the downward transitions become more balanced. Think 'uphill' so that the horse can round his back in both the downward as well as the upward transitions. It will be some

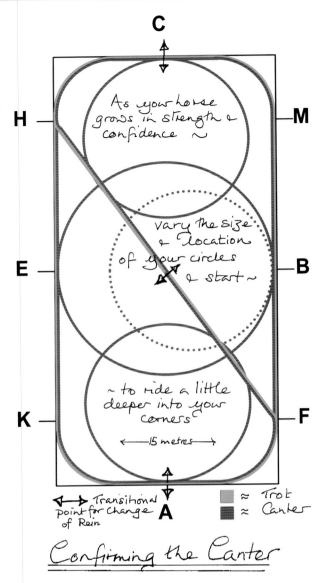

As your horse grows in strength & confidence ~

vary the size & location of your circles & start ~

~ to ride a little deeper into your corners

←—— 15 metres ——→

↔ Transitional Point for Change of Rein

▨ ≈ Trot
■ ≈ Canter

Confirming the Canter

time before the horse is sufficiently muscled up in the back to take a strong seat to make his transitions. Remember the closing, dampening down action of the legs is just as important as that of the seat for downward transitions. As for the hands, their action on the rein should always be secondary to the seat aids and they too must close, never pull back.

Once the horse is producing nice canter transitions to and from the trot, we may advance to upward transitions to canter from walk. (Downward transitions to walk require much more collection, so the latter should not be attempted at this stage). Again, these are

In walk to canter, beware of shortening the rein, which may set your horse against the hand (above). Instead, confirm bend to the inside and allow your horse sufficient length of rein to stretch his neck into canter (left). Here, the inside rein could be a little softer but the rider's position is exemplary.

best produced from the circle: the half-halt feeling through the body will become more important to their successful completion.

The canter from walk will depend upon an increased engagement behind as well as the all-important bending. Some horses actually find it easier to jump into canter from walk, but if there is any sign of hollowing, it should be set aside until later. Those horses built more 'downward' and inclined to lean on the fore-hand naturally find it more difficult and, at a later stage, it may be helpful to encourage the weight back from a few steps of rein-back. There is no hard-and-fast rule as to when either of these exercises should be introduced, but if the horse is showing signs of resistance, or if in doubt, it may be wise to leave the walk to canter transitions until after some lateral work has been introduced.

As in walk and trot, suppling work on the canter circle or half-circle prepares and improves the horse for all his straight work:

- l5 m canter circles can be introduced gradually, but only after the first three months of cantering bigger circles
- as before, do not ride circle after circle in these early stages of canter
- always follow up the figure work with straight line work in between
- it is good idea to return to the circle again for the downward transitions.

On springs! After only seven months of schooling Fabuloso rounds up and offers me his back in canter. Now, I can afford to sit up erect, well aware that lightness and balance are elusive qualities which can be lost as swiftly as they come. With some horses the wait may have to be much longer. For the time being, however, the feeling is fabulous!

Working in this way, progressively, will encourage bending, straightness and forwardness. We can never achieve real forwardness without engagement behind and there is no doubt that these transitions will do a great deal to increase the weight-bearing capacity and flexibility of the quarters and hind legs.

Naturally!

Canter is a wonderful gait to enjoy and helps us to understand a little better what we mean by that elusive quality of lightness in our riding. In canter, the horse should naturally elevate his shoulders, stretch up and forward with his neck and carry the poll at the highest point, which are all requisites for lightness. *Naturally*, the hind legs should engage much further under the body and take weight further back to push the forehand up and forward. *Naturally*, the horse should give the rider a feeling of rounding and lifting through the back.

If all these factors can be offered by the horse naturally, it is clearly incumbent on us to learn how to let these qualities shine through. How we ride and school in the canter is therefore very important and perhaps this, of all the chapters, should be read and studied again and again.

PART FOUR

The Work Proper – Novice Level

CHAPTER VII

Two Different Trots
Building Impulsion through Transitions

Long strides and freedom of the shoulder result from strong haunches and elastic hind limb joints.

Whilst concentrating and building up on for-wardness and balance through all three gaits, we have, to date, only used progressive transitions from one gait to another in order not to impose too many constraints on the young horse. Now that he is growing in strength and confidence and the aiding process has been well understood, we can work towards greater accuracy. At this stage, the rider should be aware that no transition can be carried out smoothly without a feeling of controlled impulsion being carried through the horse's body from the rider's legs to the rider's hands.

Although this may sound paradoxical, the sensitive rider will be aware that the flow of energy should only be *redirected* in downward transitions; never completely broken off. The horse must always want to move forward again when he is released from the slowing down or stopping aids. In this way, both the downward and upward transitions will look 'together', smooth and natural, so that the rider can request these regularly and at specific points, with a greater degree of balance in the horse's posture throughout.

From the working trot, therefore, try introducing just three or four steps of medium walk, then go straight forward to trot again with the emphasis on immediacy and activity and a feeling of 'oomph' from behind.

The Value of Transitions

With the young horse, it is better not to work on trot to halt transitions as yet, since the back is rarely strong enough to cope with these demands. However, repeated trot to walk and walk to trot transitions are perfectly acceptable at this stage and should reinforce forward thinking. Once the latter can be obtained smoothly and easily, we may take the upward transitions a stage further, interspersing them with the halt to trot transition from time to time.

Both types of upward transition will encourage impulsion provided we ensure that the horse remains 'off the leg'. The downward transitions are very useful for calming an excitable horse who tends to get faster and faster in the trot, but they also encourage the horse to take weight behind, and improve general balance and attentiveness to the aids.

In the early stages, these transitions are best practised on a 20 m circle or just after a corner on the short side of the school at A or C. The reason for this is simply that it is always easier to control the horse out of a bend, when the weight of the horse will be a little more on his hocks. The downward transition should encourage the horse to step more under with the incoming inside hind to 'catch' the balance.

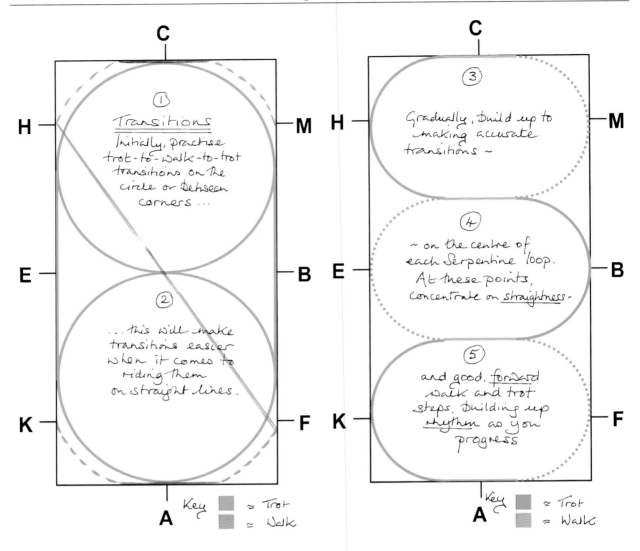

Key ▦ ≈ Trot   ▨ ≈ Walk

Diagram annotations (left arena):

① Transitions
Initially, practise trot-to-walk-to-trot transitions on the circle or between corners ...

② ... this will make transitions easier when it comes to riding them on straight lines.

Diagram annotations (right arena):

③ Gradually, build up to making accurate transitions ~

④ ~ on the centre of each serpentine loop. At these points, concentrate on _straightness_.

⑤ and good, _forward_ walk and trot steps, building up _rhythm_ as you progress

---

The return to trot should subsequently show greater engagement.

After five or six circuits and an equal number of transitions made in this way, the rider should allow the horse to stretch down in walk on a long rein and then change the rein. The whole process is then asked for again on the other rein. On a 20 m circle it would be counter-productive initially to ask for more than one transition on a whole circle, but gradually you can work up to a three-loop serpentine, with a transition made every time you cross the centre line.

Always decide how many walk steps you are going to ask for in advance, and count these out loud to start with. 'One-two-three-four... and Trrrrrr-ot!' Giving the horse a sense of timing through your voice in this way is far more valuable than you might think. It also helps you to measure and control your own body movements.

Downward Transitional Aids

Too often, we see horses hollowing in their downward transitions. This is generally a result of too much hand, too early, or too much pressure exerted over the back of the saddle. If you want to keep your horse's back up, with the hind legs stepping well under in the transition, here are some ideas to consider:

Trot to walk

When the rider braces against the stirrup in the down-ward transition, the seat slips back taking the contact with it. This creates hollowing and resistance.

Instead, centralise the seat and gently resist through squared shoulders, a firm waist and with the legs asking further back. In this way, the horse will step into a closed contact which almost immediately gives again.

- Always stretch up tall with the upper body to 'receive' and make room for his back.
- Simply think of ceasing the movement of trot through *your* back – just as you would on the ground – for example, from a jog, you draw up to walk again.
- Place both legs a little further back than normal and close into the horse so he can step forward and *through* from behind into your receiving hands.
- Support and 'contain' the movement by squaring the shoulders, resisting with the elbows, and closing the fingers around the rein – remember, no pulling back...
- Visualise the transition happening at the exact spot you want; remember – this is a much more powerful aid than you would imagine.

Upward Transitional Aids

Often, when the horse is asked to trot forward again, the rider unconsciously puts him straight back onto the forehand by giving away too much through hands and body. Once the horse knows to go forward from the leg, we can start to keep him more together in the transition. The first step *up* into trot is very important if the horse is to be encouraged to push from behind, so the time has come to ask more positively.

- Feel on the rein with soft, inviting fingers to gather the horse together as again you stretch up tall – but this time with a sense of opening and lift through the pelvic floor.
- Allow your legs to drop forward to the girth, so they 'hang' long and unconstricted, ready

Walk to trot

(Left) As your horse moves off into trot, use the upward phase of your rising trot to square your shoulders, 'ask' with the fingers and introduce a moment's suspension, before...

(Above) ...softening the contact to allow a more forward trot to emerge.

for action.

- Open and square the shoulders, with a sense of unlocking your back and yielding your elbows.
- Now, in one swift action, brush forward with your legs and really ask for go!
- As your horse moves off, allow your supple back to carry your hands forward with a soft, opening feel of the fingers, but try not to drop the horse in front.

All these transitional aids should be quiet but positive. The opening-up or freeing of the rider's upper body will be felt instantaneously by the horse if the rider is sitting quiet and central, since this raises the centre of balance. Thrusting into the back of the saddle for a tran-

sition is quite incomprehensible. In the downward transition such action will hollow the horse's back, leaving the hind legs trailing. In the upward transition, harsh driving will drive him onto the forehand.

Once the horse is familiar and easy with these transitions, the rider can start to think about transitions within the same gait. The idea is to bring about a change whereby we show the horse how it is possible not only to increase and amplify impulsion, but how he may retain it in reserve without in any way losing activity.

Comparisons, Comparisons...

Gradually, we have helped our horse build up the power which his body will require to meet our increasing demands. Control of power leads towards collection when he has the strength to remain fully on the aids without unleashing everything at once. Full collection is still some way off, but there is no reason why, at this stage, we may not give the horse a taste for what is to come later. Developing further kinetic energy allows the horse to hold and store impulsion for whatever task may come his way. It is a mistake to think that a slower, more collected gait needs less energy and activity; the contrary is in fact true.

Since the all-important lateral and longitudinal bend have been steadily developed through riding corners, circles, serpentines and so on, the foundation stones for this coming together of the energy forces have been well laid. Impulsion and the desire to move forward in active (but not rushing) strides has been radically improved with the transitions; the horse is also better organised to change down a gear or halt without losing balance. Now it is time to bring about changes *within the gait* which will strengthen the back by working the various muscle systems in different ways.

We have already taught our horse to understand the difference between a brisk medium walk and an equally active but more ground-covering 'open' or free walk on stretched reins. Our work on upward and downward transitions will have prepared the horse for what now lies ahead – achieving two contrasting trots – one more open and forward, the other more rounded and contained, all without losing balance.

It will be the feeling of *comparison* that assists us to measure just how much energy we will allow him in each movement, and how much we should retain. The horse will also benefit from these sensations of contrast. The change within our own bodies is our only way of telling him what type of trot we are looking for. Vicariously, he will soon experience the different feelings for himself. But first there has to be impulsion! Without impulsion we have nothing with which to work.

Impulsion not speed

Even at this stage, too many riders still tend to associate impulsion with speed. Because their horse naturally offers a speed-driven trot, they are afraid to lose forwardness by imposing controls which might diminish that sense of free forward movement. Thus, their idea of a working trot is relatively fast, whilst a collected trot is by comparison not only slower but stodgy! In their mind, a medium or extended trot would thus be very fast indeed and yet if we have ever watched good dressage, we must know that this is not the case.

In fact there should be little or no difference in the tempo of the different trots, but what does happen is that the length and quality of the strides will differ. How the horse delivers these strides will also differ. They may come from hocks that are more deeply flexed with the horse's back more bunched up, so the stride is shorter but springier, or they may come from a looser, forward feel, with a greater sense of stretch and overtrack behind. All these factors will make a difference to the shape and balance of each movement and of the gait and, of course, to the horse's general outline.

Outline

Outline is, of course, a very useful word to employ when correctly understood, but generally I tend to steer away from it as much as possible since so many travesties of riding are committed in its name. Indeed, for the unknowledgeable, the constant pursuit of outline can become a battleground between horse and rider. Because it is too much associated with a feeling of weight in the reins, generated by the amount of contact in the rider's hand, the entire point is missed. Outline should have less to do with weight in front and much more to do with engaging the hind legs to transfer weight *behind*.

However, even amongst experienced riders, trainers and judges alike, there is still the

Balance

Small or big, human or horse, we are all governed by the same law of gravity

Two people can balance one see-saw very easily ~

– for one unbalanced person, there will be difficulties ...

but for another, with concentration and control ~ balance is attainable

SL.

Once we find the centre – we can then change the balance with the tiniest weight adjustments

Showing a difference

Here with Fabuloso I use the rising phase of the trot to check and gather him a little – more with the body than the hands, for he is not yet fully on the bit...

...now I use the sitting phase of the trot to ask more from the leg to encourage greater pushing from behind without speeding up. The result shows a pleasing engagement.

misconception that if one end of the horse is loaded, the other has to feel the same. For this reason, their vision of good outline tends to be of a horse who is overbent and compressed together. Generally, such a horse will look 'downhill', with the weight on his shoulders. No wonder the rider talks about so many pounds of weight in the hand!

And yet, all this is flawed thinking –

- The horse is not a seesaw carrying two people at either end to maintain a balance; he is better described as a seesaw with one person in the middle – the rider!
- From the centre therefore, the rider can change balance either to load one end and lighten the other or vice versa.
- Both ends cannot be loaded at once! There will always be a light end – and Nature decrees that this should be the front end.
- Therefore, a horse on the forehand will look heavy in front and lightweight behind – *not* a good idea if we want more impulsion...
- The horse on his hocks will look (and feel)

elevated and light in front, with deepness, stability and power behind.

Because of these misunderstandings over outline, I generally prefer to ask my more novice students to think of the shape of the *gait*, rather than the shape of the horse when first carrying out any changes within the gait.

Shape and Showing a Difference

In this vein therefore, I suggest that the horse's normal working trot should now be looking fairly horizontal. If it is not to be 'downhill', the horse must be pushing forward nicely from behind and stretching over the back and neck to reach into the bridle and accept the bit without leaning on it. For this, the poll should be more or less the highest point, with the head now coming towards the vertical.

By containing some of the energy, we can begin to look for a rounder, more 'uphill' trot. Here the horse will continue to push from behind, but gentle restraints through the rider's body will mean that he covers the ground in shorter, springier strides. Again, the poll should be more or less the highest point, but the whole neck and back should take on a more convex appearance.

If the rider is not to block the horse through stronger hands, upward support must come from elsewhere. The idea is for the horse to merge his activity and balance with ours. Therefore, when we draw up through the abdominal muscles, in a similar way to which we did for the downward transitions, only less so, he draws up a little more too. In the meantime, the leg continues to say 'forward' so the rhythm is only altered, not broken.

By contrast, when we think more 'horizontal', letting the movement go *through* us by allowing more with both the rein and our bodies, but still asking with the legs, he follows with longer, flowing strides.

The sooner the horse is made to think about and feel for himself these contrasts in trot, rather than sticking in the same rather flat, unchanging rhythm, the more he will begin to listen for them.

Changes Within the Gait

Now that we understand the idea, we should use the natural boundaries of the school to make it plain to the horse just where and how these modifications will take place. Remember, at this stage we are not looking either for collection or for extended strides – these will develop later. What we do want to show to our horse is that he is quite capable of offering us two contrasting trots – one more open and forward, the other more rounded and contained. Both of them will require concentration and activity behind.

A good way to introduce this exercise is to develop the more ground-covering 'open' trot down the long sides, while we make our steadier, rounded trot on the two short sides. The idea is to improve the quality and clarity of both trots. This certainly does not mean that we kick on hard and allow the horse to gush

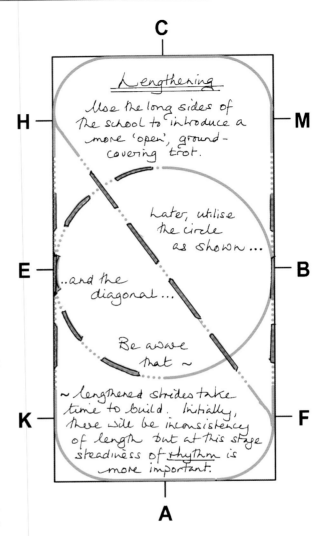

down the long side on the forehand. Instead, we prepare him through our contained trot on the short side to bring more impulsion and swing to the bigger working trot and only go for a few lengthened strides past B or E.

At all times, our inside leg must continue to support the horse through the corners by deepening into the stirrup, whilst our outside leg should be encouraging him to stretch his body as he moves into the straight. Real impulsion can only develop from light but positive leg aids correctly applied. The hands must take sufficient contact to channel that energy into longer, rhythmical strides so that the horse works from back to front and retains his balance. In this way we build up the rhythm, tempo and shape of these changes within the gait.

After a few weeks, the rider may start to introduce these changes on a 20 m circle. As the horse becomes more familiar with the work, he will note the small signals within the rider's body and tune in to what is required. By now he should be seeking the bit more consistently as he sustains a feeling of uphill activity in the transitions from one gait to another and also within the gait.

To bring him even more to the aids, our next exercise will be to ride one half of the circle in the more forward trot; the other in the more contained trot. Both lateral bend and longitudinal suppleness will be developed, but the more demanding the exercise, the more help the horse will require from his rider. It is time therefore to become more aware of how centrifugal force and gravity can assist these changes provided we take appropriate steps to aid him correctly.

Too often the horse is blamed for falling out through the shoulders when this is rarely his fault. The time has come to be more *specific* concerning the framing aids, so that the parameters of the frame can be drawn in a little more here and there or, if necessary, opened a little in other places. Then it is just a matter of riding the horse through these parameters – but how?

Changing Parameters

At this stage, to think merely of framing the horse through the leg, seat and upper body will be insufficient. We must now also be aware of:

- feet and ankles
- knees and inner thighs
- seatbones to the rear
- seatbones to the front
- hips, waist, etc

Never forget that every single part of us, whether in direct contact with the horse or not, exerts pressures and weight aids. Many of these are transmitted to the horse's body quite unconsciously as, for example, in the crooked rider, who will be tighter through one side of the ribcage, one hip joint, one thigh, one knee and so on without even realising it. Nonetheless, since the balance of the horse is radically influenced by these constrictions, we must at least become aware of them.

No one wants to get bogged down in too much technical detail when they ride. It is generally counter-productive to tell a rider to tighten one adductor muscle and relax another. What we can do is improve the posture of our upper bodies, which will release tensions below and free us up. It is then clearer how we may effectively support in order to increase or contain impulsion and how we may give an opening aid, when we really mean it.

One principle we should never forget is that every opening provided by the rider's body, whether conscious or unconscious, will represent an invitation to the horse. Therefore, on the right rein, a loose thigh to the right may cause him to lean onto his right shoulder, particularly if the left thigh is pinching and pushing him that way. Similarly, a slack lower leg may allow the quarters to fall in or out. The natural inclination of every horse will always be to move into a space and away from tension. In this way the weak areas of the frame will quickly be exposed, so as riders we must be very disciplined about the way in which we use our body if we are to remain in control. Tone and suppleness in the muscles are as important for us as they are in the horse.

Happily, this tendency of the horse to fill or move into empty spaces can be used to *help* us once we become aware of how to use the frame to our advantage. In this way, we have to be very clear about which openings we *mean* to provide, for example, an open inside rein, or a softer inside thigh to invite the turn inwards. As one side of our body makes way, the other side should act to support, check or close – for example, the supporting outside rein, or the firm closing press of the outside leg. Opening

Rounding and outline

(Right) Outline can differ enormously from horse to horse depending upon type and breed, but without impulsion it is worthless. Here Thomas's trot has become much more rounded after several weeks of work in transitions. Jodie's position frames him nicely.

(Above) This Andalusian, at a more advanced stage of training also shows impulsion, coupled with elevation. Again, Vaughan's position helps contain the energy. However, both horses should have their noses just in front of (not behind) the vertical with the poll the highest point.

up and closing down a little may also take place through the rider's seat and back.

This concept is very important as we teach the horse more and more to respond to the mildest of seat aids for making changes within the gait. For example, when freeing up the trot, both legs placed a little more forward at the girth will stimulate greater reaching through the horse's shoulders. In complementary fashion, the rider should raise the diaphragm and bring the shoulders just behind the vertical for a few strides to let the movement swing through. This action relieves downward pressure away from the centre of the saddle which 'opens the door' of the seat and, provided impulsion is present, the horse will want to lengthen his stride with greater verve.

By contrast, the coming together of the gait is effected by the rider drawing up very erect and thinking a moment of pause within each stride. With both legs placed slightly behind the girth rather than in front, there is a sensation of holding through the pelvic floor, which rechannels some of the outgoing energy. Now the door feels somewhat less 'open' than before and in consequence the horse takes shorter, more measured strides.

When these subtle aids are taken to their logical conclusion, it becomes apparent that there is nothing more counter-productive to good movement, than to allow every part of us to open or yield at once. A very slack, uncontrolled body will produce a very slack, uncontrolled horse. Impulsion will never be gained by allowing all the energy of the horse to spill out in all directions and no serious rider can ever wish this! It is only by firming up on certain sections of the frame, and opening doors in other places, that we may send the energy in the direction we choose.

Support not Tension

Some riders work so hard and with so much steely tension in their arms, seat and legs to achieve a rounder frame, that instead of amplifying or rechannelling the flow of energy, they end up by closing every door and extinguishing it. When there is little room to manoeuvre, the horse will become heavier in the hand and laboured in his movement.

In such a case, the rider has stifled the impulsion before it has had a chance to blossom. We all know the scenario; the horse is blamed, strenuous leg aids are applied, sharper spurs, more stick and so on. The whole thing is so sad and self-defeating. It can never get better until the rider lightens up, but how many trainers will tell them this?

Containing the gait, which gives us the introductory feel for collection, should never be confused with laboured movement. Instead, it should be associated with lightness. So, merely:

- think what you want
- see yourself doing it
- and tune into those small nuances of posture which are second nature on the ground.

It is simply a question of measuring the degree of impulsion you decide to let through.

Physical Demands

Finally, it is important to recognise that the horse needs as much energy to raise his back and shorten the stride with an increased flexion of the hind limb joints as he does to lengthen his frame and flow on more. For those of my students who have difficulty with this one, I ask them to run quickly and loosely with big strides

across my yard; I then ask them to try covering the same distance on tiptoe but with obviously shorter, higher steps. For this they must hold themselves much more erect, which actually requires more poise and balance – just as it does in the horse. Very soon they discover that they need just as much, if not more energy, for the shorter, measured steps.

As always, in the early stages of introducing transitions or changes within the gaits, the rider must be careful not to use any seat aid too strongly. For this reason, it is important to learn to make transitions off the horse's back as well as by sitting down into the saddle. I always recommend that my students do not make transitions from the sitting trot until the horse is well established in sitting trot generally. *It is perfectly possible to ride two or even three different types of trot both rising or sitting.* (The masters taught that, with finesse, one could produce at least fifty different trots from the same horse!).

In the Rising Trot

It can be a big mistake to ride the working trot rising and the more collected trot sitting in the beginning, since it may send out the wrong message to the horse. If one is not very careful, the horse will learn to associate sitting with a shorter frame, so problems might emerge later when one wanted to achieve lengthening or medium trot whilst sitting, and so on.

For this reason, I prescribe that in the beginning the transitions are probably best done in rising trot alone. Later one can alternate the rising and sitting and finally all the transitions, including that from full collected trot to the ultimate extended trot, can be achieved in sitting trot alone – by which time the horse will be fully muscled and strong enough behind to cope with this amount of seat.

Since the influence of the seat is obviously lessened with the rider largely off the horse's back how, therefore, may we indicate to the horse that we wish for a slower trot whilst still rising? This is where an understanding of projecting or

Working outside can be enormously beneficial to the horse's acceptance of the aids. Espada is much weaker through the back than Fabuloso and it has taken three years for him to engage and accept the sitting trot easily. Here, on a gentle slope, I use a big circle to shorten and lengthen Espada's strides. The slight bend invites more flexion from the inside hind leg; while the slope provides a feel of 'uphill' which he clearly relishes.

sending on energy as opposed to storing it comes into play. In the slower, contained trot the rider should weight the stirrups a little more, close the leg more against the horse in the sit phase of the trot, and again feel a moment of pause and support within his or her own body to invite a slower trot from the horse.

Everyone has their different way of thinking about these matters, but we can now see how the idea of pulling back on the rein and 'shortening' the horse through the neck need never feature. Instead, everything is controlled through the *centre of the horse*, long before all the energy seeps 'out of the front door' to the forehand.

In the Sitting Trot

Once the horse has begun to tune into these changes within the gait, it is time to test them out in the sitting trot. Start this work on the large circle again as, with the horse slightly bending to the inside, it is easier for the rider to influence the horse more to the aids of seat and leg. A soft bend from nose to tail encourages the horse's inside leg to step well under, which causes the inside hip, stifle and hock to gently lower, bend and take weight behind.

Sitting trot should only be undertaken when the horse has developed this capacity to bend and flex. With the hind legs further underneath the body mass, the horse's back is supported and, with care and good posture, the rider should now be able to sit the trot without the horse losing balance. If the horse should hollow and disengage, the rider should return immediately to rising trot. Initially, the sitting trot should be performed for half a 20 m circle only, with the rising trot adopted again without any change in rhythm, tempo or balance.

Riders must be careful not to let their seat slip to the outside by caving in during the trot circle. Sloppy riding leads to sloppy and also precarious circles. When circling, the horse's legs should remain vertical, but leaning in will actually push the horse onto the outside shoulder, so his forelegs have no option but to lose verticality and slant inward to prop up the bodyweight.

Let us therefore look at the reactions of the same horse ridden by two different riders in the same situation. From sitting trot on the right rein past A the horse is required to show an 'open', more forward-going trot down the long side of the school from K to H: then to proceed to a l5 m circle at C in a rounder, more contained trot; finishing with a transition to medium walk on returning to C. We start with the uneducated rider and consider the difficulties that the horse will face:

THE HORSE'S THOUGHTS (uneducated rider)

- I've just left A but it's hard to stay out on the track as I go past K because there's little support to the inside and the right rein seems very short. At the same time, I am losing my quarters because my rider is pushing back with her right leg. If only she would let go – I could straighten up!
- I guess I'm supposed to go on more as we pass E because the reins have been thrown forward and there's a lot of kicking. Sadly, I can't seem to get going, because my rider squeezes so hard, she inhibits me. Also, these busy, busy legs make everything so unsteady; I feel a constant shift of balance in the saddle. Nonetheless, I try my best...
- Now we're at H, she shortens the rein and slows me down (there wasn't much to slow...). I hope she'll assist me round the corner with a nice supporting leg on the girth but no! She's more intent on pushing my quarters out. With no support for my shoulders, I fall in through the inside one – she's even turned her knee away! This means I'm not very straight when we approach C.
- I'm just about to carry on past the marker when I feel a further shortening of my right rein. It seems a circle is on the cards and suddenly I am hauled round with the bit and made to twist my neck. I labour round with difficulty. The only way to bend on the circle nicely is to get one's hind legs under, but now there's a feeling of jack-knifing and it seems quite unsafe.
- We made a semblance of a circle but I felt unbalanced and awkward and I was losing my quarters, which I hate – if only she'd sat centrally, given me inside leg support and helped me round with her outside leg.
- Now it's walk time and I can feel the signal coming long in advance as she scrabbles up the reins and prepares to lean back. She sits down hard and pushes her seatbones right down and into my back. At the same time I come up smack against the bit... Of course I stop instead of walk!
- It was all so strong I had to drop my back – something I hate – and I simply fell out of balance. Now I can't even take good steps forward again because she's still wedged on the back of my saddle. If she would just sit up, I might be able to squiggle my hocks underneath. Oh dear – I've just been punished for going sideways... You just can't win...

With care and step-by-step schooling, Fabuloso is able to offer good lengthening within his first year of schooling. Here he has lengthened the entire frame, having the strength and muscle tone to maintain roundness and stretch all at the same time. An imaginary vertical line can be drawn from the tip of his nose to the foremost front hoof. The thrust of the hind legs matches the reach of the fore. Biomechanically and classically, this shows promise of a good medium trot.

Now let us look at the same horse with a completely different rider:

THE HORSE'S THOUGHTS (educated rider)

- As we leave A, I bend snugly into my corner as my rider's inside leg nudges me a little more out to the track than usual. The outside rein keeps me steady as we pass K and then she lets me straighten before going on rather more than usual from light but insistent legs.

- Approaching E, there is a definite feel of release through her seat which makes me want to flow on even more. Her legs relax as I respond but her back is so supple I want to move ever forward in partnership. At the same time, there's a nice, positive, quiet feel about the reins, but although I draw balance from the bit, I don't want to lean on it because her leg keeps me just ahead of that temptation.

- As we come to H, I feel her sit up a little more and there is a feeling of holding through her back. At the same time, I feel her weight deepen in the centre of the saddle, which steadies me. Through the corner, her inside leg supports me in the bend and because she sits tall, I can get my inside hind well under. Her outside leg keeps my quarters in line, so I feel quite balanced as I approach C.

- Now we are at C and there is a change. As we decrease pace, she deepens her seat again, but her upper body supports me upward and again, her legs say forward. She gives little warning feelings through the fingers which make me shorten my stride...

- Before I know it we are on a 15 m circle at C, but I wasn't even aware that she had taken me there because I just came around at C with her. I guess it was because I was already around her leg from the corner and the rest was easy. She deepens the weight into her inside stirrup and her inside leg becomes a pillar for me to bend around. It's easy to push more from behind too, because her outside leg clads me behind the girth and encourages all the time.

- Now back at C, everything is suddenly quiet. She is no longer moving with me but she draws up firm and steady as though about to close the door. As her hands close on the rein, there is a closing pressure in her seat, thighs and knees so there is nowhere to go except to walk. I want to leave my hind legs out behind – as that's the lazy way out – but I can't do so because her lower legs send them on. This gives me the feeling that I'm all up together and balanced in the walk. It's as though we're joined up and – actually – I rather like it!

CHAPTER VIII

To the Bit

Flexions, Half-halts and Roundness

Poll flexion is natural to the young colt in animated movement. The connection from hindquarters to forehand resembles a bow.

To date, we have talked about achieving a nice, even contact on both reins as the young horse moves forward with impulsion from the leg to meet our hands. In the beginning, the general contact was positive but 'allowing' to encourage forwardness. Gradually, we began to discriminate between the two reins, softening to the inside to encourage bend, whilst using the outside rein in a more supportive way, particularly in changes of direction and changes of gait.

The Collecting Aids

With increasing maturity, the time has come to introduce a new phase. We wish to introduce an element of restraint which will gradually bring about collection, but how can the contact of the reins remain elastic, some people may ask, once the horse is brought to the bit? Also, I am often asked 'What did Nuno Oliveira mean when he talked about the "push, take and give" to introduce collection?'

Most people know what a well collected horse looks like, but too many people are afraid to try for collection since they recognise the dangers of constricting the horse's neck and pulling him onto the bit. Of course there must be no question of pulling; we are merely asking the rider to send the horse forward into hands which, by momentary passive resistance, act as

a gentle check in a similar way as when making a transition.

So, if you think of collection as being a state somewhere between an upward and downward transition in terms of the aids, you will be closer to achieving it than you might imagine. In car terms, it's rather like changing down a gear, not so much to slow down but to negotiate corners and turns with power and greater revs. Because, make no mistake, collection has to be about increasing power.

Refining Feel

We have already touched on making a difference within the gait through changes in the seat and legs. We are now ready to assist these changes through the rein, provided we remember that passive resistance has to emanate from within the rider's body. The legs have said 'forward', but the quality and length of the steps is determined by how much impulsion the rider's seat allows through.

To change down a gear and store power rather than let it all go, the rider must brace the back by squaring the shoulders, and feel a sensation of hold or check through the abdominal muscles and pelvic floor. We want to draw the hips forward towards the pommel, which lightens the weight on the back of the saddle but ensures a deep, central position of the seat. By closing the thighs slightly as the horse moves forward, we narrow the channel through which the energy of the horse must pass, so the horse is encouraged to round the back and transfer weight to the quarters by bending his hocks.

Now we are ready to educate the horse to the fact that the hands as well as the seat and legs may take and give almost in the same breath. Until now, these aids have been more associated with go-and-stop or go-and-slow down, but by using them more subtly, the horse is encouraged to remain in the same balance with well-engaged hocks, without either speeding up or slowing down. Collection, after all, is about retaining impulsion rather than al-lowing it to go powering onward as in extension.

The feeling of *take* and then give is made by the fingers through a very gentle squeezing or vibrato on the rein. Once the hands have learned to work with the body in a collecting or filtering way, the horse very quickly switches in to this silent language. Since we give only after he has gathered more, the horse soon learns that he can earn a pleasant reward and is eager to offer more. In this way the horse is encouraged to transfer more weight onto his quarters and, as a consequence, becomes lighter in the hand. As the shortened forward steps grow more active and springy, he learns gradually how to reward himself.

However, never forget to relax your horse on the long rein in between. Initially, only ask for short, intermittent periods of work on the bit. Two or three minutes at a time is quite sufficient to start with, but you can gradually introduce these periods more frequently during each schooling session, and the horse will always tell you how much he is comfortable with. Taking time always pays off.

In our anxiety to experiment with these feelings, we must be careful never to move the hand back or give two contradictory instructions simultaneously. For the horse to be encouraged to come to the bit, both leg and hand must know when to act and when to yield so that he never feels trapped in between!

Listening to the horse in this way develops split-second timing and finesse which no one can teach you except him. However, you can help yourself by improving your posture and utilising your own joints! This will keep the rein controlled but still elastic. We shall shortly be discussing greater finger mobility for half-halts and flexions, but to ensure that the hands do not block – yet refrain from giving away too much – the feeling should be slightly upward, supported by the body.

Upward Support

Opening the shoulders and drawing them down and back not only strengthens position, it also enables the elbows to slot nicely into place. With the seatbones engaged further forward it is easier for the rider's chest and abdomen to expand to lead the horse more 'uphill' and forward from a supple lower back.

As the rider's entire seat and upper body remain central to, and part of, the movement of the horse, the hands will then be carried forward as a pair and part of the whole. Hands that bob in the air can be very harsh; steady, supported hands can learn great sensitivity. Always keep the elbows bent, but do not pin them to your sides. They must retain the capacity to 'breathe' gently so they can complement the hands to resist or allow as appropriate. They must also absorb movement in the same way as they would if you were carrying a tray of precious glasses, but without spilling a drop.

The horse's mouth is equally delicate, but many people allow for this too much, which may drop the bit against his teeth. 'Following the movement with the hands' is not desirable in collection, but it may assist the walk on a long rein or encourage the extended gaits. However, too much movement will definitely discourage the horse from finding a better balance, so the rider must exercise self-discipline in order not to move the goalposts. *At this stage*

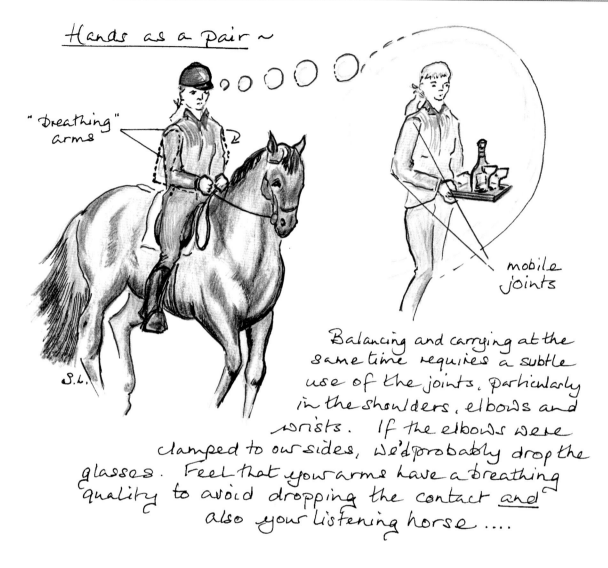

Hands as a pair ~

"breathing" arms

mobile joints

S.L.

Balancing and carrying at the same time requires a subtle use of the joints, particularly in the shoulders, elbows and wrists. If the elbows were clamped to our sides, we'd probably drop the glasses. Feel that your arms have a breathing quality to avoid dropping the contact <u>and</u> also your listening horse....

we should be bringing the horse to the hands and not the hands to the horse.

Gadgets and Blocking Agents

With the horse already longitudinally supple, the mobility and strength of his quarters will increase as he now makes his transitions with the hocks more deeply bent. Provided the rider allows the neck to remain forward and arched, never pulling the head behind the vertical, topline muscle will develop. Unfortunately, some people believe that the use of gadgets may speed up this process, but in fact the contrary is true.

Biomechanically, too much pressure applied to the head and neck of the horse – whether from an unfeeling hand, stiff arm joints or a fixed leather contraption – effectively breaks off the flow of muscular activity which emanates from the hindquarters. The interaction of all the muscle fibres from the psoas to the longissimus which facilitate impulsion is thereby interrupted.

Hollowing through the back and, noticeably, in front of the withers is an obvious symptom of the horse being held in front. Blocking occurs over the trapezius muscles so the horse is forced to compromise elsewhere. This creates tension in the splenius muscles (see p.116)

Two examples of creating an outline through gadgetry
which places artificial pressures on the muscle systems

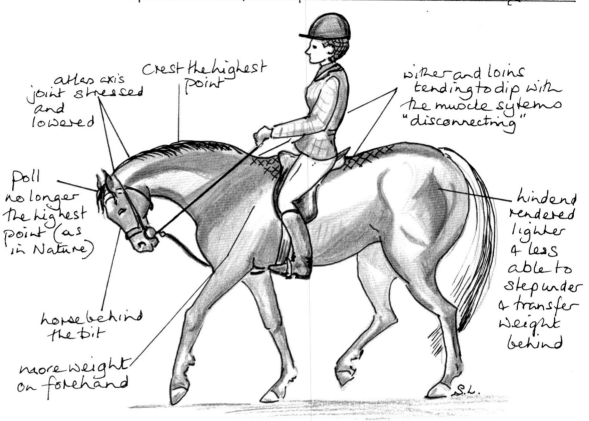

atlas axis joint stressed and lowered

Crest the highest point

wither and loins tending to dip with the muscle systems "disconnecting"

Poll no longer the highest point (as in Nature)

hindend rendered lighter & less able to step under & transfer weight behind

horse behind the bit

more weight on forehand

S.L.

The horse's muscle systems are incredibly complex in order to be so dynamic. Muscles develop over time with use but a restrictive force will stress some muscle pairs while leaving others idle. Tissue may wither and die if blood flow is interrupted. Who is to know which set of muscles need to be employed at any one time? We are kidding ourselves if we think we can produce Nature's balanced results in a shorter timescale through gadgetry.

which clothe the sides of the neck. *When muscle tone develops in the wrong places, the action behind will be severely inhibited.*

Horses schooled in gadgets tend to shorten their frame, although sadly not by advancing their hocks. Instead, there is a tendency to 'telescope' the neck downward, with the horse overbent and subsequently hollow through the loins. This often leads to a lot of movement (known as 'punting') out behind, which will impress the ignorant, but the lack of bend in the hocks gives the horse a heavy 'downhill' appearance. Too much weight in the shoulders creates an imbalance which stymies the free interplay of the muscle fibres over the entire topline. This, in turn, leads to severe resistances at a later stage in training, when resulting muscle spasm or pain builds up under or just behind the saddle where the horse has braced himself. Tail swishing, head-tilting, teeth grinding and general overall tension in the topline or gullet are all symptomatic of rushed or incorrect training.

A horse worked in this way can never be light in hand. That precious fine-tuning of energy and muscle power between horse and rider will remain a distant dream. Instead, the rider will feel a need to match power with power, which is a very different sensation from filtering energy. *Too strong a contact downgrades riding to a matter of physical strength.* It precludes the horse from ever being able to transfer sufficient weight from the forehand to the quarters.

The classical rider recognises that weight behind has to be counterbalanced. *Nature's way is to increase the engagement of the hindquarters so that self-carriage and collection can evolve.* For this reason, it is very important that we understand these simple mechanics. Time taken to work the horse naturally will not be wasted. Quick-fix methods may lead to early success, but few horses trained this way continue into higher-level training without developing physical or personality disorders.

Forward, Calm and Even

As a result of our work, our horse should now feel quietly steady in the mouth, with the head and neck fairly stable. The poke-nosed, flat-necked, horizontal appearance of the very young or inexperienced horse should have gradually given way to a more compact, rounded outline with the line of the face approaching the vertical.

Purposely, we have omitted talking about flexions of the horse's poll or jaw until now. Often these are practised incorrectly and if introduced too soon may confuse the horse. The all-important objective of encouraging our horse to *move forward* to take the contact and join up to the rider's hand needed to be instilled clearly. This is still our objective, but now we can make things pleasanter for both horse and rider by asking the horse to join up but to lighten onto the bit.

This may have happened naturally for many, but for those who still feel the horse harden against the hand rather than 'giving in the mouth' the time has come to look at things more closely. To quote Sara Wyche again: 'If the lower jaw is locked, then so are the muscles around the poll. Suppleness at the poll is essential to the suppleness of the back; you can't have one without the other.' We are therefore now seeking two definite responses:

- a yielding or unclenching of the jaws
- a softening and yielding of the joints and muscles around the poll.

Both effects will bring about a state of relaxation over the tongue and jaws, often referred to as chewing on the bit, which is the hallmark of true submission. This will also encourage salivation from the parotid glands. However, none of this can happen if the horse is winched into a tight noseband which clamps the jaw together.

Feeling your horse's mouth has nothing to do with forceful or busy hands. In the words of Udo Burger: 'Before he can allow himself to induce the mobility of the mouth, the rider must teach himself to feel it and to accept it passively.' Hopefully, some riders may already have achieved this without even really thinking about it.

Yielding Through Every Joint

Up until now, we have focused on the overall bend through the horse's body required for our turns and circles. To date, this bend has been relatively mild. As we progress towards smaller circles and lateral work, we need to become aware of the importance of keeping the horse vertical, while still helping him to bend. This will only happen when the horse has the confidence to yield through the poll and jaw, otherwise the head will be tilted – which would set up a chain of resistances elsewhere.

The effects of bringing the horse to the bit are not by any means isolated to the carriage of the head and neck alone. A chain reaction through all the joints influences the entire equine body to mobilise in sympathy. Gradually the back, hindquarters and hind limbs learn to free up until, finally, superior engagement is achieved with a feeling of softness and ease.

To the Bit

Here are some pointers to clarify these very natural phenomena:

- If the head is not correctly balanced over the atlas/axis joint, a whole chain of resistances is set up in the horse's back.
- Visualise the horse in freedom, particularly in canter or trot; remember how, when animated, he raises and extends his neck, drops his chin and carries his head just in front of the vertical (he only pokes his nose if sniffing the air or in full gallop for economy of breathing).
- Remember that the easy carriage of the equine head, neck up, nose down, chin and jaw relaxed is similar to human posture; discover how you carry your own head when you dance, skip or jump; feel how your chin

drops naturally down whilst the crown (poll) of your head remains uppermost.
- Be aware that tension in your jaw can cause tension in the horse's jaw. Move your tongue around if you suffer from a dry mouth and consciously let your jaw relax. Some of the best riders in dressage today ride round with slack chins!

Once we appreciate how the correct and easy balancing of the human head and neck allows the spine to articulate correctly, it is not hard to put oneself in the horse's shoes and imagine how deeply uncomfortable it would be to have the chin pulled down and back toward the chest. Once we acknowledge this, there is little temptation to place the horse's head into a false position through force.

While some horses come to the bit quite naturally, others with conformational difficulties find this initially harder. Heavy shoulders, a long back, weak loins all make it difficult for the horse to round up, raise the neck, flex from the poll and drop the chin with our weight on their backs. Sometimes, therefore, Nature needs a helping hand to restore that natural balance.

Before we learn to be more specific with our aids, we must remember that no rein effect will be of value if there is no impulsion. Impulsion therefore is a prerequisite at all times.

Rein Effects – Two Different Terms

Working complementary to our body aids, rein action can stimulate the unlocking of the horse's poll and jaw. Two important concepts to recognise are half-halts and flexions.

The Half-halt

The term *half-halt* (in French arrêt) has become very commonplace in today's dressage lessons. Many trainers use the word repeatedly, almost as a cure for all. While the half-halt has great validity, there is no doubt that unless the horse is forward-going and obedient to the leg

To the bit: the three stages of progression

First year: the young Espada is encouraged through the forward seat to reach into an elastic contact. The outline is naturally horizontal and angular.

Second year: the horse accepts more seat and a more positive contact from the rein. He answers to my leg not simply by going forward, but by raising his back under saddle with a softer more 'together' outline..

Third year: Espada now accepts my weight, full seated (classical vertical position). The contact takes on a collecting nature as I ask more from the fingers. With much less repetitive aiding from the leg, Espada now engages behind and elevates the forehand into a rounded frame. There is greater power but it is contained.

Resisting and yielding

In the early days, Milo was very prone to crossing his jaw and hardening against the hand in response to any feel on the rein, however slight.

With loving patience and tact, Allegra has won Milo's confidence to soften and yield to her hand. Note the asking effect of the fingers and of the leg closing firmly against his side ('nutcracker' action – see p.55). Once he complies, both these aids will yield.

and seat aids, and the rider has a totally independent seat, its frequent employment can be harmful. Working with the body aids, the half-halt indicates a checking restraint on the rein which is a different action from that involved in flexion.

Flexions
Although flexion through the whole of the horse's body is demanded in dressage, the term *flexions* (sometimes known as bridling) general-

ly indicates a response to a rein aid. To flex simply means to bend – in this case bending (or giving) through poll and jaw. In contrast to a checking feeling, the term 'flexion' indicates more of a touchy-feely sensation, so that the horse is gently invited to drop his chin and bend into the rein.

Although this term was constantly used in German, French, Portuguese, American and British dressage circles until the 1970s, its specific mention appears, at least in Britain, to have fallen from grace. This is odd, since good riders subconsciously carry out flexions all the time. Unfortunately, few instructors take the trouble to explain how to start the process off and often there is confusion between these two contrasting rein effects.

Skilfully used, both rein effects will assist us in bringing the horse towards that advanced state of collection known as the *rassembler*, with arched neck and rounded body, where the support of the rein becomes minimal. Both half-halts and flexions demand a sensitivity in the rider's sense of feel and timing, not just from the hands and fingers, but from the entire body – but we must understand the nuances between them.

Only with practice and knowledge, will students learn to understand the two concepts and to recognise which action does what to the body of their horse. It will take time for you and the horse to recognise the subtle differences.

Employing the Half-halt

Although this is a rein action, always think of it in terms of a change within the entire body and never of the hands alone. As previously explained it should consist of a momentary check of energy achieved by sitting up a little more, straightening or bracing the spine and squaring the shoulders, coupled with more effective leg action. Drawing up in this way whilst producing more energy behind, allows us to rebalance and prepare the horse for whatever changes we wish to make. Isolated hand action may lead to an inadvertent jab in the mouth.

- A half-halt should never, ever imply pulling the horse's head back.
- It should merely indicate a calling to attention, a confirmation that the horse is on the aids, through a light, momentary steadying or checking of his energy through the hand on the rein.
- The fingers close and, if anything, the feeling should be more upward than backward, as though the rider gently relieves the fore-

hand of much of its load, before releasing forward to allow the horse to flow into a more balanced rhythm.

- Lasting only a *split second* in its entirety, this action may be applied on both reins but is probably more commonly applied on the outside rein as, for example, in the canter depart.
- The half-halt is used primarily as a collecting aid, and its function becomes particularly relevant to gather the horse a little more together.
- A half-halt on the outside rein acts on the entire length of the horse's body to compress the energy; so, for example, in canter, the horse can bound more confidently into the gait from the energised outside hind leg.

Remember that it takes time to introduce these new ideas to the horse and great patience must be exercised, with the rein being given if any problems are encountered. Although we are working towards a feeling of gentle restraint, be careful not to quench your horse's desire to move forward. The half-halt is merely used to help us conserve energy as described in Chapter IV, so as to release it forward into a more *concentrated* form.

Employing Flexions

There are two types of flexion and it is therefore important to know the difference.

Direct flexion occurs when:
- The horse yields or flexes at the poll, drops his nose and brings his head towards the vertical (the head should never be behind the vertical).
- He must also flex or relax his jaw in response to the asking of the fingers on the rein so that he softens *into our hand*, which remains steady.
- We do this by repeated squeeze and release requests as though squeezing water out of a sponge.
- Our legs mimic our fingers by asking and

releasing and asking again at the girth. The 'asking' with the leg involves closing rather than squeezing; the inside of the leg or ankle bone should connect with that most sensitive part of the horse's side, the intercostal nerve, stimulation of which has the ability to lift the horse's back if sensitively done.

Lateral flexion occurs as:

- The horse yields or bends at the poll to look either to right or to left.
- This unilateral aid requires the head to turn into the asking rein by a subtle feel through the fingers of one hand; we may also turn the wrist and hand together with the fingernails uppermost (see photograph opposite) for more emphasis.
- The application of the leg at the girth on the same side encourages the bend, whilst the outside leg stops the horse falling outward with the quarters.
- Lateral bend enables the horse to look, encurve or be supported into the required direction – just to the inside for a turn or a circle; just to the outside for say, counter-canter.
- The feeling from the relevant rein should be enough only for the rider to see the glimmer of the horse's eye and the outer edge of the nostril; the other rein supports passively.

Collection, leading to the rassembler which involves the elevation of the horse's forehand and a constant bridling into the rider's hand, cannot take place until the horse is able to carry out both direct and lateral flexion with ease and without resistance. There can be no real collection without a degree of direct and lateral flexion present, whether on straight lines or in figurework. The feeling will be one of lightness as the horse willingly submits to the leg and rein effects and carries himself from increased engagement behind.

In direct flexion, the idea is not to pull the horse's head back into his body, as is too often seen in some arenas around the world today.

Instead, it is to work the horse's body towards the hand by energising the hindquarters. From a light acceptance and consequent submission to the rein, the forehand will become more supple and light.

Personal Confirmation

To be absolutely sure in your own mind what the horse feels in both types of flexion through the poll and jaw, put yourself in the horse's shoes and try the following simple exercises.

Direct flexion

- Stand up tall with hips forward and shoulders square and level; the neck should feel erect and balanced between them.
- Now, simply drop the chin – no more than a nod. Place the fingers to the atlas/axis joint at the back of the neck, and feel exactly where the hinge effect of the flexion takes place – this is similar to the mechanism in the horse's poll.
- The head should have dropped naturally by its own weight, supported through the stem of the neck.
- To complete the picture, relax the jaw and move the tongue around loosely with the mouth closed but never clamped. Everything should feel totally natural.

Indirect flexion

- Draw everything up tall again, and make sure the neck remains to the back of the collar.
- Nod downward again and then, without forcing anything, simply turn the face a few degrees sideways to right or to left, as though about to look over your shoulder. In so doing, try to keep the jaw relaxed and the stem of the neck erect.
- The simple act of turning the head very slightly to right or left, enables us to look where we wish to go.

Practising these two exercises together gives us a very good idea of what the horse will feel. The slight nodding down of the head (direct

(Above) Incorrect flexion: here Thomas shows both direct and lateral flexion to the left, but too much inside rein has 'shortened' his neck and his nose is behind the vertical, which blocks impulsion from behind.

(Left) Correct flexion: here, Jodie demonstrates a soft 'asking' feel on the left rein coupled with leg action to obtain correct direct and lateral flexion. Note in particular how Thomas's neck remains forward without 'breaking' in front of the wither (as so often seen). This will allow impulsion to flow through.

flexion) prior to turning actually makes things very much easier for the sideways lateral flexion (as with us).

Flexions put into Practice

How are these flexions achieved on horseback without pulling back? Initially, experiment gently with your horse standing square in halt, and think merely of inviting attention by squeezing the rein. The old masters described the action of the fingers like the 'vibrato' on a musical instrument. If the horse sets his jaw and seems unwilling to give, keep the hands quite low initially, one on either side of the base of the neck, slightly turned in. By resting them against your horse's skin, the horse feels secure and there is

less temptation to move the hand as you move the fingers.

It is always the finger action of the third, fourth or fifth (little) fingers playing or teasing on the rein, with the thumb securing the top of the rein in the normal way, which persuades the horse to 'give' through the mouth. The horse should enjoy what he feels going on in his mouth, as we cause the bit to move gently over the tongue and massage the bars.In this way, the horse is *enticed* to relax the jaw and lower his nose *into* the contact.

In direct flexion – he merely nods down, as though acknowledging the invitation of both hands.

In lateral flexion – he bends into one rein or the other, without twisting his neck.

Lateral flexion (without the rein) should come very naturally to a horse who has been frequently rewarded. However, only a fraction of the bend shown here will be required in movement.

In response, the rider then reassures the horse immediately by ceasing the action on the rein and allowing the hands to become passive again. This, kind words and a stroke show the horse he has responded correctly.

In Movement

We are now ready to start work on a big circle which will involve both types of flexion, the one complementing the other. The legs and seat must continue to aid normally and there must be *sufficient* contact with the rein for the horse to feel the fingers in the first place. Reins with no traction will hang limp in the horse's mouth and he is unlikely to notice any difference between the asking or yielding hand. Once the horse learns to flex and yield too, he *rewards himself* every time he softens to our touch on the rein.

Many books suggest that the rider's hands should be held high at this stage, in order to allow the horse to raise his head and neck, prior to flexing down from the poll. In my opinion, this depends very much upon the type of horse. If the horse is heavy in front and tends to carry himself on the forehand, with a lowered neck and poking nose, this advice may help. However, many young or novice horses carry their head a little too high and tend to hollow away at the first signs of a change of contact from their rider, and will stiffen up through the gullet and resist through the topline. With such horses it is better to keep the hands relatively low, closer to the shoulders than the wither. Turning the hand in can settle a nervous mouth.

Whether the hand is held high or low, the action of the fingers for direct flexion will remain the same. There should be a light traction on both reins as the fingers of each hand squeeze and ask, complemented by the legs. The moment the horse complies by nodding his head downward from the poll – however slight the offering – the fingers must soften and reward, to allow the horse to move forward from the leg, thus filling the rein again.

Once the horse understands these concepts on the circle, it is time to think about flexion on straight lines. Direct flexion may be more difficult initially when the horse remains on the track, since there will be less bend through the horse's body to help us – but this is very natural. Do not, therefore, try to force anything, just concentrate on improving the lateral flexion and gradually, as the horse becomes more ambidextrous, he will start to put himself on the bit.

The proof, therefore, that the flexion aid has been understood in this very early stage, is when the horse continues in his work with a relaxed poll and jaw, quietly maintaining the position into which the rider has placed his head without in any way leaning on the rein. The neck and back of the horse should flow as one continuous piece, with the horse's poll

This shows the moment of 'give' through the fingers. As the horse lightens, so must we if we are to encourage more of the same. There should be no subsequent loss of outline or engagement if the horse is truly in self-carriage – the proof of collection.

generally constituting the highest point.

Correct flexion has nothing to do with displacing the head and neck from the horrendous but all-too-common practice of see-sawing hands. The rein action should be imperceptible – merely a secret shared between horse and rider.

Decreasing Circles

Decreasing the circle, whether in walk, trot or canter, will require a greater degree of lateral flexion from the poll commensurate with bending in the body in response to the leg aids. We have already discussed the important influence of the outside supporting rein in smaller circles in Chapter V, so be careful that, in seeking lateral flexion to the inside, you do not overemphasise the action on the inside rein to the detriment of the other aids.

Since the horse is required to be more flexible

Now that Jean brings her horse together with asking legs and both hands together, her horse begins to come 'to the bit' showing a moist mouth, which is the result of softening and yielding through the joints.

in the smaller circles, initial requests may be answered by blocking. If the horse continues to resist, simply try again but make shorter, quicker squeezes with the fingers and more urgent requests with the legs, always remembering to relax the pressure in between.

The moment the horse responds by yielding the jaw and rotating his head slightly to the inside – a few degrees is sufficient – reward immediately by softening the fingers and making the hand passive, even if it means losing the bend. You should then stroke the horse and praise him. If difficulties continue, it may be that previous mistakes made in schooling have created resistances. A good way to encourage relaxation and bending from the poll is to stroke or rub the horse's neck, particularly close to the poll area. Never expect direct flexion until the horse can flex laterally first.

Often, this gentling with the hand creates an understanding of what is required. For greater emphasis with a very 'tight' horse, the rider may go a stage further by rotating the inside hand and wrist together as one piece, so that the fingernails begin to show uppermost before squeezing again. This puts a little more pressure on the asking or opening rein, but again the hand acts in a forward direction. This aid was prescribed by the great eighteenth-century master, de la Guérinière, for the shoulder-in.

Always help the horse by turning your own head, but only as much as is required of the horse. The human head weighs just under a stone (6.35kg or 14 lbs, US.) and I have seen previously uncomprehending horses move into the asking rein, after just a mild turn of the rider's face into the required direction. It's as though they say '*Now* I understand! – why didn't you do that before?' The effect of such aids says much for the sensitivity of horses. No wonder top dressage riders always look exactly where their horse is looking.

Rounding

As the horse learns to flex through the poll there is less likelihood of his falling out through the shoulders as he works through from behind. In the meantime, the neck will have become more muscular and arched. As with our own bodies, the equine neck must be firm and supported, never floppy.

From now on, the horse should be able to maintain a uniform bend throughout the entire body whilst remaining secure, balanced and upright. On every straight line and in every circle, turn or change of rein, the rider should just be able to see the glimmer of the eye and the outer edge of the nostril, no more no less. It is all a matter of correct aiding and sensitivity with the fingers. Once the horse knows how to yield into the rein, everything will seem lighter, more flexible but infinitely safer.

There is now no excuse not to keep the position of the neck in front of the withers. The horse's ears should be level in all the turns and there should be no 'shortened' or 'broken' necks. Colonel Podhajsky of the Spanish Riding School specifically warns against rubberising the horse's neck since, as with the

Note how flexion through the poll and jaw complements the flexion of the hind limb joints. Having obtained good flexion in this collected trot, Suzanne employs a gentle feeling of half-halt through her body, which sets Vaidoso momentarily back on his hocks to rebalance. This aid is much more to do with the rider's seat than her hands. The horse should remain in a pleasing outline, with his neck forward and arching softly upward towards the poll.

human neck, the entire structure must be upwardly stable. Everything should therefore flow forward in a soft, unbroken line from the hindquarters to the poll as a mere *extension of the horse's back.*

Roundness comes when greater engagement or 'sitting' behind allows the forehand to rise and the back and loins to take on a convex appearance. Correct aiding from light touches of the lower leg on the girth encourages greater freedom of the horse's shoulder. Correct bending allows him to move in one *supple, flowing but connected piece* in all forward work and in reining back.

Minimising the Rein Aids

Once the horse has responded to these requests, try not to go on asking and asking. Feel that your hands merely indicate the general parameters, but after that the body, seat and leg simply maintain the horse in the desired direction, frame and rhythm. When the horse is truly on the aids, it is as though the horse puts himself on parole with 'non-interference' the name of the game. Soon the asking phase will lessen, the allowing phase becomes longer and, when every aid is minimalist, we know our schooling methods have been correct.

CHAPTER IX

Stiff or Hollow?
Improving Both Sides of Your Horse and Turns on the Hocks

Every creature favours a particular way of travel; the dominant side prevailing over the passive.

One of the greatest difficulties for the conscientious teacher, and for pupils, is the number of instructions and counter-instructions that will need to be issued during a dressage lesson. 'More inside rein!', 'More outside rein!', 'More inside leg!', 'More outside leg!' and so on. Riding is full of apparent contradictions.

To date, I have warned of the evils of pulling on the inside rein, which destabilises the horse's neck, concentrating instead on flexions from the poll which complement the gentle bend from nose to tail. In so doing, I have spoken of the outside rein supporting the outside of the horse and preventing too much bend to the inside.

I have also touched on the collecting effects of the half-halt, particularly when applied on the outside rein. Whilst all the above is valid, and will bring a great deal more prowess and control to the movements learned to date, we should also be conscious that it can be tempting to overdo things to the outside as well as to the inside. At the end of the day, a light even-handedness will be our ultimate goal, with the action of the rein passing through the entire body of the horse in every stride.

Despite this, we must recognise that, even with the perfectly balanced horse, there will be times when he will feel softer on one rein than the other – and this is not necessarily wrong. On a circle, particularly a smaller circle of say 10 m, it is logical that the more the horse bends through his body to the inside, the lighter he will feel on the inside rein. Indeed, he makes his own softness because of the degree of bend which ensues from the stepping under of his inside hind leg. This also has the effect of shortening the frame to the inside. The classical masters warn against blocking the incoming inside leg by taking more contact on this rein, since this could destroy all the good things being offered.

Conversely, as this process occurs to the inside, the outside of the horse's body must stretch and lengthen relative to the shortening to the inside. We have already compared the working of the equine muscles to those of the human, the action of the triceps and biceps being a prime example. In flexion to the right therefore, the horse's left side will require sufficient freedom to stretch in order to *accommodate* this bending effect. If we are to help rather than hinder this natural process, the rider must at this stage be very careful not to block the horse with the outside rein either! *Instead it should ease or allow so the horse is encouraged to fill it.*

Too Much Outside Hand

The principle of riding inside leg to outside hand is a useful concept to help keep the horse out to the track and from falling in on the circle. Taken to an extreme, however, too much action with the outside hand can actually prevent the horse advancing correctly round a corner or circle and it may lead to head-tilting and crookedness. Many horses lead with their croups when attempting voltes.

In order to help the horse move correctly in these tighter manoeuvres, the rider must offer a momentary respite from the outside rein. Once the rider becomes more aware of this need on behalf of the horse, feels the right moment and acts upon it appropriately, the whole picture becomes more flowing. *Momentarily allowing* with the outside hand, to release the horse's outside shoulder a little forward, is therefore just as important as giving with the inside rein to free the inside shoulder. Again, it is all down to awareness and timing.

If riders find this concept difficult, they should use their eyes to see when it might be necessary. Prior, say, to turning down the centre line, the moment will present itself through the corner as the horse bends around the rider's inside leg but extends to the outside. Watch as his outside shoulder advances; all at once there is greater pressure on the outside rein as the horse stretches like a bow. If the rider were to take more rein in this case, the horse might jack-knife sideways and lose balance. A momentary release forward with the outside hand *allows* that outside shoulder to come round smoothly. Only then will the centre line be accurate and straight.

Blaming the Horse

All dressage students worry about their horse's hollow or stiff side. Too often the horse bears the blame for this, but crooked riders make for crooked horses and my first priority with a new student is to ascertain whether the fault lies

In flexing right, the horse's left side will need to extend in order to accommodate the bend. By correctly allowing her left shoulder to ease round in the half-circle with the horse, Andrea has reduced pressure on the left rein which allows the horse to turn easily.

with the horse or with their position. Nine times out of ten, the rider will have a tendency to sit more heavily to one side than the other. The fashionable excuse is for the rider then to say 'my horse throws me this way'. On the other hand, it could be that the horse is merely moving into and under the uneven load -– in other words, he kindly picks his rider up and then gets blamed for it!

Right-handed riders have a tendency to draw back with the right hand, which twists their body in the same direction so that the inside hip moves back and slightly towards the left of the saddle, instead of remaining firmly on the right of the twist. Since this creates a weight aid to *the left*, the horse cannot be blamed if he then finds it difficult to turn right or to circle right in balance. Until a rider is aware of his or her own inconsistencies – and this generally involves a commitment for life,

In this circle right, the rider demonstrates the error of leaving the outside shoulder behind (a common fault among dressage riders). Clearly, this puts more pressure on the outside rein so the horse, unable to stretch the outside of his body into the right bend, tilts his head uncomfortably left.

since we can never forget for a moment our own weaknesses when we ride – the horse will take on our problems as well as his own.

So while it cannot be denied that each horse, like us, has his dextrous and his less dextrous side, we must first work on ourselves. This means self-examination at all times, particularly when our horse finds it difficult to carry out what should be a simple request. More often than not, he may be unable to give us what we want because our body is telling him something quite different.

These are small checks which every serious rider should go through as soon they are mounted and in motion. On a straight line therefore:

- Are my eyes and ears level?
- Are my shoulders square and on the same level one to the other?
- Are both sides of my waist tall and erect?
- Are my hips level?
- Are both my seatbones on their correct side of the saddle?
- Is there equal pressure in each?
- Are both my legs hanging down evenly?
- Are both my knees and both my feet pointing forward?
- Are both my stirrups correctly and evenly weighted?
- Are my hands evenly placed on each side of the horse's neck?

(Even in turns and circles, the levels should remain equal, but by remaining in balance with the horse, the pressure may alter accordingly).

Only when all questions can be answered in the affirmative, should the rider address the problems which may exist in the horse. As with the human body, most forms of unevenness can be vastly improved once the rider teaches the horse to stretch correctly.

So many horses tend to hold themselves rigidly through one side of the body and compensate by overbending the other way. Once the work on the long rein is introduced as a regular daily work-out, with equal and generous time given to stretch exercises on both reins, these difficulties will gradually iron out. Certainly no horse should be allowed to develop in such a way that his natural crookedness becomes more marked.

The hallmark of a good rider is one who is able to show a horse who appears ambidextrous; who bends equally on both reins or is equally straight in every exercise. By now, an onlooker should have to look pretty hard to assess which side of your horse is stiffer and which more hollow. Once these tendencies

Checking levels: work without stirrups can often help eradicate human error and make us more ambidextrous. Here, Jodie remains absolutely square to her horse, much helped by a good hand position.

have been eradicated with stretch exercises, the rider can concentrate on increasing flexibility on both sides with the help of the more collected exercises. *Always ask for a little more position of the forehand on the stiff side, and rather less on the hollow.*

Early Collection

The 10 m circle or volte, required in dressage tests from Elementary level onwards, not only creates a more malleable horse, but is the best preparation for lateral work. Although this is demanded in trot at competitions, it is often incorrectly ridden with the horse hauled round by the inside rein, which disengages the hind legs. For this reason, it should be started in walk as the first step towards introducing the horse to the collected work. Although many authorities advise caution when introducing

Checking for stiffness: temporarily removing the contact will very quickly show us which side of the horse is the stiffer (in this case, the left). Here, by not giving him the inside rein to lean on in a left circle, Jodie is teaching Thomas to become more responsible for his own balance.

From a half-circle left at K, Allegra rides Milo back to the track and finds that the right rein has become more important than the left. This, together with her right leg, creates a framing effect for the horse.

As well as assisting bend, it is important that the inside leg also gives impulsion to the walk. The rider must feel that the horse moves forward in a good four-beat rhythm, nicely framed and channelled within the circle by the rider's whole body. The outside leg will make sure that the hind legs do not stray out of the circumference of the circle. They must keep the quarters engaged and the hind legs marching forward.

After a couple of voltes, the rider should move on up the track towards the A or C end of the school, still in walk, and return to the track by riding half a 10 m circle to the centre line and progressing diagonally back to E or B. Since this manoeuvre will require a change of rein, the rider should again be aware of the role of the outside rein.

It may even be at this point that the rider feels the influence of the outside rein is beginning to *supersede* that of the inside. This is no deception of mind; neither is it a product of faulty training. The truth is quite the opposite, for subtly used the outside rein has become an *indirect rein* aid and is responsible now for returning the horse to the track.

Back at E or B, the new inside rein takes over and the horse is flexed gently into the new direction. The outside hand remains in a passive, supporting role until another turn, change of direction or circle is asked for.

Directional Aiding

We have now seen how an indiscriminate use of both the inside rein and the outside rein may block the horse through the shoulders. We have also seen how each rein, acting independently, can discriminate and help the horse in

the collected walk, it is my view that this is the easiest way for the horse to learn to move forward and in balance from behind.

Collecting the walk encourages deeper engagement, elevation in the shoulders and lends a cohesive strength to the whole structure. As the rider brings the horse off the track and into the circle with the inside (opening) rein asking for a little flexion with the fingers, it will soon be found that the outside rein has a greater part to play to keep the horse *out* to the circumference.

This is more important than ever when the circle is small since the all-important tracking must be maintained. At this stage it is too easy for the horse to avoid working behind by leading with the inside shoulder, falling in with the quarters and 'skating' round. This is where flexion becomes so important and one visual indication that the horse has not overloaded one shoulder or another is when the ears of the horse remain level throughout.

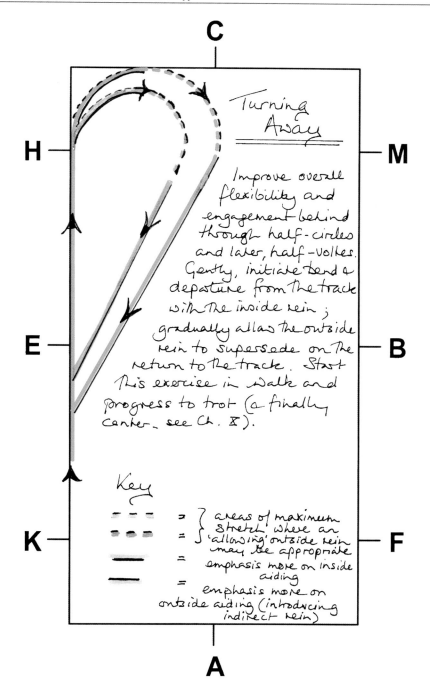

C

H — **M**

Turning
Away
‗‗‗‗‗

Improve overall
flexibility and
engagement behind
through half-circles
and later, half-voltes.
Gently, initiate bend &
departure from the track
with the inside rein;
gradually allow the outside
rein to supersede on the
return to the track. Start
this exercise in walk and
progress to trot (& finally
Canter - see Ch. X).

E — **B**

Key

K — **F**

- - - = ⎫ areas of maximum
- - - = ⎬ stretch where an
      ⎭ 'allowing' outside rein
      may be appropriate
──── = emphasis more on inside
      aiding
──── = emphasis more on
outside aiding (introducing
indirect rein)

A

his different tasks. If we are going to ride in subtlety and lightness, with the horse happy and submissive through mouth and body and able to bend, straighten and stretch at any given moment, the time has come to give names to these more specialised aids.

Up until now, we have always talked about the inside opening rein for turns and flexions.

From now on this may be referred to as the direct rein.

As we have learned to appreciate the influence of the outside rein, not only through the half-halts but also with general support to the outside, we have discovered that the outside rein can be instrumental in confirming direction. For that reason it may be referred to as the indirect rein. Both the direct and indirect rein act on the forehand.

The term 'indirect' implies that it acts from the opposite side of the required direction.

If this sounds confusing, let me remind the reader that we spoke at the beginning of the chapter of many apparent contradictions in riding. One of the greatest of all is that you can turn your horse to the right with the left hand! But in reality, is it so confusing? Not when we examine it step by step. For example, if working right:

- First focus right and make sure your body, seat and leg aids are also thinking right.
- Now, in one quiet action, move *both* hands a little right – into the direction of the movement.
- This will have slightly opened the right (direct) rein to provide a little space (right) for the horse to move into.
- At the same time it should have closed the left (indirect) rein up to the base of the neck – that is, you close any gap to the left.
- All together now, the whole horse is moving right!

In this way, the *combined effect of the reins* has turned the horse.

More on the Indirect Rein

Western riders use indirect rein aids all the time. Perhaps more sensibly, the term is known as neck-reining. In the classical school, neck-reining is never mentioned; nevertheless with both hands remaining at the wither, the outside rein creates a totally unobtrusive nudging sideways effect. The flexed position of the horse's head to the inside is thereby helped by both direct and indirect aids.

Nowhere is the use of the indirect rein more appropriate than in spiralling down exercises. Once the 10 m circle is established in walk, we may think about similar work in trot. It is better by far to do this gradually and progressively.

Spiralling downward from a 20 m circle to a 15 m circle and then gradually reducing the

On a tighter half-circle right, Lesley allows her left shoulder to ease round and then uses the indirect (left) rein to prepare Vaidoso for a return to the track (right). It acts against the base of the neck but must never cross it.

circle in size, until the horse can move into a volte all with the same ease and balance, will again demonstrate the value of the indirect rein encouraging the horse ever inward. It is important that the horse is not hurried in these circles, since a greater sense of collection and engagement will be required. The horse will need to encurve more to the inside and the joints of the hind legs will sustain more pressure to cope with the increased flexion. So as not to tire him, or put too much stress on these joints, the rider should initially ride the horse back out and onto the larger circle after a couple of attempts. Now the outside rein will act in an opening capacity.

(Below) Do not sit too heavy in the trot to halt transitions. Jodie is preparing to halt at A from a circle. Correctly her lower legs move back to close around the horse and she will draw her tummy forward and up in the moment of halt, hopefully looking up too!

(Right) Make sure everything stays neutral once the horse has halted. Straightness is more important than perfect squareness at this stage. Sit tall so that your weight flows naturally down. Do not push!

Trot to Halt Transitions

At this point the horse should be ready for balanced trot to halt transitions. You may have tried these earlier, but it requires real engagement of the hind limb joints to do these well. As with all the transitions to date, start this work on a big circle. Initially, don't place too much importance on the horse standing perfectly square. The nature of the circle will tend to place his inside hind more under his body than the outside so it would be wrong to discourage this. Later, you can ride some half figures-of-eight joined together by a straight line and here, in the centre, it would be fair to ask for a square halt once the horse has got the idea – but take time!

The point at which the circle touches the track is the easiest place to start developing these transitions. Always think of your outside rein checking (half-halts) rather more than the inside. Remember, however, that the rein aids are very much secondary to those of the seat and legs. If your progressive transition work has been correct, there should not be much difficulty in achieving an obedient halt, but if your horse suddenly swings his quarters to the inside, it may well be that you have used your outside leg more strongly than the inside. All he is doing is moving away from the pressure. This is a common fault, so correct it with a little more inside flexion and by keeping a feeling of inside leg to outside hand.

Centre Line Transitions to Halt

When you come to do these transitions on the

centre line, you will have no bend or outer walls to support you, so everything must feel very 'four-square'. Halts are quite a personal thing, but for me, the sequence of events prior to halt at X is roughly as follows:

- I think of sitting tall as I approach X, but I keep my horse's hind legs active, with both legs asking for impulsion.
- The downward transition aid is as much *thought* as anything, but somewhere I check through my back and tummy before checking with the reins.
- Letting my weight down through the front of my thighs, I close the lower legs slightly further back than normal, keeping the seat-bones well forward to make space for the horse's back.
- The idea is to ride the horse *up* into halt, so I stretch an inch taller still at the moment of halt. This creates a feeling of resistance through the shoulders but the horse is given the room for the hind feet to step well under.
- I yield with the fingers immediately the horse obeys and my legs relax and drop back to their normal place.

Always remain proud but unresisting after the halt; if you bear down, the horse may well step back. Riding this way is very much in keeping with the Spanish Riding School motto: 'Up the body; down the weight!'

More Bend and Less Bend

One of my favourite suppling exercises to utilise both the small and the big circles is to progress onto a 20 m circle at either the A or C end of the school. Initially, the horse is then asked to make a 10 m circle off the circumference of the 20 m circle at the two sides – just after K (M) or just after F (H). Having completed each small circle, he is then immediately brought back onto his big circle encouraged by the outside hand. In this way, he gets used to moving inward and outward; this makes the

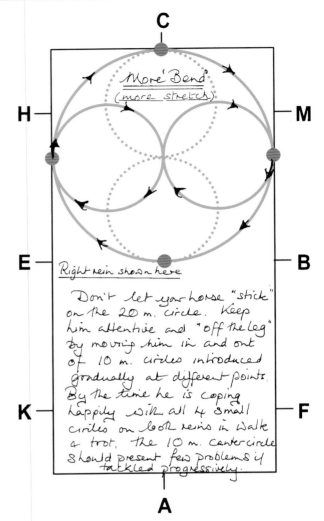

bigger circle feel really easy after the effort he has had to make to produce more bend for the smaller circle. In other words, returning to the 20 m circular track constitutes a reward.

Gradually, as the horse becomes more adept at changing from the small circle back to the bigger one, he can be asked to make four 10 m circles at the four 'points' of the big circle (see diagram). Do not ask for this too quickly, however, and make sure that the rein is often changed so that he does not linger for too long in the same bend. As the old adage says – a change is as good as a rest – and so it is for horses.

If the horse finds it easy to bend to the inside because we are working him on his hollow side, it is better to ask for rather less position with the forehand. On the horse's stiff side, we will ask for soft flexion and more position with the forehand. Working the stiff side to achieve more bend, helps the hollow side to take more contact, provided it is always backed up by the correct leg aids.

Diligent work of this nature on both reins, with the rider always retaining a feel through sensitive hands for the balance of the horse in every exercise, should soon eradicate major signs of crookedness. Never ride the horse more on one side than the other, and be aware that sometimes, through technically skilful training, the horse can change from being hollow on one side to hollow on the other. While this might be encouraging to the extent of proving that you have made a difference, it reinforces the message that all training should be even-handed. If real difficulties are encountered with contact, it may be the rider has forgotten to return to basics. The answer is always the same – if you come up against a problem, do not present the horse with more of the work which he finds difficult; instead let him chill out. The work on the long rein and in particular the stretch, will almost certainly iron out the creases.

Turns on the Haunches

The time has come to find another exercise which will reduce one-sidedness by accentuating flexion to the inside and greater stretch to the outside. Performed with a proper contact and asked for on both the horse's stiff and hollow side, it is a great leveller. The turn on the haunches is also known as turn on the hocks or the quarter or half pirouette. At this stage it will be done in walk (although at a much higher level it can be developed in canter).

This exercise teaches the horse more collection in the walk, helps him to turn from well-engaged hind legs, and encourages him to remain in 'one piece' while flexed to the inside. Performed correctly, it promotes lateral bending and so it really helps one-sided horses. As

described by the FEI: '*The forefeet and the outside hind foot move round the inside hind foot which forms the pivot and should return to the same spot or slightly in front of it, each time it leaves the ground*'. It has the added advantage of freeing up the shoulders by bringing the weight of the horse further back.

Everyone should start with the quarter pirouette since the half or demi-pirouette is generally considered quite an advanced movement. The quarter pirouette consists simply of a turn through 90 degrees, and is ideally comprised of two steps, with the horse remaining bent around the rider's inside leg. While the front legs take two well-defined forward-and-sideways steps, the hind legs, by pushing well under the horse, take much smaller steps.

In a half pirouette, four steps will be taken (in a full pirouette – generally ridden in canter – there will be eight). The forehand moves around the hind end, with the radius equal to roughly the length of the horse, while the hind legs describe a small half-circle, no bigger in diameter than a dinner plate. There should be no stopping prior to the movement and no swivelling on the hind legs. Instead, increasingly active and collected sideways steps will be taken, but always thinking forward.

Once understood and ridden correctly, the quarter pirouette is very useful for turning away from the track to make a change of rein across the short side of the school. Frequent practice will prepare the horse for better turns in trot (say at E or B in a test from Elementary level upward) since the aids will be similar, particularly the use of the half-halt.

Ideally, the turn on the haunches should be introduced to the horse after riding a correct 10 m circle in walk to ensure lateral bend to the inside. The number of steps may vary with each horse, but it is a bad fault to step out behind. Since the turn requires deeper engagement, a feeling for flexion through the poll and jaw is vital. However the exercise itself improves flexibility, so as with most things – it's a chicken and egg situation.

Introducing the left quarter pirouette (walk)

Preparation: think left, look left, flexion left; weight into left inside seatbone and stirrup, outside (unseen) leg moves back.

Outside leg acts, indirect rein nudges left, maintaining tempo and collection, rider's outside shoulder edges round with horse, inside leg invites and supports bend.

Repetition of each aid, but inside leg is sufficiently allowing for horse to step round and into it; so is the inside rein.

(The number of steps can vary at this stage depending on the capability and collection of the horse.)

Riding a Quarter Turn on the Haunches Right

RIDER AIDS AND THOUGHTS (prior to turning at H)

- From an active walk, I ride a 10 m circle between E and H, with my horse flexing softly into the inside rein and bending around my inside leg.
- Back on the track, I straighten my horse but keep a soft feeling of flexion right through the fingers and inside leg.
- Although I want my horse to turn right (away from the track) at H, I know I mustn't take more right rein, since the circle already gave me flexion; instead I advance my inside (right) seatbone and slightly increase the downward pressure into the inside stirrup.
- As I do so, I sit up, straighten the spine, and half-halt very gently with the outside rein to put my horse more on the hocks.
- I then ask the horse to move right from the haunches by stepping away from the pressure of my outside (left) leg, which has moved back to act behind the girth.
- As the horse turns, I take my outside (left) rein gently to the right to help his shoulders move right.

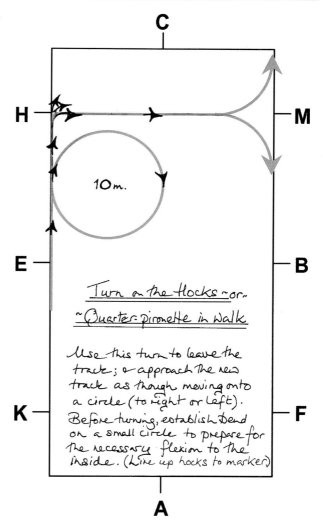

Turn on the Hocks ~or~ ~Quarter-pirouette in walk

Use this turn to leave the track; or approach the new track as though moving onto a circle (to right or left). Before turning, establish bend on a small circle to prepare for the necessary flexion to the inside. (Line up hocks to marker)

The rider should always think forward and into the turn in two definite steps. Thus two press and release aids are given with the outside leg. As the horse responds to these requests, the outside (left) rein acts as an *indirect rein* by moving towards the wither.

The contact with the left rein should feel *positive* since, by giving away too much, the horse might be tempted to fall back onto the track. At the same time, this rein must never pull back, since it has to accommodate the longitudinal stretch of the horse's body to the outside. Nevertheless, it is the indirect action of the outside rein which has taken the horse right. The inside hand, having asked for flexion in the circle, has mainly done its job, although

the fingers may continue to invite. The idea is that the horse will always *want to move into the softer, more passive rein* and into the weight aid of the inside leg.

Having completed the two steps to the right, the horse should now be looking straight across the short side of the school to M on the opposite track. This is where mistakes are invariably made as the rider allows the inside leg to move back with the thought that the turn is complete. Unfortunately, the horse is usually still listening to the influence of the outside leg and may fall onto the right shoulder unless the right (inside) leg supports on the girth and actively and immediately says forward! This, therefore, has to be the next aid if the horse is to arrive straight at the centre line.

Let us examine what actually happens to the horse as he makes his quarter turn on the hocks. First, we show just how easy it is to make mistakes:

THE HORSE'S THOUGHTS (uneducated rider)

- I've been circled right, but my hindquarters are not quite under me as I return to the track because my neck has too much right bend.
- 'Outside hand!' the trainer calls, and now I receive a sharp backward tug on my left rein which they call a half-halt! It's more like a halt to me, because it stops me altogether for a second!
- Suddenly my rider draws her outside leg back and pushes me hard sideways.
- Because my neck is still twisted, and there's no support from the inside leg, I fall onto the right shoulder, but I find myself looking to the left since the outside rein hasn't allowed me sufficient room! It's most uncomfortable...
- I want to move forward with my hind legs, but the sideways push has really caught me off balance so I step out and back with my right hind to save myself and spin round.
- I try to go straight to M but my rider's outside leg is still clamped on, so I wobble violently to the right and receive a big boot in both ribs! This turn on the hocks is a beastly exercise...

Yet, with patience and the correct aids, this exercise is one which horses generally love since it allows them to turn comfortably and naturally. Let us try again with an educated rider and see how her body movements will help the horse to remain secure, confident and balanced in his turn.

THE HORSE'S THOUGHTS (educated rider)

- I have just finished circling and am now moving up the track prior to the turn right. My rider's inside (right) leg restrains me from falling in but I feel a soft bend through the poll and ribcage, even though she has straightened my neck with the outside hand.
- Suddenly, everything changes! She sits up taller, deepens her weight to the right and changes the straight-and-onward feel to one of checking and change of direction. It's almost a juggling act of rebalancing my energy!
- Now I feel her bodyweight takes me right. I can feel the downward pressure through the inside (right) stirrup and the inside rein is soft and inviting, so I feel I want to step into this opening – shall I?
- Now I get a real signal! There's a quite definite tap from her outside (left) leg behind the girth. Her outside knee and thigh are nudging at my outside shoulder and I take one step to the right and then another. I keep my balance because she sits so firm and erect and the inside leg is like a pillar!
- With each step I feel the outside rein encouraging me in the turn; my rider's left hand is close to my wither and it's as though she is nudging my forehand around my quarters – it feels quite surprisingly natural...
- Suddenly I am facing straight across the school. For a moment I almost lose my balance and wiggle as we proceed to M, but her inside leg is there at the girth to catch me! I have nothing to fear and go straight across.

As can be seen, we are now getting to a stage in our riding where everything we do can either help or hinder our horse. Every aid we have learned to date is being reinforced at this stage but, without constantly examining the reasons behind each move and appreciating how the horse feels us on his back, our work will be flawed. Try always to feel and listen to him, and as much as possible, put yourself in his shoes as I have above. It can really make a difference once we think like this *all* the time.

PART FIVE
The Work Proper – Elementary Level

CHAPTER X
Building up to Counter-canter, Canter Transitions and the Rein-back

CHAPTER XI
Lateral Work from Leg-yield to Shoulder-in – the Key to Collection

CHAPTER X

Building up to Counter-canter, Canter Transitions and the Rein-back

All horses can counter-canter quite naturally if left to their own devices.

By now our horse should be feeling far more connected through the reins, softer and suppler through the back and more impulsive behind. As both horse and rider become more familiar with the influence of the indirect rein aids, previously tricky manoeuvres such as turning straight across or down the centre line will be much more accurate.

The riding of squares in walk is another exercise to be developed from the quarter turn on the hocks. Start with 15 m squares and gradually decrease these to 10 m using the centre line or quarter lines as your guide. In the trot serpentine, think of riding onto the track as part of a circle and depart from the track as part of a square with an indirect rein aid.

We can now take the theme of the indirect rein a little further as we prepare for counter-canter. This should only be started when the horse is able to make balanced transitions from canter to trot and back again. There must be no sense of rushing. Riding the canter transitions in the same way as we approached the trot transitions in Chapter VII by thinking 'uphill' and inviting through the seat will achieve a feeling of roundness under saddle.

The most important aspect of the canter transition is to keep the horse engaged without overuse of the rein, which will merely 'shorten' his neck. For this reason, we have refrained from asking for accurate canter transitions too soon. It is all too tempting to concentrate on the front end and stop the movement through the neck, but the reality is that the best transitions are made centrally, over the point of balance and this can only be brought about by weight changes exerted through the seat and legs.

Consistency

For this reason, the rider must always think forward in the canter, even when slowing it, and the most flighty horse must learn to accept the leg. This does not imply gripping on, but the leg should be close to the point of application, *always at the ready* to reinforce the aid. Thus, the 'canter position' of inside leg close to the girth, outside leg behind the girth, will remain in place. Removing the leg once canter is achieved, with the idea that this will steady or calm a very forward-going horse is a mistake. Every vestige of balance and direction will vanish and it is almost an invitation for the horse to freefall in canter. Without the continued subtle use of the leg, the channelling effect of the rider's body will be lost.

Once the horse is confident, forward-going and accepting of the rider's seat and leg aids in normal canter, it is time to introduce...

...more collection. Once this is achieved without the horse losing balance or leaning on the forehand, we are ready to introduce the counter-canter.

So how can we make accurate transitions in the canter without the horse leaning on the hand? The first thing to remember is that in every change of pace, change of gait, change of direction, we have to think how the horse draws support from our aids. By now he should be accustomed to a real consistency in the way we ask for things. Therefore, once a request is obeyed, he should remain in that particular way of going, until we make a change. Nowhere in riding is this consistency of the aids more important than in the canter.

Reinforcing the 'Canter Position'

If we have followed the accepted guidelines for canter, the horse should by now be well accustomed to the feel of our body as well as our legs in the *canter position*. To recap:

- The rider's inside leg position should complement the placing of the inside hip a little more forward in the saddle.
- There will be fractionally more weight in the inside seatbone and inside stirrup.
- Likewise, the outside leg will be placed further back – not simply from the knee down, but the whole leg.
- The outside hip should have released to accommodate this position; some trainers call this the 'opening' hip, which will be placed fractionally further back in the saddle.

Provided that nothing changes and the legs and seatbones remain in the canter position to freshen up the gait, the canter should not change.

Canter circle right

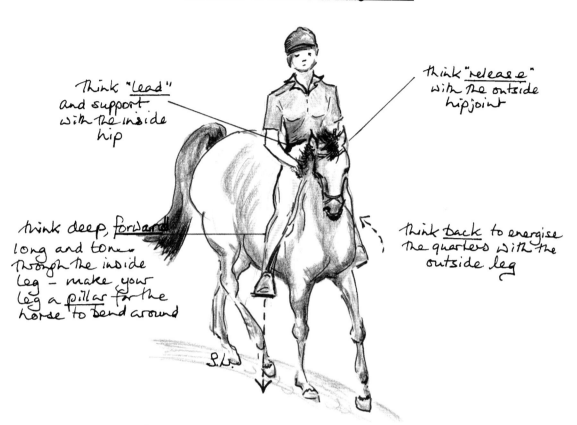

Think "*lead*" and support with the inside hip

think "*release*" with the outside hipjoint

think deep, *forward*, long and tone through the inside leg – make your leg a pillar for the horse to bend around

think *back* to energise the quarters with the outside leg

S.W.

Check your "canter position" at all times and make sure you are giving your horse the feel of canter through your whole body.

We are now entering a more refined phase of riding as we consider the effects of deliberately changing these important leg and weight aids. Most people are aware that, in the flying change, the rider's 'canter position' reverses itself, in other words the old outside aid becomes the new inside aid and vice versa. However tempting it may be to move onto teaching the horse changes of lead in canter at this stage – particularly since so many horses enjoy this and offer long before asked – it is important to desist for the moment. To start with, concentrate on obedient changes of lead through trot.

Transitions

The first thing to ensure in these downward transitions is that the horse understands adequately when he is no longer required to canter -– in other words, when he is to return to trot – and I am not implying a pull on the reins. We are now at the stage of thinking *less*, rather than *more* to refine all that has been achieved to date.

In this context, I ask my students to sit up firmly to stay in balance, but to think of *releasing* the horse from the canter to make a smooth downward transition. To achieve this we must release ourselves from the canter position while still riding forward. This involves allowing the inside leg to drop fractionally back while the outside leg, previously behind the girth, drops fractionally forward so that both hang roughly parallel to each other to act again in a bilateral way. Since this will also affect our weight aids, the horse no longer 'feels' canter so, depending on the accompanying body and hand aids, he should assume trot or walk.

In this way, the horse is required to learn nothing new; it is simply a logical response to move out of canter once the 'canter position' no longer exists. Coupled with a checking feel through the seat and rein, most horses will automatically move forward into trot. Canter to walk transitions will require much more collection and greater engagement behind, but the process is similar. *Remember, however, that you must still ride forward and through in all these transitions.*

Simple Change of Leg at Canter

British Dressage rules define this as: '*A change of leg where the horse is brought back immediately into walk and, after three–five steps, is restarted immediately into a canter with the other leg leading.*'

Although the upward transition from walk should pose few problems, many horses are not yet strong enough through the back to offer sufficient collection for an accurate canter to walk. Although dressage tests demand these transitions at Elementary level, my feeling is that it is better to ride the downward part progressively at this stage if your horse is struggling. Nothing is worth doing badly and many will agree this is quite an advanced and arduous requirement.

Whether proceeding immediately to walk or through trot, the legs should effectively return to a *neutral position* to guide the horse through those intermediary forward steps after the first canter. Before the canter depart on the new lead, the rider should apply an extra half-halt

from the 'new' outside hand (to warn of a change) and then clearly assume the new canter position with reversed aids.

Few textbooks explain just how sensitive horses are to these small shifts in balance, but many riders may now begin to appreciate why their horse sometimes breaks in canter when they least expect it. If the horse is truly on the aids, moving the supporting inside leg back during a corner or canter circle is enough to make the horse feel quite insecure. The safest and most logical response for him therefore will be to return to trot, and he should not necessarily be blamed.

The opposite case is the rider who experiences difficulty in coming out of canter. By failing to release the horse from the canter position and then trying to salvage the downward transition with the hand and seat alone, such a rider may simply drive the horse onto the forehand. It will thus be difficult to make accurate transitions in a specified place.

Counter-canter Loops

Once we have shown the horse real *consistency* with the aids of direction, support and impulsion, we are ready to tackle the counter-canter. This should be done in stages and should present no problem to either horse or rider. To help the horse prepare for his first attempt at full counter-canter, where he literally goes round the track with 'the wrong leading leg', we may wish to slightly exaggerate the downward weight aid of the original inside leg. However do not start with this, but build up the exercise progressively.

Probably the best way forward at this stage will be to introduce some shallow loops, as shown in the diagram. Always start these exercises after a big circle at the A or C end of the school to establish forwardness and bend. Proceed now to the next corner and invite the horse to move in from the track and ride a 3 m loop towards the quarter line. This movement involves very little extra aiding other than

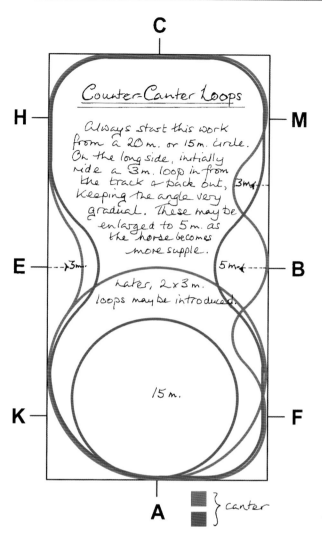

Counter-Canter Loops

Always start this work from a 20 m. or 15 m. circle. On the long side, initially ride a 3 m. loop in from the track & back out, keeping the angle very gradual. These may be enlarged to 5 m. as the horse becomes more supple.

Later, 2 x 3 m. loops may be introduced.

Once the horse is confident making 3 m loops in from the track, the loops may be ridden deeper. The more testing the loops, the more accurate you must be with your aids, so do not ask for too much too soon. You must try to keep your body in alignment to the figure you are making, but in the shallow loops this will be very slight. Only in the deeper curves will there be a more noticeable turn of the body, but the basic 'canter position' must still be held. Simply look where you are going (and no further!) and your body should take up the correct alignment – but do pay attention to the inside hip position.

In a 60 x 20 m arena, progress to two loops (as shown) for extra suppleness. During these exercises try to maintain soft flexion to the inside so that, even when the horse is returning to the track, he is still a little bent around the inside leg and flexes from the poll and jaw to the inside rein. This is important if we are to be able to progress to the full counter-canter, where the correct bend around the leading leg will be maintained whilst going large.

Half-circle to Counter-canter

When the horse is confident in his loops, introduce counter-canter from a half-circle, returning to the track in counter-canter.

- Start from a 20 or 15 m canter circle at A or C to establish forwardness and bend. Now canter normally down the long side to M or H, F or K with a gentle feeling of flexion on the inside rein.
- Just before the chosen marker, make a smooth, rhythmical 10 or 15 m half circle to or beyond the centre line (the smaller half-circle reduces the angle of return, so is ultimately easier for the horse). Think central and sit tall and be careful not to pull on the inside rein or to allow your horse to fall in by leaning in yourself. You will need more outside leg to get yourself round.

focusing with the eyes on where we want to go. Simply allow your body to take the horse off the track and back again in the same way as you would ride a meandering path out hacking.

If we are to be analytical, the idea is simply to weight the inside stirrup a little more and bring more sideways pressure against the horse from the outside leg. A little indirect rein aid will also help. Remember most of these aids are minimal and should be quite invisible to anyone watching. If the horse does not want to move off the track, it could be that the rider is blocking him with too much tension in the inside thigh. Think of allowing the whole inside leg to relax downward to release him from the track.

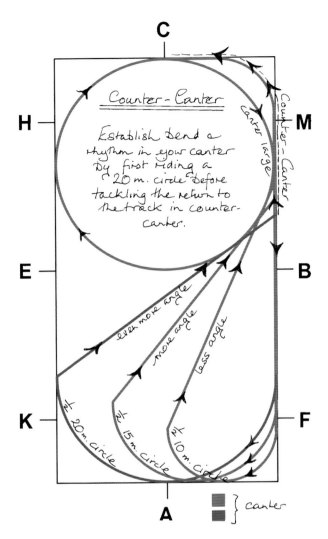

Counter-Canter

Establish bend a rhythm in your canter by first riding a 20 m. circle before tackling the return to the track in counter-canter.

Counter-Canter

canter large

even more angle

more angle

less angle

¼ 20 m. circle

¼ 15 m. circle

¼ 10 m. circle

canter

that was the leg you started on and absolutely maintain the aids for that canter. You may need to slightly reinforce the downward weight aid into your inside (now on the outside) stirrup.

- If your horse manages to straighten out on the track and maintain canter, still flexing from the poll into the original rein, for a few strides of counter-canter, release him from the canter position and return to trot before the next corner comes up.

It is very important that you do not threaten his confidence by asking too much at this stage or you may risk the horse losing balance and going disunited, which is something to be avoided at all costs. If he has done as you asked and managed even one step of counter-canter, make much of him and praise him lavishly. If, on the other hand, your horse fell back to trot before you ever reached the track, reassure him and try again, making sure that your aids are really consistent throughout the exercise.

If he has tried, but gone disunited, do not blame him; the fault is more likely to be rider-related. Try again, but if the problem persists, it could be he is not ready for this work. Perhaps the building blocks to date have not been sufficiently laid and he is simply too weak or not yet established on the aids.

Counter-canter should not be attempted by a rider whose own position is insecure. Moving hands, changing bodyweight, a rocking sensation with the upper body all constitute major disturbances to the horse's equilibrium, so be honest with yourself. Do not attempt to teach counter-canter until you yourself are very confirmed in your own canter work.

Once the horse is able to cope with one or two steps of counter-canter, more can be requested. The time will come when the counter-canter may be carried on past the corner and on towards A or C or beyond without the horse wanting to break. The rule of thumb is always to focus on the true canter, so that when it becomes counter-canter, you give no

- You will now return to the track on the diagonal line, aiming just beyond E or B (well before the next corner) in counter-canter, but beware of making the angle too sharp. This is where the support of your indirect rein aid is important. Feel that your outside hand takes the horse back to the track by keeping his quarters under control and guiding the forehand.

- As the track comes up be careful not to turn your head suddenly into the new direction; instead, remain looking over your horse's leading leg, which will now be to the outside. *Do not change your 'canter position'.*

- Although travelling in the opposite direction, keep thinking 'canter right' (or left) if

As I prepare Fabuloso for counter-canter on the right rein from a 10 m half-circle off the track, I press a little more downward into my right stirrup to assist bend round the right leading foreleg.

In returning to the track for counter-canter, I think up and forward and continue to support my horse at the girth with my right (unseen) leg, whilst keeping him active behind with my left leg encouraging well behind the girth. (Later the emphasis on the differentials of leg position can be reduced.)

indication to the horse that anything is different. Even highly experienced riders on highly experienced horses need to keep reminding themselves of this fact. A little voice keeps saying 'Look to the inside, sit into your inside seatbone...' all the way round, particularly as one approaches the track. *The fact that the inside aids will shortly become the outside ones is irrelevant; think like a horse and into the leading leg.*

Counter-canter Benefits

As horse and rider become more confident in counter-canter, different exercises can be introduced. There is no doubt at all that counter-canter improves the normal canter and leads to greater collection and balance. In the classical school it is considered the best exercise for working the loins, leading to more muscle tone just behind the saddle. Once corners are being ridden without difficulty in counter-canter, the rider may move on to counter-canter on the circle. Again, make the work progressive,

Here we see Fabuloso accept the counter-canter with all the ease of true canter (compare with the photo on page 144). The aids remain clear and Fabuloso looks confident as well as light and springy in front.

It is better to make your transition to trot while everything is easy and forward-going.

(Above) Here, Lesley and Palomo demonstrate counter-canter on the left rein. Once the horse understands your aids, you should be able to pick up counter-canter at any given moment, at least on straight lines.

(Right) This photo of Vaidoso shows me just looking into his leading leg in counter-canter on the right rein; this is a much more important aid than people realise. With the weight aids of the 'canter position' clear to the horse, there is no reason why horse and rider should not be as straight as in normal canter.

starting with half-circles before full ones are ridden. Always be aware that the more testing the exercise, the more supportive your posture must be.

When the horse is totally attuned to the weight aids of seat and leg, which may take several months of practice, the rider may straighten the horse more in the counter-canter. This is done by releasing the old inside (new outside) rein so that the horse is no longer so flexed over the leading leg. By now, the horse should be so attuned to these clear but discreet leg aids that he may even be asked to flex to the opposite side – that is, to the inside of a counter-canter circle. This is a marvellous exercise to stretch the back in a rounding way and eradicate any last vestiges of hollowness – however, do take time over this work.

Eventually, you should be able to ask for counter-canter directly from trot or walk on either rein and from wherever you are in the school, without the horse swinging his quarters. Remember, above all, that straightness

and forwardness remain the name of the game.

Of all the movements, counter-canter perhaps tests the trust and acceptance of the aids between horse and rider more than any other. If you can cross this hurdle without any difficulty, you are well on your way to the higher work and can give yourself a pat on the back because everything is looking promising.

One word of warning however; use counter-canter sensibly. It is a great exercise but try not

to overdo it. Certainly, never punish a horse if he changes when you have not asked – after all, this merely shows sense on the part of the horse, for your work to date has all been in 'normal' canter. Remember, there will come a time when you will want your horse to offer the flying change, so ride this exercise in moderation.

Opening out and Lengthening

With such improved balance, the rider can now think about lengthening the frame with some strides of an altogether bigger canter. A superior medium canter will not evolve until there is a greater degree of collection, but hopefully this is building quietly on its own as the horse grows in strength and suppleness behind.

When people talk about medium canter, it is very tempting to go hurtling down the long side of the arena with lots of impulsion. However, corners have a habit of presenting themselves quite quickly and it is far better to introduce some lengthened strides progressively as you pass E or B, but to move back into a steady working canter as you approach or leave the short ends of the school. Three or four steps really onward-bound and then back again, all in the same rhythm, can gradually be built up, without interruption to balance and harmony, and it is better to stay against the rail rather than to attempt the diagonal in the first few days. Horses have a wonderful way of interpreting open spaces as a signal to open up a little too much!

Generally, people need only think 'open up' for these bigger, more open strides to be shown and the aids should be as unobtrusive as ever. A little more opening and drawing back of the rider's shoulders and a corresponding raising of the diaphragm and pelvic floor is often all that is needed. The main thing is not to interrupt movement with a pushing seat or squeezing legs. Provided that the rider's back is supple, the shoulders moving back will actually drive the seat a little more forward if the rider is sit-

ting correctly, so no more seat movement is required. As for the hands, they should yield to accommodate the stretching of the horse's neck, but they must never throw away the contact as is sometimes seen. Neither should they pull back.

The legs can often assist by moving a little more forward as though stimulating the horse behind the elbow. Clutching on to the horse further back may put him into backward-thinking mode, and is to be avoided. If this advice seems confusing, all will be made clear when we discuss the aids for the rein-back – another exercise which works very well when used in conjunction with the canter.

The Rein-back

This is a movement which can be introduced at an earlier stage if the horse is strong through the back and unresistant through the jaw. For others, after all the unlocking and stretching work has been accepted, this will prove a more appropriate time, but it should not be left much longer.

Although the horse is required to move backwards, the very last thing we should be thinking of is pulling him backwards with the hands – so their role is minimal:

- always think forward into halt;
- always think forward into rein-back.

The position of the rider's hands is the same in the rein-back as it is for all forward work. The hands should remain as a pair at the base of the neck, with sufficient contact for the horse to yield through the poll and jaw. If the reins are too long, there may be a temptation to bring the hands back to the waist, whereas a good rein-back should always be ridden, waist towards hands.

Just as a correctly ridden halt will increase the bending of the horse's hind legs as the horse steps underneath himself from behind, so too will the rein-back increase the suppleness and engagement of the joints; hip, stifle, hock

Practise counter-canter equally on both reins, on the straight, in turns and on the circle. As the horse becomes more sensitive to your aids, the leg position will become less exaggerated, until each aid is only a nuance. Note in particular the stretching of Espada's loins as we ask for some medium canter out of the counter-canter in the photograph lower left.

and fetlock. In order to bring his weight back smoothly and easily, the horse will need to round his back, so there must be absolutely no sense of him leaning on the reins. For this reason it is very important to:

- Lighten the seat over the back of the saddle by sitting deeper into the thighs, which has a collecting effect (see p.113).
- Think of the position of the pelvis when you walk backwards yourself and mimic it; if this puts you a little more on the fork, compensate by stretching tall through the waist so that you do not sit heavy.
- Reach down and back with the lower legs to place them against the horse's sides behind the girth and, by closing them, ask him to step back.
- Ask only for one step at a time and then release the pressure before closing again.
- At the beginning, pause and reward after each step taken.

The horse is required to step with his legs in diagonal pairs: he must clearly lift his feet and not drag them back through the sand. To help him understand this, the rider specifically asks with both legs for one step at a time. Stretching tall and remembering to pause and reward will prevent the horse from rushing backward. Gradually more steps can be introduced, but remember that overdemanding legs and a heavy seat are highly detrimental. Too often, the horse will drop his back with the hind legs camped out and ineffectual.

Difficult Moments

With a horse who has never reined-back before, it may be helpful to have someone on the ground for the first few sessions. It is surprising how helpful a gentle hand on the horse's chest can be. Be content with very little at a time, even half a step is a good start, and don't worry if he swings out a little – this can be corrected later. Any progress should earn much praise and an immediate relaxation of rein, seat and leg. Use of the voice is also important; horses very quickly respond to the word 'Ba-ack!' if accompanied by a gentle prod of the assistant's hand close to the breastbone.

The rider's hands should squeeze the rein in much the same way as required for the half-halt to ask the horse to yield in the jaw. There is simply no point in even asking for rein-back until the horse has flexed gently from the poll. Trying to force a rein-back with a horse poking his nose and above the bit is to risk damaging his back.

Once the horse moves back easily, one of the most difficult things for novice riders and horses is to perfect straightness in the rein-back. All too often the horse will fall out to one side or the other, This may be caused by the rider using one leg more strongly than the other; stiffness in one or both hocks, or the horse simply avoiding taking equal weight behind. Initially, it is wise to start this exercise against the edge of the school, so at least the horse has the mental and physical support of

the wall. Now he will only be able to go crooked to the inside, so a way to correct this is to ask for gentle lateral flexion to the inside initially. This will help to keep the inside hind more underneath him and encourage straightness behind.

Far from feeling more tension in the reins in the rein-back, riding this movement should create a greater feel of lightness in the hand. We will know that our aids have been successful when the horse softens into the bit and steps back as though simply walking back with his rider. In so doing the action of the rein is carried right through the horse's body.

Forward Again!

After one or two steps have been made in this way, go forward immediately to trot to keep the horse forward-thinking. As with counter-canter, don't overdo the rein-back sessions, especially in the early stages. The transition to trot should be seen as a reward, but it will also serve another purpose. The very fact that the horse has learned to move his weight back in the (diagonal) rein-back should have improved the trot immeasurably. It may be only now that the rider discovers the first real sensation of collection.

When the horse becomes more confident in the rein-back, these transitions can be used more regularly to improve all the gaits, particularly if the horse tends to be rather strong in the hand and in the habit of running on.

Rein-back to Canter

As the horse becomes more muscled and more established, the rider may feel it is time to improve the canter from the rein-back. The rein-back should now be offered without resistance, with a nicely rounded back and clearly defined steps. In this case, the rein-back to canter is not nearly so difficult as people imagine; again this is done in Western Riding as a matter of course, yet in dressage tests it is

Rein-back should be performed regularly on both reins. Three or four measured steps are far better than several steps, rushing back. The rider's hands should never move back; instead they ask and give to induce flexion of the poll and jaw as weight is eased off the back of the saddle. Here, the right rein-back looks a little softer than that shown on the left rein although the walk steps are less generous. It is important that the horse bends his limbs in the rein-back and as with all movement, the neck should still arch forward into the rein so that the head remains just in front of or in the vertical; if I had slackened off the curb rein in the left rein-back, this would have been achieved.

considered a fairly advanced movement.

The fact, is many horses really enjoy and benefit from the rein-back to canter. For horses who bore a little on the forehand, or who are proving difficult to canter on a given rein, two steps of rein-back first can help enormously. Often, it is just a question of getting the rider to think more 'together' and contained. The rein-back gives the rider time to take stock and rebalance the horse before applying the canter aid, which gives the horse time too. Too many horses are allowed to run into canter from an over-anxious and often unbalanced body aid. Since rein-back demands a proper acceptance of the bit and a good posture from both horse and rider, the canter is much improved and the horse is able to make the transition with the hocks more under.

Let us now look at a sequence involving; a) the rein-back to canter; b) true canter down the long side and into a half-circle; c) counter-canter back to the track. First, let us appreciate just how much can go wrong:

THE HORSE'S THOUGHTS (uneducated rider)

- I've been brought to halt. Unfortunately, my hind legs are not quite under me, and I don't feel settled into the bit, but my rider is demanding that I go back. I know this because of the strong backward tug on the bars of my mouth and she is squeezing tightly on my sides with her calves. There is simply nowhere to go but back, but I do so reluctantly because she is pushing down so hard I can't raise my back to bring my hocks under and it's painful.
- I make the obligatory few steps as best I can and suddenly I am being firmly kicked into canter. At least my back is relieved as she leans forward, but I feel all my balance go as she drops the contact quite suddenly and the bit bangs against the back of my teeth.
- Down the long side we go and all is well until a corner comes up and I am expected

to make a half-circle right to the centre line. This is hard because I am definitely on the forehand but can do little about it, since there is no solid support to the inside of my body and my neck is pulled round by the inside rein. I'm afraid I take the turn in a very awkward fashion with my hind end swinging out alarmingly.
- We are now facing back to the track and I am still in canter right with my head firmly held this way. There's no way I can hold this canter and turn onto the track at the same time because the rein stops me from stretching – it's a physical impossibility...
- Now my rider has turned her body to look left, so I thankfully change in front. At least the left rein provides an opening for my left shoulder to go through. I'd like to change behind but she bears down so hard on my back I simply can't.
- We're now heading back to where we started so I go back to trot. It seems a lot safer than staying in this very peculiar canter. I receive another pull in the mouth, because clearly – as usual – we have done it all wrong. If only it wasn't so difficult and uncomfortable all this dressage...

The above may sound an over-exaggerated scenario, but is far closer to reality than one would hope. Horses are asked to do things all the time for which they are ill-prepared. Until we can teach people to feel what their horse is feeling, and understand a few essential biomechanical truths, there will be many casualties.

Now let us look at a happier picture, where the horse is prepared correctly for what is about to happen:

THE HORSE'S THOUGHTS (educated rider)

- My rider has brought me to halt. I shuffle slightly but she flexes me gently to the inside and since she is square, I square up too. She sits up – there's a moment of pause for us both to organise ourselves and then she squeezes on both reins and I drop my nose; she squeezes again and, since her legs move back and I feel her shift her seat more forward and deep as though closing the front door, I step back into an inviting space behind me.

- I make three steps in this way, encouraged by her legs, which seem to step back too. Because there is room to bring my back up and the rein-back sets me on my hocks, it's easy to respond to her clear canter aid which comes a moment later. I know the canter so well now because it's always the same. Her inside leg steps down as her inside rein lightens and I jump into it, much encouraged by her outside leg starting me off behind.

- We canter right down the long side of the arena ahead of us; I am looking slightly to the inside but the left rein prevents me from falling in. Just as well, since we are about to make a half-circle to the centre line and I need all the balance possible. The outside rein eases as it brings me round and I feel my inside hind able to take more weight in the turn – this helps to keep me upright!

- We are now facing the track diagonally and it's always a temptation to drop back to trot when one sees the wall coming up. But my rider keeps her outside leg stroking me forward from my outside hind; and since she herself feels nice and onward-bound, I just keep going with the flow. Now I'm being drawn to the fence by a feeling of weight through her right leg and happily she allows on the left rein so I can really stretch through and into the turn.

- We are now heading back up the track to where we started; my rider feels as though her body is just looking right, so I stay that way too as it's the only way to be in balance – I hate it when we are physically at odds with each other. Her left leg is still encouraging my canter to continue in every stride and, because nothing has changed, I feel quite happy to canter right on the left rein.

- The last corner is now approaching and I think she wants me to return to trot, but I feel so confident I offer a few more strides in canter right and all of a sudden we are back to A where we started, although this time the other way round! She seems over the moon, we return to walk and she flings down the reins and hugs me. It's nice to be appreciated – apparently I've just done something rather clever but *all I did was follow her!*

CHAPTER XI

Lateral Work

From Leg-yield to Shoulder-in – The Key to Collection

In shoulder-in, the forehand lightens, the poll is the highest point, and the angle obliges the inside hind foot to step across.

It is only when we start 'the work proper', as aficionados call it, that the collection or *rassembler* of the horse's body will begin to emerge. The first exercise designed for real collection is the shoulder-in, invented by de la Guérinière of France but acknowledged by him to have been inspired from work achieved by the Englishman William Cavendish, Duke of Newcastle, a brilliant horseman and the personal tutor of Charles II. The main difference between the two types of shoulder-in was that the French developed theirs down the manège wall, whereas the English duke had started his on the circle.

It is interesting that in many Iberian circles, Newcastle's version of shoulder-in is often used in preference to that of de la Guérinière. The problem with the circle version is that, unless you are a very experienced rider, it is too easy to allow the horse to fall out on the outside shoulder instead of taking more weight onto the inside hind leg – which is the main purpose of the exercise. For this reason, most people ask for very little sideways movement in their 'shoulder-fore,' which is the term generally used for working on the circle.

Leg-yield and Turn on the Forehand

In the leg-yield, too, there can be a tendency to push the horse onto the outside shoulder. This must be avoided. As a schooling exercise its value is similar to that of the turn on the forehand. Both require that the horse move away from pressure, in this case that of the rider's inside leg.

Turn on the Forehand

The turn on the forehand is generally introduced first at the standstill, when the young horse, being halted and stood up square is asked to give way or to yield his quarters one way or the other. It should only be asked for when there is no resistance in the horse's mouth.

To turn to the right:
- a gentle flexion right is requested;
- the rider's right leg moves behind the girth and presses against the horse's side;
- the horse moves his quarters to the left away from the pressure (weight aid);
- the horse's right hind passes in front of the left and he steps sideways;

158

Personally, I like to teach the horse to move or yield away from the leg in a natural environment with flexion to the inside as in shoulder-in. Moving the horse sideways can easily be introduced out on a hack and may prove invaluable when it comes to riding past a spooky spot.

- the rider's outside (left) leg remains close to the girth, ready to ask the horse to move forward the moment the turn is complete.

A turn on the forehand may comprise 90, 180 or even 360 degrees – although the last is not advised. Even if several steps are asked for, the turn on the forehand should never consist of a pivot round a grounded leg. While the off fore is the pivotal leg, it must mark time by lifting in place as the hind legs move around the forehand, with the horse ready to move forward at any given moment.

The turn on the forehand should not be seen as an end in itself. It tests the sensitivity of the horse to the leg aids and is very useful for opening gates. At this stage of riding however, it should be used sparingly, more to reinforce a past lesson than to develop new ones. Some trainers miss it out altogether.

Leg-yield

Some trainers also omit leg-yielding and personally I do not teach this as 'a movement' in itself. However, to help those who do, the following points need to be considered:

- In leg-yield, the horse's head is flexed slightly away from the direction in which he is moving.
- The body should be relatively straight as he move forwards and sideways away from the rider's inside leg.
- The inside legs pass and cross in front of the outside legs.

The idea is only to ask for a very slight bend away from the direction of travel and to keep the horse's body as parallel to the wall of the school as possible. Therefore, when he arrives on the opposite track from whence he started, neither his shoulders nor his quarters precede the other.

Leg-yield should not be a very difficult exercise to teach, particularly if the horse bends nicely on the circle.

Too much time spent in leg-yield may produce confusion when half-pass is introduced, since the half-pass is also generally ridden diagonally across the school but with the horse required to look and bend *into the direction* in which he is travelling.

For this reason, the leg-yield is not deemed to be a classical movement, since every classical movement is destined to teach the horse something that helps him onward to the next stage – i.e. nothing learned should be changed or undone. Since both leg-yield and half-pass are generally required on the diagonal with different bends, it can all become very muddling for the horse and rider. For this reason, Podhajsky advises that leg-yield should only be used in walk and not in trot: 'The Spanish Riding School has always used this yielding to the leg only to a *limited* degree' (*The Complete Training of Horse and Rider*).

I should, however, add that another school of thought prefers to see the leg-yield ridden up the track (in the manner of shoulder-in). In this way it could be viewed as a useful precursor to the shoulder-in. However, to my mind, it generally makes life simpler for both horse and rider to think 'shoulder-in' from the very beginning. Most early attempts at shoulder-in will take the form of a leg-yield anyway, until both partners can refine the work and produce sufficient lateral suppling, but by calling the movement 'shoulder-in' from the outset – even if it is not textbook – a great deal of confusion could be avoided.

The Classical Shoulder-in

We shall now concentrate on the French version of shoulder-in, which was developed by the Spanish Riding School and adopted pretty much universally. Most serious dressage riders and trainers acknowledge this movement to transcend all others in terms of suppling, balancing and teaching collection. To my mind, its value is beyond measure but whereas in competition it makes its first appearance in trot at Elementary level, I have very strong reasons for starting the work in walk, as we shall see.

Shoulder-in, or shoulder fore (with less angle) can also be ridden in canter, but this is only suitable for a more advanced horse. Generally, shoulder-in is initially ridden down the long side of the arena with the visual support of the wall to help, and later, on the centre or quarter lines.

In shoulder-in, the horse is bent around the rider's inside leg, looking away from the direction of movement. His inside foreleg passes and crosses in front of the outside leg; the inside hind leg steps in front of the outside hind. (British Dressage Rules)

Ideally, the shoulder-in should be ridden at an angle of approximately 30 degrees to the wall. The horse should mirror the rider's posture with both shoulders and the face turned to look slightly inward. The difficulty in the early days is to maintain this angle without losing impulsion, so it is better to start the work in walk, with only a mild angle required initially.

Benefits

During this time, the rider must really concentrate on the feeling of what is happening under saddle. The first purpose of the shoulder-in is to increase strength and athleticism behind and general suppleness throughout. As the inside hind leg engages and steps more deeply under the horse's body, there will be a lowering of the inside hip and greater flexion in the stifle, hock and fetlock joints. Performed with equal diligence on both reins, the movement will have far-reaching beneficial effects as it works and engages the horse's back, loins and quarters.

It is axiomatic that the more the hind end flexes and deepens in this way, the more the forehand is encouraged to rise. The horse's shoulders should become freer and a well-executed shoulder-in will have an 'uphill' appear-

In a good shoulder-in, the horse should be stepping laterally forward, whilst remaining calmly bent around the rider's inside leg, without the quarters falling out.
(Left) We see Vaidoso in a three-track shoulder-in ridden on the right rein in walk.
(Above) From a different viewpoint, Palomo offers the same movement in trot; note good engagement from the hind legs and crossing in front, coupled with suspension and lightening of the forehand.

ance. The bonding effect of the whole horse working with greater engagement behind, strengthens and supples the topline and increases support from the strengthening belly muscles below.

Ideally, the poll should remain the highest point; however, in the early days, allowances should be made and a lower position may be necessary to start with. It is important, however, that the horse arches and flexes nicely into his bridle both laterally and directly and there is no resistance. Too much neck bend to the inside is undesirable since it blocks the inside shoulder and will place the horse on the forehand.

Tracking and Terminology

The steps should be even and regular and the horse should be able to move laterally forward while still keeping a good rhythm, whether for the four beats of walk or the diagonal beats of trot.

There are two ways of riding the shoulder-in; either on three tracks or on four. Both are deemed correct by the experts but the very skilled riders of the Spanish Riding School favour the four-track movement with their advanced horses. However, in the early schooling of the horse and in competition, a three-track shoulder-in is generally advised. The

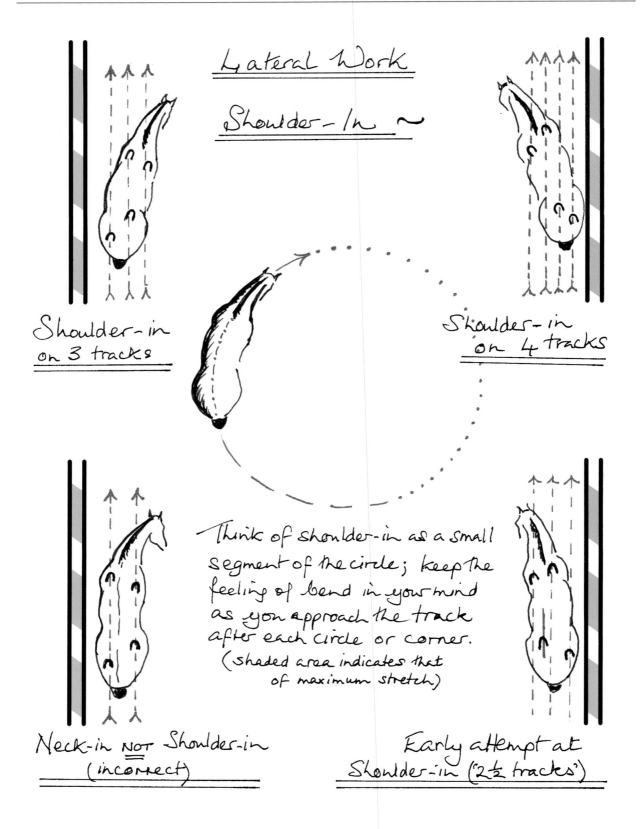

Lateral Work

Shoulder-In ~

Shoulder-in
on 3 tracks

Shoulder-in
on 4 tracks

Think of shoulder-in as a small
segment of the circle; keep the
feeling of bend in your mind
as you approach the track
after each circle or corner.
(shaded area indicates that
of maximum stretch)

Neck-in NOT Shoulder-in
(incorrect)

Early attempt at
Shoulder-in ('2½ tracks')

horse has to be very supple indeed to make the four-track movement without the quarters falling out.

In discussing three or four tracks, it can be confusing in the extreme when lateral work is often summed up under the term 'two-track work' in some manuals of horsemanship. In normal circumstances, the track is always composed of a double set of hoofprints (two tracks); on the other hand if we move the quarters out and encourage the forehand in, we will end up with four tracks clearly visible. Let us therefore abandon the term 'two-track' for now, leave the four-track shoulder-in to a more advanced stage of schooling and concentrate on the more attainable three-track shoulder-in. To do this, we need to be very clear in our minds exactly what is involved.

Important Factors

As with all lateral work, the horse is required to bend around the rider's inside leg. In shoulder-in right, the horse will be on the right rein and bending around the rider's right leg but moving away from it at the same time. In fact, although on the right rein, he progresses left. Shoulder-in is actually the only *classical* movement where the horse actually moves away from the direction in which he is bent.

Just as we ourselves pass one leg in front of another if walking sideways at a similar angle to shoulder-in, the horse, too, is compelled to step through with his inside hind. Initially, even with sympathetic riding, the feeling is almost as though the horse is catching himself from losing balance in every stride by passing his inside hind leg *further underneath* (see photos this Chapter). The inside foreleg will actually cross in front of the outside foreleg, which gradually brings about a feeling of lift to the shoulders.

By remaining flexed to the inside, the horse should move fluently forward and sideways away from the direction of bend. It is important that the horse remains in the same angle and maintains the same number of tracks,

whatever the rein.

Basically, we are looking for three distinct lines of hoofprints all travelling forward in a clearly marked, unwavering sequence. This will be a testimony to the fact that the horse has not only suppled his body to the inside, but also engaged his inside hind to the extent that it can step into the track made by the outside fore.

- The first of these tracks will be made by the inside fore, which is brought away from the wall and is closest to the centre of the school.
- The second track will be the inside hind, which should reach into the print left by the outside fore, these two feet thus forming the middle track.
- The third track will be that of the outside hind which again describes its own track and is the one closest to the wall.

It is better to ask for rather less angle initially and content oneself with a fairly modest shoulder-in when teaching this to the novice horse. Even 'two-and-a-half'* tracks shows a good start initially.

In Practice

Riding the shoulder-in sympathetically and in such a way that the horse does not feel he is being pushed off balance is very important. Let us think ourselves onto the left rein in walk as we approach the long side after riding past A or C and take it from there.

- Always introduce shoulder-in by first riding away from the track into a small circle of roughly 10 m at F or H, which will give you most of the length of the school to work up. The circle is important in order to introduce bend and to establish the idea of bringing the shoulders inward from the track before starting the lateral movement.
- On returning to the track, instead of straightening your horse, retain lateral flexion to the

*This term is not an accurate description of the tracking, but is used to convey an image of less angle and bend than the 30 degree movement.

inside and merely think 'forward' as though to circle again. As the horse moves forward as though to leave the track on the first step of a circle, now is the moment to sit up, apply a gentle feeling of half-halt and give a gentle pushing aid sideways. This is done with the inside leg drawn slightly behind the girth and more against and into the horse than usual. A definite tap is more effective than a hard, prolonged push.

- The sideways movement requires that the rider's body be turned a little more to the inside, so that he or she, too, assumes an angled posture of roughly 30 degrees. Thinking sideways must not induce a collapse to the inside. For the circle, the rider should have been sitting a little more on the inside seatbone but stretching tall at the same time. This is also correct for the shoulder-in, particularly in the introductory phase.

- As the horse responds to the pressing or tapping aid of the inside leg by moving away, the rider encourages the horse to continue up the track with an inviting but supportive contact on the outside rein.

- To prevent the horse from falling back to the wall, the outside thigh and knee turn in to support the forehand in its new angle. In this way, the horse finds himself moving away from the influence of the inside leg and into the outside rein without lurching onto the outside shoulder.

- In this quiet, clear and unhurried way, the first sideways step is taken and the rider should warmly praise and stroke the horse.

Step by Step

It is tempting to continue and try for two, three or more steps, but much depends on the sensitivity and willingness of the horse concerned. Some horses take to shoulder-in like a duck to water, others find it extraordinarily difficult. There is no doubt that horses who have been used to working well into their corners, as well as moving away from the leg to open

gates, etc. will get the idea quicker than others. Initially, the shoulder-in may seem more like a leg-yield, but this is to be expected.

Every time the horse offers one or more sideways steps it is important to keep bend and forward flow going, so always ride back onto another 10 m circle before trying again. In this way, we can build up to several steps, liberally interspersed with circles all the way up the long side. Upon reaching the top of the school, reward your horse by allowing him to stretch his neck and body and change the rein in the next corner.

Initially, one side will feel much easier for the horse than the other. Generally, horses prefer shoulder-in right, but every horse is a little different. Some horses overdo the sideways feel by moving obligingly away from the leg but falling out. Others over-hollow to the inside and bring the quarters in. The most common fault is too much neck to the inside, caused by the horse never really bringing both his shoulders in. This may be unavoidable at the outset, but if allowed to continue, can result in a two-track movement with the horse locking the inside shoulder rather than stepping through behind.

Rest assured these are common faults, but if you take time and perfect the necessary basics in walk, the problems can be sorted out before the transition to trot. After all, we want this to be relatively problem-free.

Some schools of thought believe that shoulder-in should only be performed in trot. There is no doubt that the impulsion associated with a nice forward-going trot will help the shoulder-in to develop flow and rhythm as time goes on. But, to my mind, there are too many examples of bad shoulder-in being performed in the dressage arenas of today to support the idea of missing out the learning process in walk. Walk gives both horse and rider time to think about what they are doing and to organise themselves. Most importantly, it allows the hind legs time to take weight and to bend through the joints in a calm, unhurried way. Riders need to

Correct tracking is very much the responsibility of the rider. Here I help maintain Andorinha in this three-track shoulder-in (right rein) through the firm inward support of my outside thigh, knee and lower leg. My shoulders give the horse 'position' (of the forehand).

First steps for the horse

(Left) Early attempts at shoulder-in (left) should be ridden in walk. The inside rein should be soft and inviting to lead the forehand off the track as though to circle again. Any attempt to bend and move away from the rider's inside leg should be rewarded.

(Left and above) A good start is made! By keeping your shoulders in the angle at which you wish to place your horse's shoulders, the horse will understand more quickly. His ears should be level as shown here.

Having worked well in walk, I ask for a few steps of shoulder-in in trot. If there is too much neck bend...

...it is better to return to walk and take a few steps across the diagonal to free and straighten the forehand before starting again (see page 169).

feel the movement. Shoulder-in requires a great deal more bending from these precious joints if correctly ridden and it is far less stressful to the system biomechanically if this is introduced in walk.

Handy Hints

Here are some tips to eradicate problems encountered in the shoulder-in.

Too much inside bend of neck with the feeling that the horse hugs the track.

Let go with the inside rein! Flexion never means pulling back. Instead, try to support the forehand with the indirect rein and correct upper body posture. Your hips should also be slightly turned in. Support with the outside knee and thigh but allow your inside knee and

thigh to soften a little to make room for the forehand.

Too much quarters out and insufficient bending to the inside.

Don't draw your inside leg back too far or apply the pushing aid too heavily. The sideways feel must be light and it should be reduced as soon as the horse obeys. The outside lower leg has an important responsibility to make sure that the outside hind works under and propels the horse along. Keep the outside leg just behind the girth and again feel a sense of support. This will help your horse to stretch his outer frame to move more around your inside leg and thus prevent the quarters falling out.

Horse becoming slower and slower in the shoulder-in.

First steps for the rider

Too much angle: this experienced rider is new to this horse. She positions him well with her upper body, but her indirect rein is a little too effective and almost turns this four-track shoulder-in into quarters out. (Photograph courtesy of Martin Date)

No real angle: riding shoulder-in for the first time requires real hands-on help. Most riders fail to turn the whole upper body sufficiently. Here, too much neck bend causes Vaidoso to resist and fall out on the outside shoulder so he remains on two tracks. Nevertheless, this rider was soon riding perfect shoulder-ins as she learned from initial mistakes. (Photograph courtesy of Maggie Lamont)

This shoulder-in shows real promise, but Edna has dropped her right shoulder, which is just enough to bring Palomo off the track and prove how important the correct weight aids are when we ride.

Remember that the shoulder-in is a collecting exercise, so you certainly do not want your horse to rush down the long side because he will avoid the required engagement behind. Nevertheless, many horses become 'stodgy' in shoulder-in because the rider tenses up and, in attempting to think sideways, forgets to sit up and ride forwards. This is why it is so important, initially, to ride only a few steps at a time and then always forward to a circle or a straight line after the movement.

Horse tilting his head in shoulder-in and bulging to the outside of his neck.

Keep your head looking in the same direction as your horse; your eyes may look up the track but the position of your head provides a mirror-image for him. Your own head may be tilting or you may have dropped your shoulder to the inside. Although your outside rein leads the horse up the track be careful to ease the rein sufficiently for your horse's poll to bend, not tip, to the inside.

Think Diagonal!

One of the best exercises to correct rider position and eradicate all the above faults is to incorporate riding the diagonal line whilst riding shoulder-in. Although we may have to sacrifice a little bend, the following exercise tests forwardness, response to the leg and an understanding of the sideways movement.

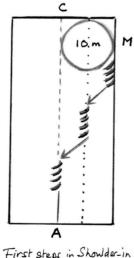

First steps in Shoulder-in (right rein)

On the right rein, ride:

- 10 m circle at M
- four steps of shoulder-in right up the track
- immediately advance diagonally to the quarter line
- four more steps of shoulder-in up the quarter line
- immediately advance diagonally to the centre line
- four more steps of shoulder-in up the centre line
- now straighten up on the centre line; ride forward to the end of the school to start all over again, either on the same rein, or by changing the rein.

This is a very good exercise in walk and in trot to help both horse and rider think more forward in their lateral work and perfect the tracking. Aiding to the outside of the horse should also become vastly improved since, apart from the first three steps, there is no supporting wall. In this way, the rider will quickly realise when the quarters are falling out too much, or if forward impulsion is being lost by a failure to hold the correct line with the horse around the inside leg.

As with all the lateral movements, building up the work in the shoulder-in has a hugely beneficial effect on the horse's lateral and longitudinal suppleness. In this way, we achieve a straighter horse, a more rounded and 'together' horse and a more balanced horse.

Real collection should now be developing, but the rider must be careful to work both sides of the horse equally and to freshen up the work with frequent transitions. Impulsion is as important as ever, but remember the steps will become shorter and more elevated as the horse collects more. Shoulder-in strengthens the horse behind and the feeling of rhythm and spring will become more prevalent after this work.

Shoulder-in to Medium Trot

Once the shoulder-in is well established, we can start to use it as a preparation for medium trot across the diagonal. By using the corner and a few steps of shoulder-in up the long side, we then use the diagonal as a way of rewarding the horse through medium trot. In this way, the horse feels as though he has been 'let off the hook', often responding with really extravagant forward steps as he is released from the lateral movement to move diagonally straight across the school.

Encourage freedom of the shoulders by keeping the waist forward with the shoulders back and aid a little more forward than normal, with both legs giving light taps or flicks just behind the elbow. Use of the voice is also help-ful – I make a special buzzing noise with my own horses...'Bzzzzzzzzzzzzzz', which I only produce for medium work. The 'B' sound makes one purse one's lips and push the breath, so pushing the word out progressively all in one breath seems to help with breath control and the horse learns through an association of ideas. (More of the medium gaits in Chapter XIII).

Shoulder-in on The Circle

When the horse is balanced and happy in shoulder-in on straight lines, we may advance to the work on the circle. For many, the hard-est thing to master is to turn the body imper-ceptibly in each stride. Unlike shoulder-in up the long side, we cannot fix the angle and then forget about it; on the circle we have to keep turning with the horse. The rider who has a heightened feel for balance may pick this up immediately; others find it very difficult. The idea is to keep the face, shoulders, chest, tummy and hips of the rider perpetually lined up with those of the horse.

To start shoulder-in on a 20 m circle, try riding a 10 m circle as before, but this time at different 'points' of the big circle (see dia-gram). Then gradually start to link these up, alternating your shoulder-in steps with normal work. After a few weeks, the small circles can be dropped until the rider can move onto a 15 m circle, riding half of it in shoulder-in and half of it normally. At a later stage still, the rider can ride

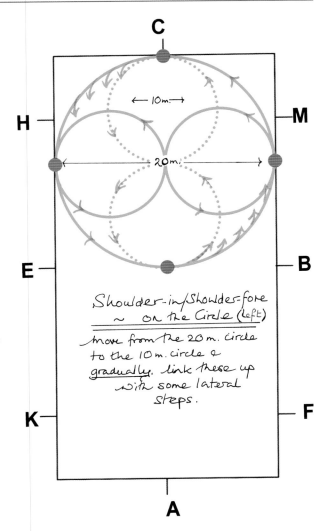

Shoulder-in/Shoulder-fore ~ on the Circle (left)

move from the 20 m. circle to the 10 m. circle & gradually. link these up with some lateral steps.

half the circle in shoulder-in and half in travers, which we shall come to in the next chapter.

All these exercises have great merit, provid-ed we always remember to relax the horse as much as possible in between. Even in the work proper, we must keep coming back to straight lines in between all the lateral work and circles. As the horse becomes more and more supple, the rider will notice a huge improvement in his general balance and straightness. Shoulder-in is a wonderful exercise to eradicate crookedness in canter.

To give more perspective, let us now look at the shoulder-in up the long side under two dif-ferent types of rider, using the corner to give position on the right rein at M.

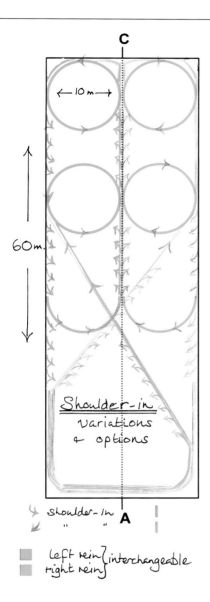

C

← 10 m →

60 m.

Shoulder-in
variations
& options

↳ shoulder-In A
　　 "　　　"

Left rein ⎫ interchangeable
right rein ⎭

THE HORSE'S THOUGHTS (uneducated rider)

- I've been ridden into the corner with a lot of inside leg to outside hand and now I feel my rider tugging on my right rein to pull my head to the inside as the long side comes up.
- I take a couple of steps to the right, but her inside leg is so strong, I am pushed back again onto the track. I simply can't bring my neck back into alignment, because she has shortened the right rein and I can feel the bit slipping through my mouth.
- I proceed up the track twisting right but my

body seems to be falling left, since her seat pulls me that way. She has turned her shoulders to the inside – I can actually see them! But she feels somehow collapsed, so my energy shoots out to the left.

- It's uncomfortable to be twisted like this but her outside heel is hard against my quarters, her inside leg is hard against my ribcage, so I have to bulge out somewhere! It feels like my left shoulder – luckily her left knee has gaped open giving me some room...
- Oh dear! Now she is tugging more with her right rein and I feel completely jack-knifed; it's not a pleasant situation and I'm getting slower and slower and heavier in front.
- I hear the instructor yelling 'Sit right!', and things improve. I struggle to move under her and keep both shoulders right, but just as soon as I do this, her outside hand shoots forward, there's no support and my neck twists round. 'Too much neck bend!' comes the shout, and I get a sharp boot in the ribs as though it is my fault!

Now we study a happier scenario:

THE HORSE'S THOUGHTS (educated rider)

- My rider takes me deep into the corner to set me up for something called shoulder-in right! Her inside leg is against me, her outside rein keeps me there but I can feel her sitting a little more into the inside seatbone with more weight in the inside stirrup so I can bend around her leg.
- As we come out of the corner, she turns her body and asks me to leave the track with a soft, opening inside hand. Her inside thigh and knee feel soft too, as though they have 'given' slightly to accommodate my right shoulder as I think about moving right; the outside rein moves towards the base of my neck.
- I am just about to straighten up and turn onto the diagonal line when I feel her inside

leg move back and press me sideways. At the same time the outside rein has a different feel, it seems to be leading me left whilst my inside (right) rein remains soft... because it's so inviting I bend into it, which is odd because I seem to be moving left!

- This all seems quite strange and it might be safer to fall back to the track, but I can't because my rider is sitting quite firmly to the inside and there's a definite sideways feel from her body. I can also feel some support to my left shoulder, which prevents me slipping back to the track.

- It seems I have no choice but to move sideways. As I pick up my inside hind, there is a definite sense of 'move over' from her inside lower leg. Just at the very moment my leg is in the air, she presses with her leg and I'm surprised to find I can step right under behind. As for my forelegs – there is a crossing sensation! It's not quite like being asked to move over in the stable, but I can't say it's unpleasant... I might even want to do more, especially after that sugar lump!

In Summary

The ultimate goal of shoulder-in is to be able to move your horse laterally forward and then straight again at any given moment. Once the aids are made clear in the way suggested above and there is no conflict in the rider's body, the horse should be able to move into his lateral work with little difference in tempo, impulsion or rhythm from his normal straight work and forward work.

One of the most important factors to remember in lateral work – as indeed in all work – is that when one aid is giving or opening, its opposite number should be firming up or supporting. Whether this is a rein effect or leg aid matters not. The only time everything should be exactly equal is when we want the horse straight as a die – generally over X on the centre line and well before the next turn comes up! Most of the time, to a greater or lesser extent, the horse is required to bend one side of his body one way, while the opposite side has to stretch. For this reason, each of our aids must accommodate this.

At this stage of training, we must do all we can to avoid pressuring the horse from every side and every angle. There is so much for him to learn, and physically and mentally he needs space. Remember the foal's first lesson of press and release! In our aids, there should by now be a moment of *give* and a moment of *take* ever-present. These nuances will be in a constant state of interplay and interchange.

It goes without saying that all should be infinitesimally quiet and discreet, a real secret between you and the horse. Nevertheless, without this fine-tuning, the horse may become trapped in the middle; there are already too many horses out there who really *are* prisoners. If we love our horse, we will discipline ourselves to give him back – as much as possible – his freedom.

PART SIX

The Work Proper – Medium Level

In travers, the outside hind has to step through and in front of the inside hind.

CHAPTER XII
Counter Shoulder–in, Renvers, Travers and Half–pass and Extending the Walk

In half-pass, with more angle, the outside fore and hind legs pass and cross in front of the inside legs.

Counter Shoulder-in

The shoulder-in, once well established, can also be used in a reverse manner. Counter shoulder-in sounds very smart, but it is simply a shoulder-in ridden with the head to the wall instead of the head looking into the school. The bend away from the direction of the movement is exactly the same as for normal shoulder-in.

Counter shoulder-in is a nice exercise to ride out of the half-pass but, for the meantime, simply ride a normal shoulder-in along the track (with your back to the wall), make a small half-volte at the end, proceed forward to the track that you have just left, then continue along it again this time head-to-the-wall without changing the bend. This will bring you back to where you started. The most difficult thing about counter shoulder-in is to maintain the same distance between the tip of your horse's nose and the wall, for the length of the exercise. It is therefore a very good exercise to improve balance and impulsion.

Counter Shoulder-in on 3 tracks

Remember that, whilst asking the horse to step sideways, the inside leg must continue to maintain bend and impulsion in the counter shoulder-in, otherwise the horse will fall away from the wall. Always release the horse from his inside flexion in good time to straighten and ride forward prior to the next (and the new bend) after the counter shoulder-in.

Renvers

Renvers is another of those movements which appears to have been abandoned from the conventional dressage tests, however it is much in evidence in displays at the Spanish Riding School and other classical academies, and is another excellent exercise to straighten and supple, as well as to improve the shoulder-in.

In the renvers the horse is required to move laterally down the track, quarters to the wall but to look and bend into the direction in which he is travelling with the outside legs passing and crossing in front of the inside legs. (British Dressage Rules)

Renvers – on 4 tracks

In France, the movement is known as croupe au mur (croup to the wall). With the rider's inside hand and inside leg maintaining the position of the forehand, it is the rider's outside leg and outside (indirect) rein which will encourage crossing behind.

Renvers is often taught after the travers, but since it is only an inverted travers and in fact works the horse's body in exactly the same way, there is a very good reason for starting it before the travers.

My reasoning is this. Since the horse is to be ridden down the wall at roughly the same angle as for shoulder-in, both rider and horse can progress to it easily from the shoulder-in. It is simply a matter of changing the bend. More importantly, it has the advantage of showing the horse that it is not acceptable to allow his quarters to fall in. Whilst travers actively encourages the quarters in, renvers (its inverted form) removes that temptation, so many riders favour it.

Perhaps the best way to introduce renvers is as follows:

- Commence with a normal shoulder-in down the long side of the arena. On the right rein, the horse will, of course, be bending right but the movement is away from our inside leg towards our left hand.
- After just four to five steps ridden in this by now familiar way, we decide to make a change. Instead of continuing with flexion right, we allow the right rein to yield more forward and start to ask for flexion with the left hand.
- In so doing, we reverse the roles of our leg. The right moves further back (to become the new outside leg) and the left, which previously guarded the quarters, moves forward (to become the new inside leg).
- Finally the original inside hand, the right one, takes on an indirect, supportive role to the outside of the horse.
- The horse is now bending left and into the direction of movement and without fuss, the

shoulder-in has turned into renvers. Be like him, look left!

It is important that we really think through this reversal of aids since this will affect the whole emphasis of the seat and how the horse feels our weight in the saddle. We must accustom ourselves to the feel of the movement itself. Provided we remember always to ride forward as we request the new bend, the new mode of travelling should present few problems if the horse is already well sensitised to the aids.

The discreet change in the rider's head position is very important. After all, why should the horse change, if we do not make the same change? If mirror-imaging your horse in

Here we see renvers ridden just in from the track. Note the use of the (right) rein as an indirect rein to nudge the forehand laterally left, and into the bend. Vaughan's right leg acts just behind the girth to ask the outside right hind to step across.

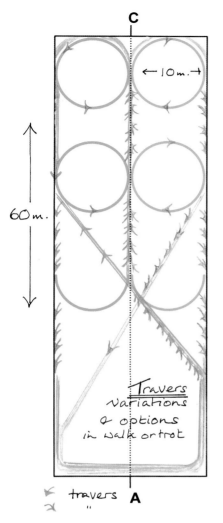

C

← 10m. →

60m.

Travers
Variations
& options
in Walk or trot

travers   A
"

shoulder-in meant looking to the inside, in renvers it is obvious that you will now turn your face to look up the track. Be like your horse and think of flexion right and flexion left, whatever you are doing! The direction in which your head hangs and how you angle your face makes a huge difference to him in terms of weight and feel. Don't underrate this additional aid; it can improve your lateral work immeasurably since your eyes subconsciously dictate body posture.

Once the horse understands what is wanted, ride shoulder-in, circle, renvers, circle and shoulder-in again to reconfirm. Renvers is a useful exercise but must be introduced gradually. It will freshen up the shoulder-in, especially if the horse shows too much neckbend – a common complaint from judges. It will also prove a good precursor to the travers.

Indeed, all these exercises are complementary one to another and the travers too will be worked in a similar way, both down the long sides and from and on the circle (as shown).

Left rein } interchangeable
right rein }

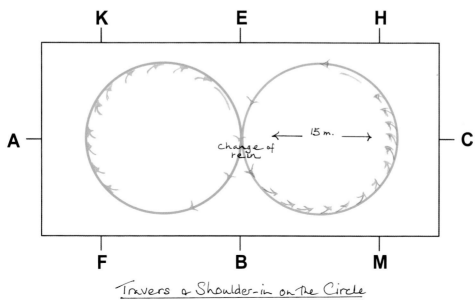

K   E   H

A   15 m.   C
change of
rein

F   B   M

Travers & Shoulder-in on the Circle

By riding a 10m circle prior to the travers, we can use the last segment of the circle as the approach for the lateral movement. Here, Lesley angles her body into the correct position for travers and two more steps will take her and Palomo laterally left provided she does not allow him to come parallel to the fence upon reaching the track.

Travers

Travers is simply renvers the other way round. It is ridden head-to-the-wall with the horse bent in the direction in which he is moving, with the quarters to the inside of the school. Many people, including the Spanish Riding School, have reservations about teaching travers but it is required in many tests from Elementary level onward and, from the suppling point of view, is a beneficial movement. By far its greatest merit is in the preparation of the horse for half-pass, with attention given in particular to the stepping across of the outside hind, and ensuring a more discerning application of the inside leg to keep the horse up to the track.

Although some trainers ask for crossing in front (as in half-pass) there is little hint of this from Podhajsky, who wanted to see 'the forehand held on the track with both reins'. In this way, the horse has to bend more in order to keep the hindquarters from rejoining the track, which is the main purpose. We should therefore be concentrating on the action of the hind legs, which involves the outside hind stepping over and in front of the inside hind, which has to bear more weight. As with all the lateral movements, this encourages the three joints of the hind legs to bend and engage so that the back and haunches are suppled.

Travers should not be tackled until the horse is calm but forward going in his shoulder-in. It can be daunting to the horse to be ridden well up to the wall in travers and, to enjoy success at this level, he must be responsive to the leg aids. As with all the lateral movement, I always insist that this is ridden in walk as, again, horse and rider will need time to organise themselves and to think!

For travers left, I have found that the best procedure to start the novice horse is as follows:

- Ride a 10 m circle at either H or F to establish lateral suppleness and flexion to the inside. As the circle nears completion, draw the forehand onto the track with a soft, asking inside (left) hand and sit a little deeper into the left seatbone.
- Just before the quarters rejoin the track in the last couple of steps of the circle, gently check your horse with a feeling of half-halt through the body and outside rein.
- This should bring the horse into a position of head-to-the-wall at an angle of roughly 35 degrees *provided* you don't align your body to the track.
- Instead, keep your upper body slightly angled like the horse to mirror the quarters-in, head-to-the-wall effect. With flexion left, your face and the horse's face should be looking more or less down the track.
- To ensure forward movement whilst still retaining angle and position, the rider's inside leg asks the horse to step forward by acting at the girth. The outside leg acts in a pushing way behind the girth, asking the horse to step sideways so the quarters are guarded from turning back to the track.
- By deepening the feeling of weight into the inside stirrup, as though leading the horse away to the inside, the rider can now invite the horse to *want* to step into the inside leg, so horse and rider move in alignment up the track.
- The position of the forehand on the track is maintained by both reins gently indicating right. Use the outside (right) rein as an indi-

Travers left: Again, as with shoulder-in, start this work off in walk. Initially the horse may feel less threatened with just a pole on the ground. The rider must sink the weight gently into the inside (left) stirrup to bend and lead the horse down the track whilst holding the angle of the movement through the upper body. Here, four distinct tracks are clearly shown.

rect rein aid against the horse's neck. The feeling through the outside fist is one of nudging fractionally sideways, while the inside rein softens and maintains flexion in the direction of movement.

With a novice horse who has never attempted travers before, try not to jam his nose up against the wall. Be careful also not to 'glue' the inside leg to the horse's side. It may be helpful to deepen the stirrup fractionally away from the girth whilst still supporting with knee and thigh. This action should engage the inside seatbone, which encourages the horse to advance in the correct direction. Try to think of the downward weight aid into the stirrup acting as a magnet! It is as though the inside leg draws the horse along with it. This being coupled with the pushing sideways effect of the outside leg, the horse should very quickly get the idea of stepping laterally into the movement.

Some trainers ask riders to lean into the travers to help the horse, but this could have the opposite effect from the one desired. Leaning may involve a degree of collapse, with the rider actually pushing the horse the other way. Instead, I ask my students to think of sitting an inch taller through the inside waist. Expanding the ribcage also helps the downward pressure into the inside seatbone without the horse losing balance.

Once the rider is absolutely vertical to the inside, he or she can think of allowing more flexibility through the outside of the body in order to give the horse little sideways nudges in the correct direction. Remember, all these subtle aids should be totally invisible to the onlooker. They involve only minute adjustments of weight and balance.

At this stage, never try to regain any loss of balance or impulsion during an exercise without riding straight forward again. It is better to go through the whole sequence, starting with a circle, rather than attempt to salvage something midstream.

Finally, always finish each exercise by straightening your horse well before he runs out of track. Never hold him round a corner in the same exercise at this stage of training.

Understanding and Preparing for the Half-pass

The travers is an excellent precursor to half-pass, but on the whole it should not be ridden too frequently. The sooner one can advance to the half-pass proper, the better. Some riders miss out on travers, going straight from renvers to half-pass. Personally, I quite like travers as a movement, but am mindful of the reservations.

British Dressage Rules describe the half-pass as a 'variation of travers' except that it is 'ridden

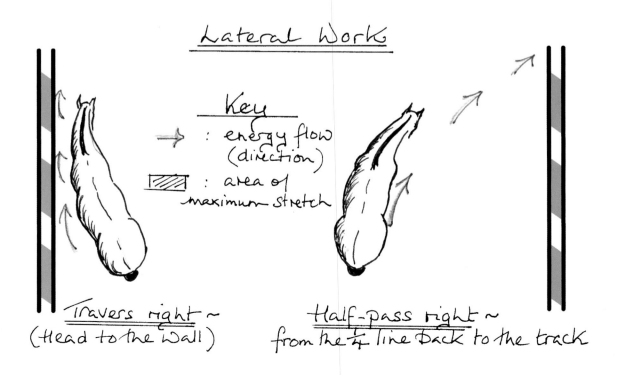

Lateral Work

Key

→ : energy flow (direction)

▨ : area of maximum stretch

Travers right ~ (Head to the wall)

Half-pass right ~ from the ¼ line back to the track

Here, my more advanced mare, Andorinha, shows a really supple four-track travers in trot on the right rein. Correctly, we see that the ears are level and her head remains to the centre of her chest, even although she is just flexing right.

on the diagonal'. To my mind this is somewhat confusing, since half-pass can be ridden in a variety of ways including alongside the track, head-to-the-wall, and head away from the wall. Moreover, half-pass requires far greater collection than travers and the crossing with the front legs will be much more obvious and clearly defined, requiring real suppleness and lift through the shoulders. The hind legs, too, will need to be more engaged.

The rest of the British Dressage definition is much clearer: *The horse should be slightly bent round the inside leg of the rider in order to give more freedom and mobility to the shoulders, thus adding ease and grace to the movement,* *although the forehand should be slightly in advance of the quarters. The outside legs pass and cross in front of the inside legs. The horse is looking in the direction of which he is moving.*

Certainly, the best way to start the half-pass is across the diagonal, either from the wall to the centre line, the centre line back to the wall or from one side of the arena to the other. The angle is generally determined by how many steps will be required. In the early days and the lower level tests, a fairly mild angle will be asked for, which requires more emphasis on forward movement. Later, the angle may be increased so the horse is required to take ever-more pronounced and extravagant sideways

(Below) Learning the feel of travers and half-pass can be quite daunting. Here, in a lesson, Suzanne shows a good understanding of the aids and Vaidoso is crossing smoothly behind as he moves laterally left.

(Right) Here we see the importance of inside leg support and how its correct application makes the horse want to move left. It is not enough simply to place the leg on the girth; the horse must feel a little more weight into both the inside seatbone and inside (left) stirrup. By keeping her loins braced forward, Suzanne's inside hip bone is seen to remain forward, keeping the seat in a balanced and cen- tred vertical position.

steps. However, in both types of half-pass, the quality will be poor without good impulsion, so half-pass should only be on the agenda if the horse is truly 'off the leg'.

Before asking for half-pass, I like to encourage my students to test out their weight aids by riding down the centre line with the horse attentive and on the bit. Then, without trying to influence the forehand, tip or lean in, I ask them merely to think of weight dropping more into the left stirrup than the right. Horses will always want to move under our weight so, if there is fractionally more pressure into that stirrup and into the same seatbone, the horse should move left. This helps to show the rider there is no need for tightness, pushing or force. By simply sitting tall, keeping everything forward-facing, they just 'let the weight down'.

Soon, the student should be able to alternate these weight aids. The horse moves down the centre line, the rider now thinks a little more weight to the right and the horse moves right. The rider straightens the horse with even pressure on both stirrups again, and then applies more pressure into the left stirrup as before. Riders are often surprised and delighted how direction can be changed at will and how naturally and without any real effort these responses are achieved.

Generally, difficulties are only encountered when everyone tries too hard. Bracing against the stirrup is a very different feeling from allowing weight to fall into it. Pushing hard on the heel may shoot the foot forward, stiffen the leg muscles, push the hip back and tighten the knee and other joints. Instead of the stirrup leather hanging vertically with the weight dropping plumb, the leather is at an angle. It is therefore better for riders to think of downward pressure resting in the ball of the foot rather than into the heel. This will help keep the hip-heel alignment which is so vital to balance.

Now the rider has greater mastery over direction, the whole idea of half-pass becomes much less daunting. Moving onto and away from the centre line in this fashion gives the sensation that *the horse puts himself into the lateral movement.* After the direction has been sorted out in this way, we are almost halfway there!

First Steps in Half-pass – How to Proceed

- To create bend and inside flexion, first ride a 10 m half-circle from the track to the centre line. Proceed straight forward down the centre line for a few metres to D or G, with just a soft feeling of flexion on the inside rein, making sure your upper body is square to axis and forward-facing.

- Now sit a little deeper into the inside seatbone with the inside hip and leg at the girth 'leading' the horse into the sideways movement with downward pressure to the inside. As the horse begin to move away from the centre line, regulate the sideways progression with the outside hand so that the forehand does not stray too much ahead of the quarters, but at the same time feel that your outside rein embraces the whole horse by acting just behind the wither in the direction of the opposite haunch.

- At this moment there should be a feeling of half-halt through the upper body to regulate and harmonise the flow in every stride. Although your face should be inclined towards the marker to which you are advancing, it is counter-productive to turn your shoulders at this early stage. Instead, keep your body roughly parallel to the track, otherwise the horse will just turn onto the diagonal line and avoid the lateral movement.

- Finally, bring the outside leg well back behind the girth to hold the quarters and prevent them from straying out. The outside leg may now give synchronised sideways nudges to encourage the outside hind leg to cross over in front of the inside. The timing of this aid is all-important, so be careful only to nudge as you see the inside shoulder advance.

(Above) Vaughan demonstrates a very common mistake. In thinking left, he has pushed his left foot too far forward to brace against his left stirrup. This in fact will push his left hip backward (instead of retaining it forward) to give the horse a misleading aid, making it difficult for the forehand to lead.

(Right) Here, we work on freeing up Bruce's left leg. Weight downward, is very different from weight against ; it is very much a case of allowing the leg (through gravity) to lead the horse into the movement.

There are many different schools of thought concerning the order of the aids in half-pass. Half-pass is not an easy manoeuvre to master, since so much is involved: the correct bend; looking into the movement; allowing the forehand to lead rather than the shoulder to bulge; keeping the quarters engaged; maintaining impulsion as well as lateral movement and all at the same time remaining roughly parallel to the track! Then there are equally important matters such as rhythm, collection and lightness in addition to correct crossing and regular steps... the list of priorities is endless.

To add to the confusion there are some horses who definitely find half-pass easier than others. To avoid the most obvious mistakes, I think we have to be very clear indeed at this stage what does what to the horse. To my mind, there is nothing worse for the horse than a cacophony of 'noisy' aids all being applied at once.

François Baucher was so right, when he wrote 'Legs without hands, hands without legs'. If we do everything at once, it is rather like revving the engine whilst crashing through every gear. In riding, we always have to find a way of taking the horse through each gear with fluency and precision and this is where a sense of timing and a moment of 'neutral' is so vital.

I therefore believe that it is important to separate the aids by fractions of seconds in their application, in the order given above. One of

Riding half-pass up the track is a good way to test forwardness as well as bend and lateral suppleness throughout. Even with experience, the intricacies of the movement require real concentration from both horse and rider.

the reasons why I think of my inside leg aid first, is because it is the most natural aid; through an opening forward weight aid, the horse is invited to move 'into' my leg and to share my space. It therefore makes sense that, just prior to this, we have prepared the horse by asking him to bend on the half-circle.

After that, one could argue that the outside leg should be applied next, but if we are not careful the forehand may have whizzed off on its own, leaving the quarters trailing, and we will have lost the half-pass before it ever began! For this reason, I ask for only a modest bend in the early days and believe the checking and indirect action of the outside rein is very important. It is at this stage that we call this *the rein of indirect opposition*. Not only does the indirect rein influence the forehand to the opposite side; it also acts behind the wither to send the haunches in the same direction (away from the rein) to drive the forehand.

Finally, perhaps our most powerful aid is left to the last. The outside leg; valuable for achieving so much – engaging the quarters, ensuring they remain under the horse, pushing the outside hind forward and through, etc. But we must be careful not to overdo this aid since the outside rein has already helped us displace the quarters, and too much outside leg can be counter-productive.

All in all, I believe this has to be the right sequence of events, for this way there will be less chance of the quarters leading or the impulsion drifting away.

Gradually, as the horse becomes more confirmed in his work, the inside leg and rein will request more bend and the horse will come more together as he crosses and moves forward with ease. For now however, we should be concentrating on the *feeling for the movement*, with the horse eager to flow with us and enjoy the new sensation that half-pass brings.

Little by Little

As with all the movements and exercises discussed to date, introduce the half-pass step by step and be prepared for it to take many months, even years, before you can achieve a really good half-pass in trot. Start in the walk and ask for three or four sideways steps and then ride the equivalent number of steps straight forward. Then advance laterally again, and so on. Once you reach the opposite track, go large until you arrive back at either A or C on the other rein. Then it is time to start down the original centre line and to work the half-pass the other way.

In the early days, always work from the centre line back to the track. There is something reassuring about the wall and the horse will be drawn there, so use it to help you. At a later stage you may try riding from a 10 m circle at F, K, M or H in half-pass back to the centre line. The moment you hit the centre line, straighten your horse and ride boldly forward to A or C. This is a very good test of balance and to check that your horse is still on the aids. If he falters and bulges out before straightening, it is likely that you are using too much outside leg. As in turn on the hocks, the inside leg must always be ready to catch the horse and send him straight and onward. Be sparing with the outside leg and try to get the horse to respond better to your weight aids.

Be careful too that your rein aids are clear – always remember that the horse should be softer to the inside and that the positioning of the forehand comes as much from your outside hand as from the inside. Think of both hands taking your horse to the right for half-pass right; both hands taking him left for half-pass left. Never let your horse end up not knowing which rein to move into and, in using an indirect aid of opposition, never, ever cross the rein over the wither.

Make room for your horse when you ask – the inside rein should always *invite* by opening and softening – and try always to keep your hands parallel one to the other as you ride waist to

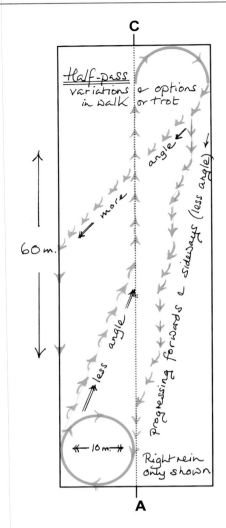

hands.

Finally, having understood the role of the extremities, do not forget that the position of the rider's upper body can make all the difference as to whether or not the half-pass is successful. Think 'into' your inside seatbone, keeping the inside hip supporting forward; think 'into' the direction of travel – try to keep your body square to axis, which means turning very little if your horse is to stay roughly parallel to the track, and don't forget the position of your head. Flexing into the same direction as the horse can make all the difference!

Exercises to Help the Half-pass

When the horse is confident in the exercises described so far, achieving fluid, accurate half-

Good lateral work should have an air of ease and grace. Ideally the horse should flow forwards and sideways, with the rider sitting tall and merely mirroring the movement with the quietest of aids.

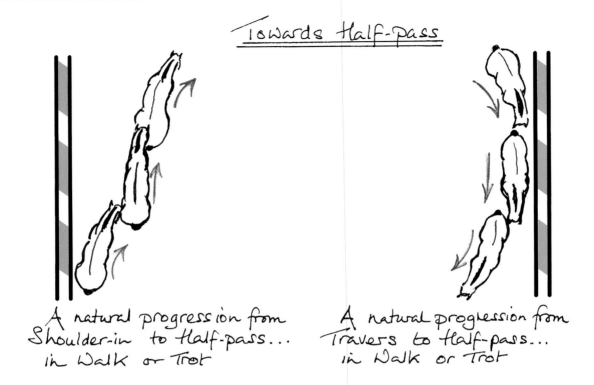

Towards Half-pass

A natural progression from
Shoulder-in to Half-pass...
in Walk or Trot

A natural progression from
Travers to Half-pass...
in Walk or Trot

passes both in walk and trot, we can start to use a whole range of exercises to enhance the half-pass.

One of the best ways to encourage more bend through the forehand is to ride a few steps of shoulder-in up the long side prior to advancing to half-pass to the centre line. Here, the shoulder-in may be picked up again, with the rider making the necessary subtle changes to re-position the upper body in addition to adjusting the aids of seat, leg and hands. In the shoulder-in the horse should be moving from the inside leg into an inviting outside rein, whereas in the half-pass the outside rein acts in an opposing way. The feel in the hands therefore will be very different in the two movements and care must be taken not to confuse the horse.

Horses who trail the quarters will benefit from some steps of travers down the wall. Here, the rider must be careful not to start the half-pass with quarters leading, so again it is important to straighten and square up before leading the horse away from the track and across the diagonal.

Another useful exercise to encourage straightness, forwardness and correct bend is to commence half-pass out of a well-ridden corner and progress to X; to advance straight to D or G; make a 10 m half-circle (on the same rein) to the opposite wall, then half-pass back again to the centre line before straightening up, and exiting at A or C before starting all over again. This movement can be played and replayed either on the same rein or by changing the rein after the exit.

Moving easily from one exercise to another; one rein to another, brings variety to the work and the horse can really enjoy himself. One word of warning; it is better not to change the rein too often with a horse who is fairly new to the work. Change the exercise by all means, but try to have long periods of stretch and relax in between. In this way, you will keep your horse sweet and happy.

To heighten awareness, let us look at what can go wrong in a simple half-pass back to the track from D on the right rein:

THE HORSE'S THOUGHTS (uneducated rider)

- I've been turned down the centre line at A but, almost immediately, I feel my head and neck being brought very firmly right. My rider's lower inside leg is pressing at the girth, but there's no support from knee or thigh and, since she's turned her hips and body to the right, I slip through and turn my body in sympathy. Perhaps I'm being set up for shoulder-in?
- I'm just about to move off sideways away from her right leg towards X when the left rein tightens and I feel a lot of booting against my left side. I look left and now my quarters are ahead of my shoulders so I set off sideways towards the track instead, not having much choice in the matter.
- Oh dear! she's pulled on my right rein again to turn my head back to where it was, but it's all very confusing, especially now she's leaning out to the left and I feel I'm being driven that way!
- Ah! now her shoulders have turned right, so I free myself out of this contortion by shooting my shoulders ahead of my quarters and diving straight across the diagonal. No stepping sideways for me, it was all quite impossible!

Or, on a happier note, how it should be done:

THE HORSE'S THOUGHTS (educated rider)

- My rider has turned me down the centre line at A on the right rein and although we're progressing forward in a straight line, I feel her gently 'asking' with the right rein, so I incline my head this way.
- She opens the right rein a little more and sponges softly and now she's drawing me to the right, but there is still this sense of staying straight because I'm well supported to the inside and her hips direct me this way.

Now her inside leg deepens and I feel compelled to step right but remain forward-going.
- As I incline right with my head, neck and shoulders, I feel a restraining hand on the outside rein. This stops me from wanting to turn my whole body to the right, but I have enough leeway still to look where we're going. Now I feel real encouragement to step away from the outside rein. Somehow I'm being urged gently sideways and suddenly my forelegs are crossing!
- Almost in the same breath, my rider's left leg is against me, and there's a definite press sideways followed by another and another! This activates my quarters and really gets me moving towards the track, which looks safe and inviting! I'm not sure quite what's happening, but somehow my hind legs have taken on a life of their own and they're now crossing too. It's really all quite pleasant!

Canter Half-pass

Many find it easier to get the feeling of half-pass in the canter long before they can master it in trot. There is nothing very wrong in this provided that you observe the same stringent rules about bend and position as you would in the walk and trot. In canter, the horse jumps sideways rather than crossing as such. The fact that this is a movement where the horse is naturally bending and leading with one side of his body allows the rider's aids to complement the sideways movement. For example, just by sitting a little deeper, the rider's inside (leading) leg can lead the horse more sideways. Just by a gentle feel to the inside and a discreet half-halt to the outside, the outside rein gives the forehand a better position.

Starting half-pass from the centre line to the wall, will involve counter-canter or flying changes if you are not to break, so unlike the trot, start the canter half-pass from the long side to the centre line. This will allow your horse to then continue forward and down to A or C on the same rein, which is much more encouraging. Since the outside leg will already be back for the canter depart, the idea of bringing the horse forwards and sideways away from the outside leg and into the leading (inside) one, can be accomplished in a few easy bounds. We should never forget that the canter is made up of a series of jumps and it is quite easy for the horse to jump sideways as well as forwards – as anyone who owns a spooky horse will tell you!

Work in the counter-canter loops will already have given the rider a good feel for the horse's athletic ability to move outward and inward in canter. The progression from the loop to those few strides further into the school to pick up the centre line is not nearly so difficult as might be thought. However, since canter half-pass should generally be left until the horse is rather more advanced in his education, we shall leave this subject for now and return to it in Chapter XIV.

Extended Walk

Having worked through all the various lateral movements in walk and trot, it would now seem a good opportunity to look at the extended walk. This is an elegant exercise with the horse well-engaged behind as he steps under and forward with the hind legs to overtrack the prints made by the forefeet in a firm, marching four-beat gait. The idea is that the horse covers as much ground as possible, with an outstretched but mildly arched neck, still answering to and seeking the contact of the rein and with the poll and jaw relaxed.

Before this gait can become meaningful for the horse, we first need to reinforce collection, which gives the horse the necessary engagement behind to really propel the walk forward. As with all the extended gaits, there can be no meaningful push from behind without coiling our 'spring' together, so in the schooling process, this is an exercise which slots in conveniently after the collected demands of the lateral movements.

Since the shoulder-in and the half-pass will have done much to liberate the horse's shoulders and elevate the forehand, it is not so much a question of teaching the horse the movement, but merely letting it develop. The main thing to remember is to sit tall and proud, with the idea that he raises himself up through the back and forehand, so that he can come 'uphill' and through into the gait, rather than dropping downward.

Just as you learned to encourage the walk on a long rein by thinking of walking through the seatbones, so it is with extended walk. The main difference is that we allow the horse to take the rein forward but not down. Instead, we ask him to stretch the rein ahead of him on a soft contact, until we really feel those ground-covering, smooth and stately strides developing for themselves.

Many horses who may have impressive extended gaits in trot and canter, lose marks in competition through poor extended walks. This is nearly always a result of tension and the fact that, in the early days of training, the rider did not take sufficient time to encourage relaxation in walk on a long rein, or do exercises in collected walk. Both are vitally important to the schooling process, even at the highest level.

CHAPTER XIII

Into the Double Bridle
Full Collection, Medium and Extended Work

Gathering himself upward, the young colt flexes his limbs to show real extravagance in trot.

Many riders fear that, in bringing about full collection, they may somehow reduce their horse's willingness to go forward. The reverse is true provided that we have always worked correctly from back to front, combining propelling power with weight-bearing ability in order to render hocks and haunches more springlike. The transitions and lateral exercises will have generated more energy, but by conserving this behind the saddle, we can control and liberate it forward at will. In this way, collected movement may be transformed into expressive and impressive extension.

At this point, the rider may wish to introduce the double bridle. The two reins encourage greater finesse and lightness as the hands act in their combined role with the leg and body aids for the collection or *rassembler* of the horse. It is always difficult to gauge these matters precisely, but generally the horse himself will make things plain. There is no hard-and-fast rule as to exactly when the change to two bits should take place. Some may turn to this chapter earlier than others; however it is generally advisable to wait until most of the lateral work has been well understood in the snaffle.

When choosing a double bridle, it is common sense to experiment until you find the combination which most suits your horse's mouth. The shape of the mouth and the length and thickness of the tongue can make a considerable difference to the perfect choice from one horse to another.

Most horses prefer a broader lower port on the Weymouth and for some, a fixed snaffle such as an eggbutt can be preferable to the normal loose-ringed bridoon, particularly if the horse is inclined to fiddle. Still others prefer a French link type for greater relaxation through the jaw and then there are the arguments for and against stainless steel with many people turning to the hugely popular Kangaroo bits. Since every horse is different and bitting is a huge and complex subject on its own, a list of recommended reading is given at the back of this book, but be prepared to take time about such important decisions.

Bit by Bit

Whatever set of bits is finally chosen, the rider should introduce the double bridle gradually, always returning to the snaffle on a regular basis in between times. This will freshen the mouth, confirm forwardness and obedience and ensure that the horse is not overly dependent on the curb. Signs of overbending and withdrawing the neck instead of extending it into the contact, should be viewed as a warning.

191

To start the work in the double, keep the curb chain fairly loose just for the first few days. Thereafter, it should be fitted snug enough just to touch the chin groove but loose enough for two fingers to be inserted. Too loose a curb will merely mean that the horse requires more action on the rein to feel its effects, and the shank of the curb should never be pulled into the horizontal.

Try to ride as much as possible on the snaffle rein initially. The horse will need time to get accustomed to the second bit, so work mainly with what he is used to. It is generally recommended that the snaffle rein is held beneath the little fingers of each hand while the curb rein is separated to pass between the third and fourth fingers. In this way, both reins emerge together through the top of the fist to be secured gently in place by the thumbs. With this method, we guard against any inadvertent damage caused by our instinctive reactions. Most people bear slightly downwards with the hand in halts and half-halts, but by keeping the snaffle rein to the outside, this rein will come more into play than that of the curb.

For all directional aiding, it will still be the snaffle rein which is used, particularly in lateral flexion. The curb is there to encourage direct flexion, acting on a sensitive point in the chin groove and at the poll. Not everyone appreciates just how vulnerable the poll is, lying at the junction of the skull and the neck vertebrae and close to the brain. Force applied here has been known to cause rearing and panic in some horses, so riders need to discipline themselves to use the curb rein with real subtlety.

It is time now for the rider to refine all the aids so that those of the hand become totally unobtrusive. In so doing, there must be much greater awareness of exactly what the fingers are doing. Real finger control permits us to ease off or allow with one set of reins whilst asking more with the other. The curb rein is used with imperceptible squeeze and release touches which, in conjunction with the snaffle, help maintain a relaxed jaw. As a result the use of the two reins should bring about a lighter feeling in the hand overall.

Differing Degrees of Contact

Some books insist that there should be the same amount of contact on both the snaffle (bridoon) and curb rein. When initially taking up the reins, I generally ask pupils both mentally and physically to slacken off the curb rein by about one inch. If this small exercise is not done, it is extraordinary how the curb rein often becomes tighter and tighter, unless the rider is highly experienced. Riders should keep a watchful eye on the angle of the branch, which should remain as close to the vertical as possible.

Riding on the curb rein alone, as seen in pictures of the classical masters, requires huge finesse and is better left to the absolute experts. Even when the horse is well used to the double bridle, is relaxed in the mouth and salivating nicely, we should not abandon the use of the snaffle bridle at regular intervals. Some people use the double in the school and then hack out in the snaffle. Others warm up in the snaffle and then compete in the double. Others do the opposite! One knows that one is on the right track when one can happily alternate these patterns of behaviour. It is important that the horse does not associate the use of the two bridles with any one particular thing.

Keep Things Simple

In the early days of accustoming the horse to the double, the rider must concentrate on forwardness, ensuring the horse remains off the leg and light into the hand. A rider who has not yet ridden with spurs may want now to introduce them for greater precision. However, it would be unfair to the horse to introduce two new things at once, so common sense should prevail as to how this can be achieved. Step by step must always be the maxim, so preferably wait until the next snaffle-only phase before introducing the spur.

Keep things simple during the first days of work in the double bridle. The main thing is to ride forward and straight whether in trot or canter. There is no reason why the double bridle should cause overbending. Ensure that the neck arches freely forward to allow a calm acceptance of both bits.

During the first month of riding in the double, the rider should refrain from carrying out the lateral work. It is better to go back to basics and confirm all that has been accomplished to date, only with much greater attention to detail. The double bridle is often known as our precision tool and we should now look for greater accuracy in transitions as well as recapitulating all the work done to date with a far greater degree of subtlety.

Now is the time to confirm collection in all three gaits, which will prepare the horse for the extended gaits. From the idea of making a difference in trot and canter we can now progress to extending the trot and the canter, for which the basic aids have already been laid down. It should now become evident why collection proper has to be established before these two states of progression will have any real flow or merit. No spring will uncoil with any sense of unleashed power or real pizazz unless it has been properly coiled or gathered in the first place.

To improve the collected trot and collected canter therefore, we must again return to the walk if the horse is to be encouraged to understand what we want in the other gaits. Again, we may come across prejudice in such a practice but provided collection grows from working the hind end forwards and not from the forehand backward, we should not be afraid to ask. Collecting the walk is made possible by an increased knowledge of the leg and seat aids, while the rider learns to hold, lift up or, in the words of the masters, 'arch' through the chest, which is the result of increased bracing forward with the lower back.

Collected Walk

This gait, if correctly ridden, should look very proud, with the horse lighter and higher in front, and the steps shorter but more energetic as the hind legs flex deeper underneath. I always tell my pupils that if the collected walk does not feel impulsive enough for their horse to offer canter at any given moment, then there is something wrong. (Later, they will learn that it is also a preparation for piaffe, which requires an equal coiling of the spring.)

To achieve collected walk, ensure that you ask with quick, light taps of the inner lower leg, rather than squeezing and dampening down energy with a tightened muscular calf. Remember that it is the subsequent and imme-

diate yielding of the legs that allows impulsion through. Whilst our light nutcracker action encourages the lifting of the back and the energising of the hind legs, the horse will only continue to move up and forward if our legs become stretched and relatively passive again.

We have already discussed the most effective place to ask with the legs. Whilst alternate leg aids help to span out and lengthen the walk, I personally find collection is only understood by the horse when we use both legs together simultaneously. Even quite dead-to-the-leg horses seem to come alive and respond when the action is swift and very light, like tiny, tiny electric shocks.

Of course, all this is a matter of feeling, but in allowing your legs to remain glued on and around the frame of the horse, make sure there is no blocking. Depending on the horse, some riders prefer a soft contact all the way through from seat to ankle bone; others prefer to let the lower leg hang free from the knee but, whatever the case, it is the short, sharp aid which causes the horse to detach his feet from the ground for the shorter, higher steps required in collection. Lingering aids only cause him to dwell more.

The rider's upper body has far more influence over the horse's posture than most people give credit for. It can actively support upward to lift the horse and make room for the hind legs or, by contrast, slump forward and drop him down onto the forehand so the hocks are left behind.

In collection, therefore, always remember that there should be a two-way stretch – long legs and tall upper body. Then your horse is given the best chance to round his back and flex his joints. As the walk becomes more 'uphill', the hands must accept this change of frame with gentle half-halts through the fingers. Provided that the hind legs are kept active and engaged (the use of the schooling whip just tickling behind the leg is useful), the horse will walk forward in a graceful, courtly way.

To sustain this feeling, a prouder or grander

posture of the rider's whole body will encourage the horse to retain a more elevated posture and, provided nothing changes, several steps may be taken in this gathered walk. As always, the horse is then rewarded by being allowed to stretch down on a loose rein again. 'Imagine you're a Spanish king!' is the analogy that seems to work for my students in collected walk; images like this really make a difference.

Now is the time to make the walk even more impulsive with short phases of shoulder-in, renvers, travers, turns and half-pass on straight lines or circles so that one movement complements and prepares for the next. The time has come to ride more deeply into the school corners so that greater bending and deeper engagement takes place.

To improve balance throughout, we can begin to introduce shoulder-in and haunches-in through corners too. As the rider turns, the horse turns; as the rider straightens, the horse simply mirrors this. The rider's hands are merely an extension of the body and, through collection, the horse himself has become part of that whole. Progressing quietly through the various exercises, the horse will grow more and more responsive. Walk gives time for everyone to think and feel and this is a time for building on everything to date; for consolidating communication lines. The horse should be listening for the merest nuance of weight change in the seat or leg or through the angle of the torso. The work must be diligent and unhurried.

Changing the Exercises

Try always to bring variety and imagination to these programmes. Visualise the progression of impulsion from quarters to poll and feel how your horse concentrates his energy into one lively ball of bubbling power. A walk ridden with real lightness, what the old masters called the school walk, is exciting! The four beats are maintained at all times, but the horse becomes catlike in his movement, moving and turning in suspension with all the ease of a ballet dancer.

Try sequences like these and surprise yourself how nicely they make the horse flow:

- Make a 10 m half-circle right and straighten down the centre line from A to D.
- Ride four or five steps of shoulder-in to X and into an 8 m circle right.
- Ride a similar number of steps of travers from X to roughly G: then in the same bend ride half a 10 m volte to the track.
- From the track, approach the first quarter line diagonally; then ride a few steps of counter shoulder-in followed by some straight steps.
- There should be just room to ride half-pass to the centre line.
- Straighten to A and change the bend and the rein and let your horse stretch down before starting the whole thing all over again from the C end of the school...

Variations on a theme create endless possibilities. Keep the steps lively and use the exercises to motivate the horse. He should feel lighter and lighter as you do them. They are there not to challenge but to make things easier.

Throw other movements into the equation. Introduce some quarter pirouettes and gradually progress to the half pirouette. A good way to start is from the walk shoulder-in on the long side, then it's only three steps to bring you round so you're facing the other way. From a straight line, ride a half turn on the haunches; instead of two steps, simply ride four. Mentally do it in two quarters; one-two, one-two. If you think four steps your horse may swivel – and beware! – the last step is always the hardest as the horse tries to avoid bearing weight on his outside hind by stepping out behind.

When you have mastered stringing the lateral exercises together at walk you are ready to move on and try them at trot. There is no doubt that the double bridle will encourage the collection of all the gaits, but perhaps in the trot it is the most noticeable. As the horse

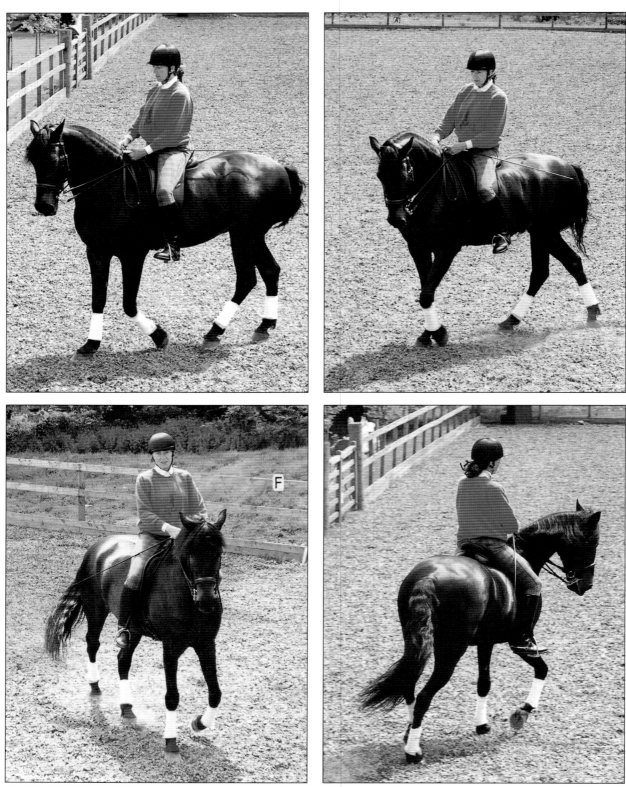

Collection in walk has nothing to do with artificially shortening the gait. Lightness develops as a direct result of suppling exercises which work the horse's hindquarters and his shoulders. Here, sitting tall and proud, I move Espada in and out of quarters-in and shoulder-in on the circle interspersed with the quarter-pirouette.

The result of the various collected manoeuvres in walk becomes obvious when we proceed to trot. The length of rein remains the same, but the horse is now very much lighter in front as we proceed to travers and then straighten out in self-carriage.

settles into the double bridle and answers to the poll pressure by flexing a little more, the rider should find that the hand aids are diminished considerably.

Gradually, the fingers take on a whispering nature; the idea of pulling or moving the hand back – never on the cards in the first place – will become abhorrent. As we yield we are aware that we never give everything away; so the tension on the rein is only commensurate with how much we want to give, how much is required. The length of rein should remain the same in each gait. Clearly, in collection, we give with our hands rather less than in extension but, in general, it is the horse who makes himself light on the rein, by lowering the croup and gathering up through the centre.

The half-halt should now be achieved by a mere closing of the fingers rather than a raising of the hand upward and, when the horse obeys, the fingers should soften but the hand remains in place. Lateral flexion is a mere vibration on one rein or the other – or an occasional turn of the wrist – but still the hands remain parallel.

The time will come when shoulder-in can be asked for almost without the inside lower leg. The moment the horse feels your shoulders and hips adopting the shoulder-in position, he just glides away from the pressure of your inside thigh. Perfected in walk, how much easier everything becomes when we progress to collected trot.

From Collected Trot to Medium and Extended Gaits

With the shoulders rendered light and a greater feeling of upwardness and roundness in the horse's back, collecting the trot to a greater degree should be nothing more than a natural progression from the collected walk exercises. Again, moving in and out of the various lateral movements will be enormously beneficial, as will the transitions. Remember always to straighten the horse before changing the bend and rein; initially, always use the voltes and half-

circles to prepare for the next exercise.

We have already seen how the shoulder-in prepares the horse for lengthening across the diagonal. Never be in a hurry to go; take measured steps as you head off the track and build up the extension deliberately by increasing the proactive forces within your own body. Remember, you too have energy and the idea is to converge and project yours with that of the horse.

Visualising a forceful jet of water rising up and passing through your centre in an arc to form a powerful projection can be helpful. This requires both legs acting at the girth, while the hands gently support the 'hose' which emanates from your waist. Instead of a controlling thumb at the nozzle, it is the tone of your dorsal and abdominal muscles which can either channel the dynamic force through collection or, by contrast, allow your horse to gush!

Here, Andorinha, ridden by my working pupil Samantha, is asked for extended trot across the diagonal. Sam's hands allow sufficiently for there to be real freedom through the mare's shoulders, while the poll remains the highest point. However, the hind legs will need to engage more deeply if they are to match the action of the forelegs, which requires more 'asking' from the fingers, seat and leg.

(Top) *A momentary half-halt to engage the hocks as we push up the slope may be necessary. Here the neck has shortened but at least Espada is not overbent — which is so important to avoid in the medium or extended gaits if we are not to put the horse on his shoulders.*

(Bottom) *Now, working on the flat, we retain that feeling of 'uphill' in the extended trot. The contact of the rein should remain elastic and the poll continues to remain the highest point.*

(Above) *Here, the trot shows more power as the horse stretches through the topline to push from behind. It is important that the rider does not block the action of the hocks by thrusting hard into the saddle as is so often seen.*

Of course, the temptation in the extended gaits is to give away too much. While we want the horse to *lengthen through the entire frame*, he would simply 'fall apart' and run if we did not maintain some form of contact and support. The latter is provided by the rider's body, and a more discerning bilateral use of the rein. This is a time to concentrate on the movement of the horse underneath you.

Good riders will alternate the pressure on the reins so that as the horse's right shoulder moves forward (for example), the right rein eases slightly to encourage the free forward passage of impulsion, whilst the left rein remains in support. A moment later, the left rein eases whilst renewed pressure on the right rein supports. Remember, however, that we are only concerned with releases of finger pressure; there is no question of pulling back with either hand and the hands must remain as a pair.

Likewise, if we are to relate the feeling in the rein correctly to what is happening behind, we must co-ordinate the legs aids with the diagonal movement. Therefore, as one leg asks, the opposite hand will give. A quick touch of the spur from say the left leg will only stimulate appropriately as the *left hind leg is about to move forward.* If it is applied when the left leg is grounded, it can have a counter-productive effect.

Think, therefore, of your horse swinging through elastic reins which, alternately, give just enough for him to punch the air with both the front and the diagonal hind foot. A freeze-frame should show the horse's nose level with the foremost front hoof if he is truly extended throughout. The action of each hind leg reaching well underneath the horse's belly should match that of the diagonal foreleg, so that the horse covers the ground with long, powerful strides.

The real benefit of using the shoulder-in to improve the medium and extended gaits is to encourage greater engagement of the hind legs so that the horse does not 'drop downhill' as is too often seen. The lateral work will have put your horse more on his hocks, and both horse and rider will already be in the correct angle to ride the diagonal.

There are many other ways of perfecting the medium trot and gradually developing it into extended trot, but always remember that there can be no real lengthening through the frame until the horse is able to work from a collected frame. Good 'sitting' and engagement will lead to an uphill quality in your work. If, however, your horse does have a tendency to tip downward – a very common fault – then clearly more work in collection is required (see previous chapter).

Rider position can so often complement or mar the potential to lengthen. In their anxiety

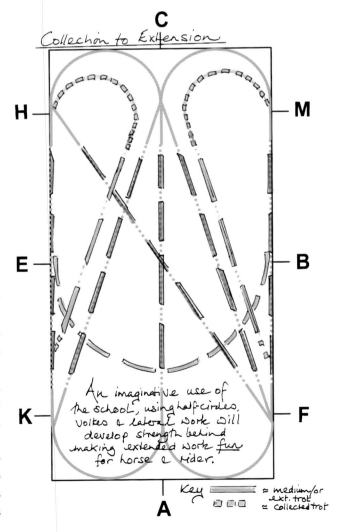

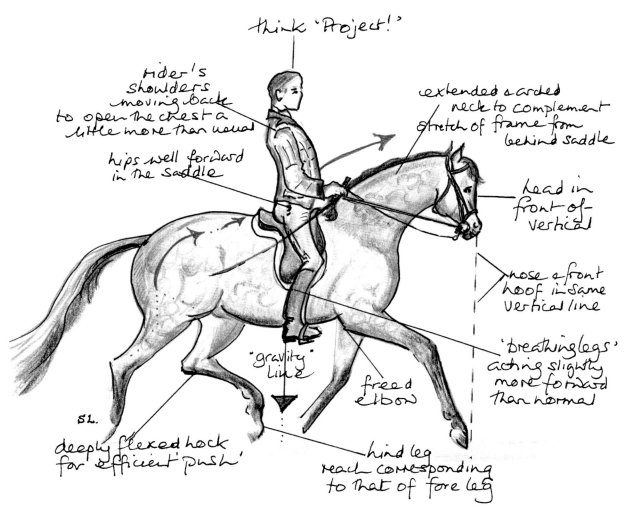

think 'Project!'

rider's shoulders moving back to open the chest a little more than usual

hips well forward in the saddle

extended & arched neck to complement stretch of frame from behind saddle

head in front of vertical

nose & front hoof in same vertical line

"gravity" line

freed elbow

'breathing legs' acting slightly more forward than normal

SL.

deeply flexed hock for efficient 'push'

hind leg reach corresponding to that of fore leg

In medium & extended gaits, merge your energy with that of the horse & project it forward through your centre in a measured & controlled manner. Think of opening your chest and pointing it skyward to encourage the opening of your horse's frame.

From Collection to Extension ~

Here, Andorinha makes the transition from medium to a very collected trot, but as she lightens onto the contact she puts herself 'on parole', drawing no visible support from the hand, but utilising strength behind and under saddle, as well as extreme flexion in the joints (note the angle of the fetlocks) to remain in balance.

to ride forward, some riders lose balance by dropping the shoulders or collapsing the waist. This is an immediate invitation for the horse to drop too – and he will. Others lean back so much that their seatbones dig into the cantle and the horse immediately hollows. The successful rider is the one who:

- continues to think 'uphill' and together in all lengthening work
- creates more forward reach from light legs applied a little more forward than usual

- keeps the hips central, whilst leaning back from the waist to send the horse on
- is able to retain energy and then project it, just at the right moment!
- allows the horse to stretch the rein.

Remember that driving with the seat is quite onerous on the horse and should only be applied for a limited number of strides. There should be no sensation of tipping backwards and forward with the seatbones; simply engage them a little deeper by the action of your shoulders moving back. There is nothing more detrimental to good extension than constant interruptions from above. The horse needs a proactive, supportive rider if he is to give his all.

Once the horse has got the idea on the diagonal and long side (see also Chapter VII), try riding medium trot from and returning to collected trot on a 20 m circle. The slight bend involved will help the engagement of the inside hind leg and your horse will enjoy this exercise as he builds up his own power and understanding of the aids.

The transition returning to the collected gait must be ridden carefully. The transition will jar and put him against the hand if you do this with the reins alone, so you must find a way of telling him with the seat to collect under you. As you think a little behind the vertical in the medium trot, make a mental note to make a contrast by sitting more upright and a little deeper in the transition to collected trot. One classical instructor I remember, with reins of silk, used to say: 'Push your navel towards the hands by pushing it out and over the top of your jodhpurs to collect the horse!' This action gently tips the pelvis into the vertical position so the weight is taken forward. If you encourage this feeling by pulling your knees down, the front of the thigh stretches deep to lighten the weight at the back of the saddle. The horse can now bring his hind legs deeper underneath to move up into the transition. The last thing we want is for the forehand to drop, the neck to shorten or the back to disconnect from unengaged hind legs. This subtle change in the seat will really help maintain the throughness of the transition.

Other people may describe these sensations differently. There will always be arguments about nuances of technique; some talented people could not even tell you what they do! What matters is that we give the horse the incentive to bring about change by making it physically possible and comfortable for him to comply. Weighting the back of the saddle and exaggerating the push from the seatbones tends to hollow the horse and drive him against the hands – uncomfortable for all concerned.

Collected Canter

There are a number of exercises, all of which help collect the canter by requiring greater engagement behind. Teaching the horse to turn down the centre line and return diagonally to the track in counter-canter improves balance immeasurably. Slowing the canter naturally on a circle by gradually spiralling-in is another.

Repeated trot transitions on a 15 m circle are excellent, particularly if you gradually diminish the trot steps from several to just one or two. Canter from rein-back, already discussed, is very effective; while asking for more lateral bend and riding shoulder-fore in canter on a 20m circle is another.

Work with the horse and do not remain for too long in any one exercise. Remember, variety is the spice of life and never forget to spend an equal amount of time on both reins. Always finish on a good note by ending with something easier, and always break up the collected work with straight lines in between, as well as plenty of stretch in walk on the long rein.

Canter to Walk

Now will be the time to perfect your canter to walk transitions. Canter becomes so much more controllable when the horse moves up and into a collected gait from the walk or rein-back. What is less easy is the canter to walk. For this, the horse should have attained a high degree of suppleness in order not to lose balance. Canter to halt is even harder and is not required in competition until Advanced Medium.

Canter to walk should not be expected of any horse under six years of age – and be prepared for it to take much longer. The horse will need to be very supple through the back and hocks to do this at the first request. Even some quite advanced horses find this

Collected Canter

*Sitting very quiet, tall & central
in canter allows the horse to grow
tall & come together for this very
balanced posture.*

movement particularly difficult.

Just as we worked on the canter to trot transitions on a 20 m circle, so we should use the same exercise for our first attempts at canter to walk. When you first ask for canter to walk it is helpful to do this on the return to the track rather than on the centre line. The horse sees

the fence or wall loom ahead and the rider uses it as a visual prop. Just as the tip of the horse's nose draws level with the fence, simply think 'walk' through your entire body and stretch up to support. It's almost a push-and-hold feeling and must never end in a pull back with the reins.

Once the rider learns to push the horse into the walk in this way – the waist to hands concept again – everything becomes much clearer to the horse. He can really engage his hind legs into the transition in this way and there will be little temptation to fall onto the forehand. However, since canter to walk is a surprisingly strenuous exercise, be happy after a couple of attempts, practise something else and get your horse thinking forward again.

Medium and Extended Canter

Now is the time to start extending the canter – in many ways an easier proposition than similar work in trot since it is mainly a question of riding more boldly forward, thinking big, ground-covering strides and going for broke. The same rules concerning contrasting seat aids as used in the trot also apply in canter. Collection comes from deepening through the thighs and relieving weight at the back of the saddle; extension is encouraged from using more seat to drive. We can perhaps be a little more extravagant in opening the shoulders and bringing them back in canter to send the horse on, but never allow your seat to slip back to the cantle, or you may hollow and string your horse out.

The overriding principle in all this work is that both medium and extended canter will never have real eye-catching, extravagant quality unless a good, upward-moving collected canter has been established first.

Here are some tips for showing the horse the way:

- Ride some full counter-canter circles, starting first with 20 m circles and then decreasing them to 15 m. Then ride all the way round the school in counter-canter and reward your horse by changing the rein and returning to normal canter on the diagonal line. Ride this in medium canter and make it bold and fun!
- Ride some shoulder-fore in canter for a few

strides after the corner, followed by medium canter across the diagonal. (Although no longer asked for in today's dressage tests, canter shoulder-in is an important old classical movement and is invaluable for suppling and straightening horses who have a tendency towards crookedness.)

- Make a 20 m circle in collected canter with a few steps of quarters-in and then normal again; second time round, some shoulder-in and then normal again; then ride the whole circle in medium canter. Make this latter a big deal with lots of pats and 'Good boys!'
- Canter some three-loop (later five-loop serpentines in a 60 x 20 m arena) without changes so you always end up in normal canter and can then ride extended canter down the long side to where you started. By now your horse will think extending the canter is the easiest thing in the world and will really want to please!

Canter Shoulder-in

For those who have difficulty with the canter shoulder-in, the principles are the same as already discussed in trot, but be careful not to draw the lower inside leg too far back, which will muddle the horse for changes. Think of the sideways movement coming much more from your upper body position, inner seatbone and thigh and you may be surprised how easily the horse will get the idea.

The canter shoulder-in simply sets the horse more on his hocks; this will help towards higher work in canter and will certainly encourage lengthening across the diagonal or up the long side. For the latter, ride a few steps of canter shoulder-in with the horse looking into the school and the hind legs stepping well underneath; then straighten your body, half-halt with the outside rein as you release the horse from the inside flexion and let him bound forward. The spring from the hind legs should give the medium canter a real feeling of 'uphill'!

The Giving of the Rein

This can have many interpretations depending upon which school of thought you are following and what is required. In the French classical school, the giving of one or both reins constitutes a reward to the horse when he is fully collected; it is a proof that he is no longer dependent upon the rider's contact to maintain position and balance. This giving away of the rein through a lowering and total allowing of the hand is known as the *descente de main.*

Unfortunately, the interpretation of the give and retake of the reins in most test situations is somewhat different. Instead of the rein being eased out slowly and gracefully, with the rider's hand remaining in place at the wither, the rider is required to move the hands forward and back again virtually all in one swift motion. This is generally asked for in canter to prove that the horse remains in balance. Since the exercise never really has the time to develop – being very shortlived – it has departed somewhat from the original purpose.

In true *descente de main,* the horse will have built up to the work through superior collection over a lengthy period of time, probably several years. The idea is that the rider then displays the horse 'on parole' for several sec-

onds or even minutes, where all aiding appears absent – except of course for a beautiful seat. The classical *descente de main* is generally accompanied by a *descente des jambes* – quite literally the letting go of the legs. This latter occurs when our legs aids have become so refined that the breathing action described on p.55 is sufficient to keep the horse attentive and forward without any need for further application of the leg during each exercise.

Usually this peaceful work is displayed in a very collected trot or canter, showing the reins hanging nonchalantly down while the horse remains in the same balance, the same attitude, round corners, across centre lines, on circles and so on. Where it finds real appeal is in the passage, that lofty, proud and elevated trot which we shall be exploring in the final chapter.

A horse who is very confirmed in the piaffe also benefits from the *descente de main.* It releases him from all possible tension and in the words of Decarpentry, 'allows him to use all the resources of his instinct to make good any local weaknesses of his muscular system.' What a pity *descente de main* in its true and original form as prescribed by de la Guérinière is not insisted upon in Grand Prix dressage today, as a final proof of trust and excellence.

PART SEVEN
The Work Proper – Advanced Level

CHAPTER XIV
*Challenges in Canter, Half-pass towards Pirouette and
Introducing the Flying Change*

CHAPTER XV
Total Lightness: Piaffe, Passage and the Icing on the Cake

CHAPTER XIV

Challenges in Canter

Half-pass towards Pirouette and Introducing the Flying Change

Changing legs is so simple for the young foal once his haunches are engaged and he is light in front.

By now, a huge rapport and fine-tuning of the aids through transitions, figure work and changes of pace within canter, should have built up both athletic ability and confidence. Prior to schooling for changes, the horse should be happy and relaxed about holding counter-canter round the entire school perimeter, on circles, and within figures-of-eight or serpentines. From rein-back he should be able to canter off on a given leg at any time and in any place, and show the same facility from the walk.

Perfecting the Simple Change

Progressive simple changes should have presented no problem and he should now be able to canter directly to walk without losing balance or straightness. In the true simple change, the horse is required to walk for only three or at the most four steps before departing in canter again, with absolutely no intermediary steps of trot. This is much easier said than done, and although this movement is asked for at Elementary level, the horse needs to be able to slow and collect the canter for at least the last three or four strides prior to the transition if the rider is not to over-aid with the hand.

Establishing good simple changes (see p146) is an important preliminary for teaching the flying change, and the rider will need to develop a sense of riding waist to hands to a much higher degree. The half-halts when applied should be much more to do with the body than the rein action. It is much more a question of 'sliding' the horse through into walk with the correct nuance of seat and leg.

Towards Canter Half-pass

In Chapter XI, we talked about the introduction to canter half-pass being little more than an advancement of the work previously done in counter-canter loops. Provided that we have kept everything forward-going and simple, half-pass in canter should present fewer problems than we might anticipate. *The weight aids will be similar to the half-pass in trot, but the very nature of canter complements the sideways movement and makes it relatively easy for the horse to understand.* The most difficult aspect of canter half-pass will be to achieve the correct bend without losing quarters or forehand. Throughout every jump of the half-pass, the rider must feel that he or she can immediately straighten forward again, so the horse must remain around and listening to the impulsion aid of the inside leg at the girth.

The aids for half-pass in canter are very similar to those for trot, but here are some extra pointers to a successful first attempt:

- Lead the horse away from the track by positioning the forehand fractionally ahead of the quarters. Use the inside (direct) rein for bend and the inside leg for impulsion and direction. An indirect rein aid will encourage the shoulders to maintain position.
- Encourage the sideways feel of the canter with the outside leg coupled with the outside rein used, if necessary, as an indirect rein of opposition to keep the horse 'together' as he advances diagonally. The nature of canter makes it all too easy to overdo the sideways push and lead with the quarters, so be sparing with these aids.
- Bend is important and will develop, but initially concentrate on keeping the horse roughly parallel to the track. Quarters which stray (either way) will prevent the horse stepping under sufficiently and engaging.
- To help the horse get the idea initially, keep your body relatively square to the short side

I never teach changes until my horse can happily canter round the whole arena in counter-canter on both reins. Here Espada shows extravagant abduction of the right fore, and this type of work will make the changes so very much easier, when they come.

of the school, but *feel* you are leading with your inside hip and inside shoulder to mirror the horse; later you may advance your outside shoulder to turn more into the movement but, if done too early, your horse may well turn too and lose the lateral steps.

Horses who are inclined to hollow on the advancing side will tend to overbend and throw the quarters in; horses who are stiffer on this side may keep the line of the half-pass better, but may lose impulsion forward and sideways.

- For the former it often helps to start the movement from a few steps of canter shoulder-in.
- For the latter, start from a 10 m circle at the first corner of the long side and try to hold the *feel* of the circle in your mind and in your body as you advance into half-pass.

On both accounts, always content yourself with just a few steps of half-pass initially and then straighten out by sending the horse up to the end of the school via the quarter or centre line. Gradually you can change the exercise to a few steps forwards and sideways, then straighten again, followed by another few steps forwards and sideways and so on. Never think just sideways alone. If you are losing bend, try interspersing the half-pass steps with a volte and then advance in half-pass again.

Whatever the pattern or sequence of events, it is important that the horse does not fall into or bulge out with the leading shoulder. Provided the inside leg is always there to bend, pick him up and straighten him out of the half-pass, all should be well. As with the walk pirouette, the horse tends to remember the sideways pressure from the outside leg even after it has ceased. For this reason, your inside leg must support at all times and, at the right moment, act more urgently and say 'No! not more

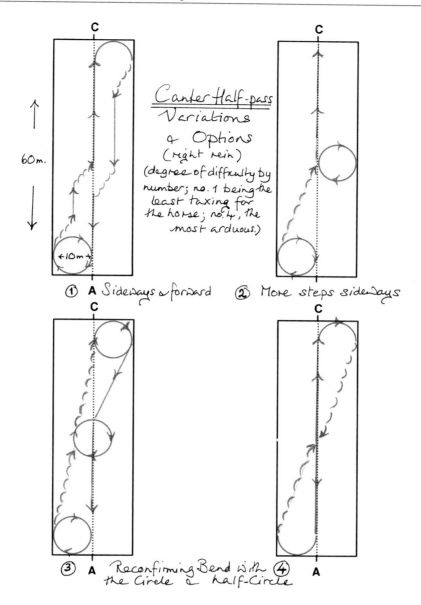

Canter Half-pass Variations 4 Options (right rein) (degree of difficulty by number; no. 1 being the least taxing for the horse; no. 4, the most arduous.)

60m.

←10m→

① A Sideways & forward

② More steps sideways

③ A Reconfirming Bend with the Circle & half-Circle ④ A

half-pass! Please now, go straight on!'

When the horse obeys these various preliminaries, do not confuse him by changing the rein or making a downward transition. Reward him by riding some medium canter down the next long side to stretch and freshen up the gait. Then canter back with more collection to where you started. You can then give him a rest if you wish before beginning again on the original circle on the same long side. Try this at least two or three times, before changing the rein and starting on the opposite side. Establishing a pattern of remembered places

and remembered requests really aids the learning process. At this higher stage of training, don't be afraid to work with the horse's anticipatory powers; you will need them! Praise frequently.

As the canter half-pass improves, try changing the angle. Ride some half-passes more steeply, others with less angle. Allow the horse to be confident to the centre line before you tackle the whole width of the school, which is very demanding. Riding half-pass back from the centre line to the track will involve counter-canter or changes.

Right   **Canter half-pass**   **Left**

The half-pass aids are merely a reinforcement of the normal canter aids. As you work towards or away from the centre line, think of your inside leg leading you into the movement whilst the outside leg simply strokes your horse a little side-ways. Here, Espada shows better bend on the right rein.

Working around Canter Half-pass

When half-pass from the track to the centre line is well confirmed, you may start to introduce half-circles to the opposite track, thus introducing the element of turning away, which will later be incorporated into the pirouette. Initially, canter half-pass from say K to somewhere between X and G on the right rein, straighten and ride forward for two or three strides, then half-circle to the opposite side, still on the right rein. The horse will enjoy this turning away aspect to the movement, so capitalise on it and with the help of the indirect rein, make the half-circle gradually slower and smaller, thinking a little quarters-in until you can half-pass back to K. As you do this, be careful not to use more inside hand since this would pull the horse out of balance.

Simply sit a little deeper onto the inside seatbones, mentally grow firm and tall to the inside and give gentle half-halts with the outside hand supporting at the base of the neck. Visualise

your body and the horse's body looking to the outside of the circle and turning in slow motion. The bend will be to the inside and you will obviously come around with him towards the centre line, but most people turn too quickly, which is as unbalancing as leaning in. Use rather less outside leg than you applied in the canter half-pass and maintain forward impulsion with the inside leg, acting on the girth. Take time! The idea is still to ride forward, but never think spin round!

Although canter half-passes are best introduced on the diagonal you can, after some months, try riding a few steps up the wall (quarters-in) or preferably the other way round, where the proper term is canter renvers. It takes time to make the canter half-pass so controlled that you can hold the line of the wall without falling in or out, so be careful your attempts do not encourage faults in the horse which may already have come to light. For example, if the horse is inclined to lead with the quarters in half-pass left, then don't ride head

Prepare the horse for the canter pirouette with some out-door riding to add zest to these difficult movements. Cantering head to the wall alongside a boundary really improves bend. Quarters-in on a decreasing circle gives the horse the idea for what is to come.

to the wall – try the renvers instead. Also, beware of the horse becoming muddled and thinking you want a poor form of counter-canter. Always be very clear in your own mind:

- what the movement should look like, e.g how much angle, bend, etc.;
- exactly where it will start and finish;
- how you are going to ride out of it without destroying your horse's confidence in the process.

Towards Canter Pirouette

Although pirouette is a more gymnastically demanding and advanced movement than the flying change, we shall leave the latter to the end of the chapter, since the pirouette is so often developed out of the canter half-pass.

Besides, at this stage we are only really considering the work towards pirouette and it would be prudent to bring in outside help before developing the pirouette up to competition level.

The FEI definition of canter pirouette is the same as that for walk (see p.137) and, again, it is most important that activity remains in the pivoting inside hind as the quarters lower and flex to carry a major share of the horse's weight. There must be no sense of spinning round.

Canter half-pass to canter pirouette

(Left) As Vaidoso moves away from the track, I free my inside leg a little away from his side to lead him into the lateral movement left.

(Below) To start the pirouette steps, I close my inside leg more against his side to give extra support in the turn. Although the inside leg acts as a pillar, my weight remains on the inside seatbone – as always in the direction of movement.

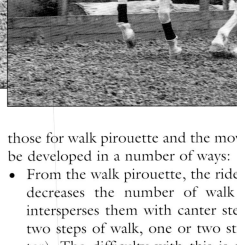

Although most judges require that the canter remains in three-time, there is a school of thought that maintains this is actually impossible. Indeed Nuno Oliveira, whose canter pirouettes were wonderfully effortless to watch, insisted that the horse would have to go to four-time if he was to keep the weight sufficiently in the hindquarters. The difficulty for most will be to keep it sufficiently collected, cadenced and slow.

The aids for canter pirouette are similar to those for walk pirouette and the movement can be developed in a number of ways:

- From the walk pirouette, the rider gradually decreases the number of walk steps and intersperses them with canter steps (one or two steps of walk, one or two steps of canter). The difficulty with this is not to lose the animation of the canter, although with the flightier type of horse, this method will have value.

- Probably the easiest way for most riders and

horses is from the canter half-pass. One way is to make a half-pass from the track to the centre line, and turn through a quarter pirouette to face the opposite track. Later as the horse grows more supple, a half pirouette is made on the centre line, and a half-pass back across the same diagonal from whence the horse started is made.

- Another way is to ride canter half-pass along the track head-to-the-wall and just before the corner is reached, the horse is asked to turn around on himself and away from the wall. This has the psychological advantage of the corner presenting the horse with no alternative other than the one we want – moving the forehand around the hocks and into the inviting space of the open school. However, such a situation can be daunting to a horse who is not yet sufficiently supple to give us what we want – so proceed with great caution.

- From the rider's point of view, probably the most popular way is from haunches-in on the circle; here the rider gradually diminishes the size of the circle. This sounds very simple but there are many disadvantages to this system, particularly if the rider is over-strong with the outside leg. First, it can lead to crookedness in the flying changes, and second, impulsion may be lost if the croup is excessively displaced.

Personally, I have found that some horses benefit from the following method. Put your horse to counter-canter (right rein) along the track (say K to H) and then proceed from H onto a 10 m half-circle right to the centre line but with the horse (obviously in left bend) to approach the track on the diagonal (say at E). Well before E, the rider half-halts and reverses the direction to the left as though turning the horse back on himself through a couple of shortened strides. Since the horse has the whole width of the school at his disposal, any difficulties incurred can be circumvented by riding across to the opposite track in normal

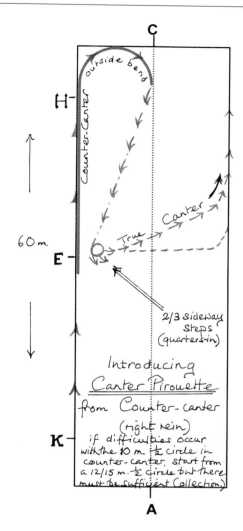

canter. In this way, the horse feels rewarded to be in true canter and we can then build things up positively and slowly.

In this way, we can collect the canter in a less threatening way through the turn. Our bodies literally take the horse round and back the way he has come. A fully engaged horse can make the quarter pirouette in two steps but be prepared at the onset to allow more; gradually you can build up to a half pirouette – but be patient! Pirouettes require great strength behind and many horses never master them.

Nevertheless all the ingredients will be in place; but again, slowing the pace whilst amplifying the impulsion will be the key to success. The rider sits very quiet and tall, weighting the

(Above) Pirouette work requires extreme collection and a shortening of the base of support as the horse gathers himself together and bends the hind limb joints to lighten in front.

(Left) Moving into canter pirouette left, Palomo (here aged twenty-one) draws support from my centred and 'growing tall' position and moves readily around my left leg.

Note that in neither picture does the horse drop the poll or come behind the bit.

inside (left) seatbone, with the inside leg supportive but active. The outside (right) rein acts indirectly and checks the forward progression, while the outside leg gives sideways pressure. Feel that a very proud and balanced seat helps stabilise the weight into quarters and hocks.

The Spanish Riding School much prefers using the renvers and the passade to develop pirouette work, but all these are matters probably best left to the individual to work out with their trainer. Much will depend upon the horse's temperament and gymnastic ability. An introduction to the first few steps of pirouette is being sought here, but it is a highly gymnastic movement, so expert help should generally be sought.

Most riders should be more than happy if they can achieve a small half-volte in canter, whilst maintain bend and rhythm which, performed without stress, shows huge progress, balance and suppleness.

Flying Changes Without Tears

To bring about successful changes, the horse should be equally balanced and straight on both reins. A willing attentiveness to the aids is vital. In the early stages, single changes are generally asked for –

- from a diagonal line, the horse making his change on the centre line, or more logically for him, just as he approaches the new track
- in the centre of a half (or full) figure-of-eight in the moment when the horse is straight
- from counter-canter on the circle.

The canter half-pass may also be used to advantage to introduce the flying change just prior to or after rejoining the track. In the latter case, a very tempting invitation may be offered to the horse in this way –

- canter normally up the long side, say on the left rein, make a 10 m half-circle left to the centre line at D or G;
- proceed in canter half-pass left back to the same side and into counter-canter for a few strides down the track;
- well before the next corner comes up – ask!

For me and my horse, the above is a definite favourite. To bring about the change, the following events should happen in the given sequence but virtually all in the one moment:

- release horse out of his left bend (i.e. from the counter-canter) and straighten neck;
- square upper body and look straight down the track;
- reverse leg, seat and weight aids from counter-canter to true canter.

If the aids have been clear to date and are clear again now, the horse released from the prospect of counter-canter through the approaching corner is only too pleased to offer the change onto the normal leading leg. Perfecting flying changes from the half-pass will lead horse and rider on towards the counter-changes of hand, but this is a very advanced stage of training and must not be attempted until half-passes on both right and left rein are highly established and the changes themselves have become second nature to the horse.

Step by Step

Before going further, let us think through the flying change step by step, for no movement carries more risk of confusing the horse. Unsatisfactory results, where the horse changes in front and not behind, can cause anguish and disharmony all round. With much soul-searching, the Spanish Riding School refused to include tempi changes in their programme at the time of Colonel Podhajsky, who regularly spoke out against their introduction in Grand Prix tests. He argued that, while some breeds were suited to the more horizontal thrust and balance, other equally malleable and talented horses would be disadvantaged because of differences in conformation. Historically, while isolated changes were employed to change the rein in mounted combat, repeated changes in sequence were not considered classical airs. Many people argued – and still do – that one- or two-time changes would never be offered by a horse in freedom and are more of a trick than natural art. Certainly, they require a highly gymnastic horse.

However, there is no reason at all why any breed, shape or size of horse may not be taught regular single changes, therefore to this end we shall discuss them.

Before you even think of teaching changes, it is highly advisable to receive some lessons on a schoolmaster horse and feel the movement for yourself. A sense of timing is vital in all can-

Good engagement in the canter is an essential prerequisite for easy changes.

ter work, and it is asking a lot to aid a horse correctly in the change without having felt it first yourself. You will, however, be halfway there if your horse is calm, totally obedient in his canter to walk transitions and always able to canter on a given leg at any time. Balance and straightness are the name of the game, so if your canter is still inclined to be a little rushing,

or the horse falls in with his quarters, you are unlikely to be ready for changes.

Assuming, however, that all is going nicely, your 10 m canter circles are round and balanced and the horse answers to your inside leg aid, not by jack-knifing out onto the outside shoulder, but by maintaining a good three-beat forward rhythm, nicely bent in collection, then the time should be ripe. We have already discussed the sequence of legs in canter, realising how important it is not to let the horse go disunited. This means that we must beware of putting the horse into a position where he might be tempted to change in front first.

The safest way round this problem is to apply the aid for change when the horse is in the moment of suspension of the canter. Only when all four feet are temporarily in the air, will he be able to reorganise his body so that he can change from one lead to the other. Remember it is not just his legs which will make the change, but the entire length of his body and, since this requires tremendous longitudinal suppleness, we must feel for the moment.

At this stage, we can see why the work on 'canter position' has been so carefully laid. The aids of the seat and leg have been made totally instinctive. The rule of thumb never changes:

- inside leg and inside seatbone forward and slightly weighted
- outside hip and outside leg opened and back.

Even in counter-canter, still think of your inside leg being the one around which your horse is bent, although temporarily this leg is to the outside. These aids should go together like sugar and spice; ham and egg – there must be absolutely no doubt in the horse's mind that right leg down and leading, left leg back and 'asking' means canter right. If this basic rule is not absolutely set in stone then we have no business even to think about changes.

Of course, some horses may already have offered a change, perhaps out of the counter-canter, because we ourselves have somehow changed our weight. Often people do this quite unconsciously and it is the normal course of things whilst hacking or jumping. The rider should always have been quick to reward such offerings and should never have found fault, otherwise the horse will remember and not wish to cause displeasure again.

However, let us assume that our horse has played everything by the rules and has never attempted to change. If this is the case, we must realise that what we are about to ask will be pretty alien. It is therefore vital that we give the horse something with which he is familiar to hang onto. That something is our upper body. By remaining quiet and square from the waist upward, we can give the horse his balancing pole, whilst all else changes below. Remember too, we need to give the horse time to 'hear' what we are going to do below the waist.

More on Bend

Another point to be considered is the position of the horse's neck. We all want our horse to bend into his circles and be around our inside leg in the canter. However, since this is often interpreted into excess neck bend which can block the inside leading shoulder in canter, I encourage my students to give a little half-halt with the outside rein just prior to the leg aids in the strike-off. Not only is this a collecting aid, but it straightens the horse's neck and repositions it in front of the withers where it belongs. You would be surprised how many horses are made to carry their necks in a 'broken' fashion, pulled sideways from the wither.

If the horse has become used to this gentle outside aid, which really should consist of nothing much more than a vibrato with the fingers, it can be a useful warning signal for the canter changes. The inside hand which has asked for flexion should, by comparison, remain soft and yielding. Some trainers advise lifting the inside hand to encourage the horse to lift through the inside shoulder into canter but to my mind this can confuse.

At this crucial learning stage, everything we do concerning canter departs must influence what happens behind saddle. After all, the first step of canter is that of the outside hind and we want the changes to start here, not in front! One of the reasons why the outside rein can be valuable here is its indirect influence over the haunches. However, the subtleties of this rein will only serve our purpose if the horse is already flexed and soft to the inside.

The time has come to feel that bend is maintained almost wholly with the inside leg so there can be a feeling of 'give' through the inside rein rather than 'ask'. This will help the canter immeasurably and ensure a smooth transmission of energy through from behind. So where is all this leading? We know our 'canter position' off by heart, we know that in the moment of change we have to keep the horse as straight as possible as we reverse the seat and leg aids. If now we can introduce two recognisable but subtle rein effects to free the shoulders a little more, we are doubling our chances of success.

Testing and Preparing

Many riders ask for their first change in the place where they would normally ride the simple change, by reducing and then missing out the walk steps. This may work with two out of ten horses but, on average, most seem unable to comply and problems at the beginning tend to multiply rather than resolve themselves. To my mind it is a pity to put the horse in a position where the odds are stacked towards failure.

A far safer way to ask initially, is on the 20 m circle. We put our horse to walk and ride some canter transitions on both reins from walk. This will be done in the usual way, outside leg back, inside leg on, vibrato on the outside rein and then give to the inside as the horse makes his depart. In this way the horse never feels himself come up against the bit, which will be most important for the change of leg.

Now we are ready to see just how clear those aids can be and how inviting we can make things for the horse. We take our horse down to one end of the school, say at A. The idea will be to use the three sides of the school to help us contain our canter circle and to give the horse a point of reference in which to make his first change. If our horse has a favourite rein in canter (say the right) we send him in that direction but put him first to *counter-canter* on his less *favoured rein*, in this case, the left.

Setting the Scene

- From A, ride a 20 m circle right in counter-canter.
- On returning to A, make a downward transition to walk and almost immediately ask for true canter right.
- The horse should offer this gladly – it's his best side and the counter-canter circle was somewhat demanding.
- In asking for canter right, reverse the leg aids clearly in the usual way; the horse must be in no doubt that our weight and gaze are now slightly to the inside – the latter is more important than one would think.
- As the horse pushes off into canter with the outside hind, soften the inside rein slightly forward, so the horse stretches *through* with the right shoulder.
- After doing this a few times and always at the same place, just before A, we are ready for the next stage when we will miss out the intervening step(s) of walk.

The Real Thing

Again, we start with counter-canter on a circle right. We are clear in our head that the change will occur on the wall at A in the same place that we rode the simple change. We know that our aids must be clear and concise and that everything will seem to happen at once. We keep the horse forward-going and rhythmic but, instead of thinking too much about collection, we send him on a little more and allow the neck to be carried slightly lower than normal. For changes, it helps initially if the balance is more horizontal. For counter-canter, we go through the aids one more time:

- left leg forward and supporting on the girth;
- left seatbone just in advance and slightly weighted;
- right leg drawn back, encouraging the horse behind the girth to spring off his right hind;
- left hand maintaining flexion, with the fingers soft and inviting;

The first changes should be ridden with the horse in a fairly horizontal frame and flowing on as freely as possible. The poll remains the heighest point.

The more collected horse tends to make higher changes but here Palomo, aged twenty-seven feels just a little over the top as we make the change on reaching the track after half-pass across the diagonal. With the more sensitive horse, the rider will need to lighten the seat to allow the new leading hind leg to jump through.

Espada comes through expressively with the new left lead after making his change from a figure-of-eight at X. A good change should always feel 'uphill' at this stage, helped by a gentle half-halt.

- right hand supporting the neck and sometimes half-halting, to the outside;
- rider looking slightly left.

Making it Happen – Reversal!

The track is looming up and we tune in to what is happening underneath, knowing what we have to do and that it is more a question of timing than anything else. If the horse is to make the change in the air, we must choose the right moment, just before that occurs. This will be in the downward (third) phase of the canter, when the left fore is grounded and the other three legs are in the air.

It is at this point that we must reverse the aids clearly and crisply so that the horse can register what is required just before the moment of suspension. Thus, by the time all four feet are in the air, he has already recognised and accepted the request to change and is in a position to respond.

For me, the defining moment just prior to the change will be the straightening of the horse's neck, followed by a subtle half-halt with the new outside (left) hand. My concern is to create the correct conditions behind saddle, and as we have seen, this checking action influences the action of the hindquarters. Thus, by energising the new outside hind, the horse is realeased from his counter-canter. As the seat and leg aids now engage into their reversed roles and as the new inside (right) rein invites and yields forward, the horse should change behind and jump into the new right lead and canter on, happy to be back on his easy leg again.

Confirmation

We must remember that flying changes require great trust as well as gymnastic ability from the horse, so timing and clarity of the aids are all-important. If you have been skipping and changing legs yourself (on the ground – a seriously good idea) you will feel the right moment. Try to do everything in a smooth, automatic way so as not to startle the horse,

and recognise that it won't be possible to get everything perfect at first – so concentrate on one particular thing.

For the novice horse and rider, the reversed position of the outside leg is probably the most important aid of all, although later it will be the weight aid involved in the moving forward of the new inside leg. The point is, although the emphasis may change, the aids themselves never change and if your horse has been conscientiously schooled up to now, he will recognise the reversal of your aids and will respond. Think positive but subtle. The inside leg moving back simply goes from toe at the girth, to the toe sliding back a hand's breadth behind, so we are not talking about a big movement (see photographs p.221).

A few extra tips to consider are:

- If the horse is truly to swing through from behind, the rider's leg must also feel a sense of 'swing' but in a light, unobtrusive way.
- Think therefore of opening the outside hip so the whole leg (not just from the knee down) slips back.
- Don't be afraid to emphasise the new aid – a quick but firm *press* well behind the girth will make everything clear to the horse.
- Don't forget to ride forward!

The nice thing about our body is that as one leg moves back, the other generally slips forward automatically, so you should not have to worry unduly about the new inside leg (after all this happens every day when we walk – as one leg moves back, the other goes forward). Your hip bones should automatically reverse their roles too, so hopefully you can (almost) forget about those!

Concentrate on sitting tall and as close to the front of the saddle as possible so that the horse's back is given a chance to work. Although the aid for the flying change to the right really will involve a reversal of all the aids listed above, it is better at this stage to concentrate on the one that works the horse's hind legs and *think yourself into the new direction –*

Canter to Halt
~ a natural progression from Canter to Walk
& all the exercises to date ~

Vienna Motto ~ 'Up the Body ~ down the Weight?..

rather than doing too much. The less you upset the horse's balance, clearly the better.

If the change happens as and when you want it the first time round, congratulate yourself and the horse. Really, make much of him, since this is quite an achievement. If nothing hap-pens at all, simply try again. Some reaction is better than none, and if the horse changes in front only, at least you will know this is a very common scenario. Ask patiently a few times, but if the horse goes on making the same mis-take, it is better to leave things for a few days and return to your transition work.

Every horse is different and there is no hard-and-fast rule why some horses find changes easier than others, but generally we find those who genuinely enjoy canter more than trot take to changes more easily. Horses with a high knee action, particularly those bred for carriage driving, may have genuine difficulties. It is also true that one method may work particularly well for one horse but not for another.

If you are unsuccessful, never belabour the point once the horse is tired. If he does well, then stop before things go wrong. It is often better to achieve one correct change and leave the school and go for a hack, rather than try again and risk a mistake. If you have really praised your horse, he will remember and will try even harder the next time.

If there have been difficulties, try to analyse what might have gone wrong. Are you trying so hard, you have tensed up? Could you have blocked him with your hands? Unfortunately, the hands are the least likely to do what we want. It is very important that both the reins remain softly elastic, particularly the inside, otherwise the new incoming foreleg may be discouraged from coming through. If the hands give too quickly, however, the horse may be thrown onto the forehand, which could result in a change in front and not behind.

When problems occur, do not be cross with your horse, but pat him to reassure, and start the whole process again, starting with simple changes and building up. Once success on the circle is established, praise should be lavish and the horse put immediately to walk on a long rein, with much patting.

The change on the circle is generally accepted as the best way to avoid rushing and disunited changes. However, if your horse simply does not understand, try asking on the diagonal just as you approach the track, either from half-pass or on a straight line.

Riding two half-circles with a change through the centre in a half figure-of-eight is better left until the work is more confirmed, since you do not want your horse swinging out with the quarters in the changes.

Few horses manage a perfect change the first time they are asked, so be prepared to put up with some fumblings and disjointed attempts. Ask fairly early into your programme of work, when the horse has warmed up but before he has become tired. Never try changes when the horse has lost his edge.

Many horses are able to offer passable changes say from right to left, but have much greater difficulty left to right, often because riders are tighter through the right side of their body and forget to allow their weight down into the inside stirrup to lead the horse into the change.

If unsure, go back to some of your earlier suppling work and take note of how your horse responds in the canter depart. If one side is proving harder than the other, this could provide the clue you are looking for.

Try varying the way you ask for these departs. Are you consistent on both reins? Do you change the number of walk steps in between the simple changes? Do you keep the horse listening and alert by changing the place and sequence?

Finally remember *all* of us favour one seatbone more than another. You may think you are leading the horse one way or another, but it is all too easy to lose the hip-to-heel alignment and for the whole seat to slip back.

Be aware! One last tip; moving your head can make all the difference to the change. Think like the horse, flex and lead him into the correct direction and allow your horse to follow you!

CHAPTER XV

Total Lightness:
Piaffe, Passage
and the Icing on the Cake

Piaffe and passage should show clear diagonal steps with the sense that the horse is on springs!

Most people think they will never ever attain a level where they may confidently ask for piaffe and passage from their horse and know that they will get it. And yet of all the movements, these are perhaps the ones which the horse will most naturally offer himself *once* he has become supple, attentive and impulsive. And there lies the rub, because the only reason we don't generally see piaffes being offered by the novice horse is stiffness in the back, lack of muscle through the loins and an inability to close sufficiently the joints of the hindquarters. Nevertheless, it is quite common to see a young horse spontaneously offer a perfect flying change on a corner, which shows that the balance is quite different.

Having said that, extremely fit horses at the racecourse often make a movement similar to piaffe before cantering down to the start, as do horses at a meet, show or parade when they are pent up with excitement and agog to go! This movement, of all the movements, is the one most likely to be given for the pure joy and zest of living and of anticipating something special. For that reason, it is vitally important that, when we teach piaffe, we never allow it to descend to an exercise which is the result of a painful spurring or smacking on the leg. In the horse's mind it should always be a fun movement, one for showing off and expressing contained exuberance.

I was tempted to include this chapter very much earlier in the book, since certainly the piaffe is a movement I like to teach my horses at home fairly soon after the collection in walk, trot and canter has been established. For me, piaffe and passage are far less strenuous or taxing on the horse's limbs than, say, extended canter, but the discipline concerning the rider's position and application of the aids has to be far greater and the sense of feel highly tuned.

However, my main reason for discussing these movements in the very last chapter is to give the reader a logical sequence from which to work. The FEI lays down that neither the piaffe nor passage will be required until Intermediare or Grand Prix level, and therefore, for purposes of ease, we have worked roughly within that established pattern.

Personally, since I was lucky enough to have learned the art of feel on sensitive schoolmasters originally, I have always found piaffe a very natural movement to teach all breeds of horse. For this reason, it is a source of great regret that a few steps of piaffe are not introduced in at least some of the earlier tests. Demonstrating this beautiful movement with perhaps an allowance for forward progression, would be a pointer towards correct and superior collection.

As previously pointed out, the order of

training procedures discussed in this book is not to be adhered to slavishly. Dressage is not just about competition and many readers will want to advance their horse's education for the pure pleasure of strengthening their horse's muscles, rendering him more athletic and light in the hand, and for enjoyment. This must be the overriding feature of all our work in the manège.

So, if you feel you would like to discuss the work of piaffe with your horse prior to some of the other exercises given in the preceding chapters, feel free! One word of warning however; both piaffe and passage are movements of high collection and to teach these correctly, the horse must be strong behind and have the facility to lower his haunches in order to sustain the necessary engagement of the hind legs. A good test is to study his balance in the canter to halt and also in the rein-back. If there is any difficulty in either of these movements, particularly if the hocks widen behind instead of bending under and retaining their normal width one from the other, then clearly your horse is not ready. Common sense has a large part to play in the training of all horses, and generally the horse will tell you – if you are prepared to listen. At this stage, I am sure you have learned to develop a willing ear.

Piaffe before Passage?

The piaffe is a highly collected, cadenced, elevated diagonal movement giving the impression of being on the spot... In principle, the height of the toe of the raised foreleg should be level with the middle of the cannon bone of the other foreleg. The toe of the raised hind leg should reach just above the fetlock joint of the other hind leg. (British Dressage Rules)

While some schools of thought prefer to teach the horse passage before piaffe, my own feeling is that piaffe should come first as, too often, horses use a form of passage to avoid releasing their backs forward in the trot. A high, over-suspended trot with the back held stiff and tight is not an uncommon sight. This is generally accompanied by hind legs which camp out slightly instead of bending under the horse and allowing the impulsion to go *through*.

Unfortunately, many of us will have been guilty in the past of not recognising the difference between this type of trot and a true collected trot, where elevation and a sense of floaty lightness can take place, but where there is genuine but contained impulsion. Certainly, for me, it has taken time and practice and the education of working with many different types of horses to recognise these differences and, quite apart from allowing the horse to kid us, we can so easily delude ourselves.

The real proof of the pudding will be when the rider can collect the trot, maintain it without a change of rhythm for some circuits, advance it to medium trot, bring it forward to collected again, and thence to extended, all with the greatest of ease and with the transitions made at a moment's notice. The horse with the stiffly held suspended trot will simply be unable to organise himself in the same way; a loss of balance will take place and the transitions will lack clarity and confidence.

Collection must therefore always involve a feeling of pent-up energy which is just bursting to go. The beauty of true collection is when the rider, without appearing to impose his or her will, can capture – as it were – that energy in suspension, shake it around so that it does not die, and then release it as required. It's rather like letting the cork out of the champagne bottle – without hesitation, the bubbles spurt out.

So it is in the teaching of piaffe. We have to build up the impulsion of the horse through either the trot or the collected walk and then allow it to be contained in an animated exercise on the spot, before allowing it to burst out again. And I use the word 'burst' intentionally, because I don't want the energy to flood or leach out; that would indicate either a lack of control or a certain lethargy in the whole pro-

A good piaffe should feel effervescent and as though the horse could go on and on, bouncing on the spot eternally. Palomo is actually quite a finely built horse, but here flexing deeply to 'sit' in piaffe, he turns into a generous ball of muscle and contained power.

cedure. The elevated steps of the piaffe must be so full of energy and bounce that at any given moment we feel the horse really wants to move forward, project and extend himself again!

Many trainers teach the horse the piaffe from the trot; and I well recognise the validity of this method which often obtains spectacular results. Personally, however, I have reservations about this method since I never want to feel I am slowing down something that is already forward-going in order to achieve the piaffe. Instead, I prefer to start with something *upon which I can build forward and up*. For this reason, I like the old Portuguese method of teaching piaffe from the rein-back with just a couple of steps of collected walk in between. Lots of transitions from rein-back to collected walk really stirs up the energy and lifts the forehand. The idea is for the walk to become so light, 'uphill' and engaged that the horse actually ends up piaffing of his own volition as he closes *the angles of the hind legs.*

In this way, the shortened four-beat steps of the walk transform themselves into the two-time beat of piaffe. It can certainly add encouragement to have someone assisting from the ground, tapping gently with a stick to indicate the diagonals, but once the movement evolves, I prefer to dispense with any outside interference, so as not to distract or concern the horse. This may come later, once the horse knows what he is to do, to enhance the lifting of the legs, but first I want all the horse's concentration to be on me, his rider.

At this point, I want my horse to be listening to every nuance, each fine-tuning aid of the seat, legs and upper body and also of the fingers, which can either give or take at any moment. When I put pupils new to the movement on my horses who already know the piaffe, they are amazed at the fineness of the definition between forwards, backwards, on the spot, and upwards. Mistakes are rarely made when doing too little; generally it is always a case of much too much.

With our untutored horse, we must therefore think 'positive' but never 'strong'. The work we have done to date in the collected walk will now truly show its value. We should ask for some shoulder-in, renvers and half-pass in walk, combined with some quarter turns and even the odd passade. This will lighten the horse considerably.

We are now ready to use the wall to encourage straightness. For this reason, it is always better to start any new exercise on the horse's easier side, maintaining a little extra flexion to the inside to keep the quarters on the track. We are now ready to ride some walk to halt transitions followed by a few rein-backs but always changing the sequence, so that the horse does not anticipate too much. Walk on five steps;

halt for three seconds, rein-back three steps (the exact number can and must vary, so long as you decide in advance and stick to that) then straight forward again to collected walk and praise warmly.

If you run out of space, simply proceed to the other side of the school, all the time thinking *forward* in a rhythmic, marching four-time beat, but keeping the steps short and light, making sure the horse is on the bit, slightly flexed to the inside and that the poll is generally the highest point so the shoulders feel elevated. Then halt again for say six seconds, this time rein-back four or five steps and then as before: immediately forward to a very collected walk but for a lesser distance before riding each new sequence of transitions. These transitions should provide a collection that feels very 'uphill'.

When all this is feeling nice and easy and the horse can comply without resistance and is clearly happy and calm, we start to think of *containing* the walk out of the rein-back a little more. So, again, we decide in advance how many steps back we are going to make but this time, we are going to introduce a feeling of hold or half-halt into the forward steps after the rein-back. We must be careful at this point that we do not lose impulsion, so our legs must be lightly active, while our fingers continue to gather and ask.

If the horse tries to trot at this gathering, it is a good sign; it shows he is already thinking of the diagonal gait that he will need for the piaffe. Bring him quietly to walk again, with the idea that we are going to change the first two or three walk steps (after the rein-back) to piaffe steps. These will not be demanded on the spot; the idea is simply that they comprise a movement somewhere between the diagonal rein-back in walk and the trot, but the steps will only advance forward about the space of a hoofprint (not a stride) at a time. How may we do this? Every horse is a little different, but for me the feeling after the rein-back will be as follows:

- Advance the seat as close as you possibly can to the pommel, with hollowed loins and straightened back.
- Stretch the knees down until you are lightly 'perched' on the thighs and bring your shoulders just in front of the vertical so that you ease the pressure on the back of your seat.
- Think of momentarily *containing the forward movement* by drawing it up through a raised diaphragm – your abdominals must really stretch!
- The lower legs will have put pressure on the horse's sides for the rein-back, so lighten them and feel they are stretching back and downwards as if to gather the horse's hind feet more under him.
- Initially, vibrate both legs together, thinking small, forward, light steps, in an on-and-off manner (press and release) to quicken the energy within the horse and detach his hind feet from the ground.
- Once you feel that you have energy, softly alternate the leg aids so that you diagonalise in time with the horse's hind legs.
- Visualise the horse dancing diagonally on the spot and make room for him to round under saddle.
- Squeeze and release the rein in the same way as you give and take with your legs – as his right shoulder moves forward (indicating left hind moving forward) give with the fingers of the right hand; and vice versa.
- Think forward but by stretching more and more upward!
- Never pull back! Remember this is not rein-back; you are releasing the horse from the rein-back into an active, forward-elevated movement.

As soon as your horse responds with even just one or two shortened steps, pat him and allow him to walk forward again, nice and calmly. Try not to allow him to go to trot proper, but if he does, do not pull back – just go quietly to walk again.

When teaching piaffe for the first time, it is very important to retain the activity in the hind legs. Here Fabuloso has walked himself into halt in front but as I ask gently with both legs applied just behind the girth, he starts to flex his hind legs and is already lifting one diagonal. Initially, I keep the rein light and prevent the horse from stepping forward or back through the weight aids of the seat.

The secret of riding piaffe in this way is that you balance the horse between the rein-back and an animated collected walk. The impulsion must remain, vibrant and alive from active hind legs. Your aids will have to be very refined in order for your horse to understand. Too much leg may block the movement. Too little may allow everything to die. Only by listening and feeling will you know how much to influence the forward steps. The most important thing is to absorb and rechannel the energy coming from the horse's hind legs. Think of impulsion like a stream of liquid, pulsing and vibrating through his body *contained* within the moment of piaffe. Piaffe should be one of the most animated and lively movements of all. It should be light and bubbly – like champagne!

The feeling of contact and the understanding between horse and rider as the hand closes and allows on the rein, must be very fine. At no time will the hand move back. Basically, the

Progression to piaffe

In this sequence, we are concentrating on activating one diagonal at a time to achieve piaffe. Slight forward progression is encouraged until the perfect balance is achieved.

rider's hand should be quietly in place at the wither, the two sets of knuckles (thumbs always on top) almost touching each other to form a nozzle or filter for the horse's impulsion. Thus the hands can either contain the impulsion and keep it bubbling on the spot with gently resisting fingers; or they can allow it forward and out again by simply allowing the fingers to unclench.

If the rein is too long for the horse to feel these small changes, the exercise will be pointless. As in the rein-back, the horse must be truly on the bit, rounded through the back as well as relaxed and giving in both poll and jaw. If there is any sign of tension or resistance, you must wait quietly until all is soft again.

If the piaffe is built up in this way, there will come a time when the whole exercise can be achieved on a very light rein. The rein feels almost superfluous as the horse recognises the restraints imposed by the rider's seat and legs. The work will depend upon the horse feeling that the rider's seat and legs can contain the impulsion, without the hands.

In all these aids, we must recognise that each and every component part of us affects another part. People talk about bracing the back for piaffe but so often this promotes the wrong picture. A proper piaffe will never emerge if the rider disturbs the fine balance of the horse on his hocks with a push or shove with seat or back.

Changes occur within the lumbar spine as a result of our leg and seat position. In short, when we bring our legs back and stretch them down and around the horse this should open our hip joints and our spine naturally slots into a more forward position, supported by the abdominal muscles. This will complement the advancement of our position towards the pommel whilst giving support to our shoulders, elbows and wrists, so that we may ride with very controlled and light hands. Nowhere are the words 'waist to hands' more appropriate.

Once the horse can move from rein-back to piaffe and forward to walk, we can gradually build the work from collected walk and dispense with rein-back. The reason it is so useful in the beginning and to freshen up the piaffe is because of its diagonal nature and the fact that it engages the hocks further underneath in readiness for what lies ahead. Gradually, however we should be able to engage the croup more in walk so the horse just 'pops' into the piaffe of his own volition.

This can also be done from the halt with hocks encouraged further underneath than normal. A schooling whip gently tickling him behind the rider's leg is very helpful at this stage. It is virtually a question of gathering up, thinking tall and the horse assumes the piaffe. Never ever let him think backward, once he is in piaffe. To avoid this, bring the shoulders gently back to the vertical whilst keeping the waist and hips forward, the moment the movement is offered.

One of the nicest things about piaffe is that it really improves the trot. If you have never experienced the feeling of a totally effortless, bouncy, round, vibrant, elevated trot, now is the time. While we should not school for the higher airs until we have mastered the lower ones, there is no doubt that correct work at a higher level will improve the quality of the basic gaits. Wonderful trots can grow once piaffe is obtained!

The Passage

The passage is a measured, very collected, very elevated and very cadenced trot... Each diagonal pair of feet is raised and returned to the ground alternately, with cadence and a prolonged suspension. The ruling concerning the height of the legs is the same as that for the piaffe (British Dressage Rules).

Thus, when the horse has got the feel of the piaffe, it is a good idea to introduce passage before he gets too established on the spot, so while the piaffe is still at its advancing stage, if he starts to offer a more suspended trot – do not discourage him. The hardest thing about teaching the piaffe first is that the horse can be daunted about making the shift from this highly cadenced, exacting exercise to the forwardness required for passage.

The mental and physical barriers which have to be crossed to make the shift in balance from one movement to the other often cause the horse to launch himself into passage in the early days, with an almost inevitable loss of balance. If he does this, bear with him – he is only trying and, like all of us doing new things for the first time, he has to work out the organisation of his limbs largely for himself.

However, do not delude yourself that things will always be that simple. Many riders make the mistake of thinking that passage will automatically follow once piaffe has been learned but with some horses, the passage may be denied for months, even years to come. Every horse is different, and whilst generally we can school for piaffe and achieve some passable steps, it has to be recognised that passage can be more complex.

I have always found that it has to be offered by the horse if it is to have much merit and he always knows best as to when he is sufficiently collected and strong enough to offer it. With some combinations it may never happen; like human gymnasts, some individuals will have their limitations and simply do not have the strength behind to offer this very beautiful movement.

On the other hand, there will be horses who want to offer a passage-like movement quite early on in their training. Let us, however, remind ourselves of the ground rules and recognise that if the horse is not straight and the hocks are not fully engaged well under the horse's frame, the passage will not be true. A proper passage is full of impulsion, rhythm, elevation and regularity.

The impulsion is as upward as it is forward, but the horse moves straight and in a perfect diagonal rhythm, with the hind legs clearly taking the weight behind. He does not overload the shoulders, or swing his quarters from side to side, or 'plait' with the forelegs as is so often seen. However there should be an appearance of his belly gently swinging. What actually happens is that, as each hip lowers through greater engagement, the horse's belly has nowhere to go but slightly outward on the other side. It was this action which caused the old masters to say that the horse would put himself into the rider's leg in the higher airs.

Passage can be taught out of the piaffe, the walk or the trot and here I have no quarrel with collecting the trot a little more, provided the upward thrust of the movement is sufficient to bring about a shortening of the steps whilst increasing their elevation. For this the horse will need to be very supple in the back and strong enough in the loins to 'sit' and contain the impulsion whilst projecting and elevating the whole frame forward at the same time.

The aids for passage are not dissimilar from the aids for piaffe, but these must be introduced quietly and in a way which does not kill impulsion. As with all these highly gymnastic movements, the horse will need considerably more energy for the passage than for a normal collected trot – although to the uninitiated it may be less obvious how he disperses it!

Working from an active but very collected trot therefore, we first enhance the balance and lightness of the horse with some trot to halt transitions, testing the horse for impulsion in between with a few lengthened strides at medium trot.

To slow the collected trot a little more, quick successive half-halts will be appropriate, with light touches from *both* legs placed slightly further back than normal which restrains the forward passage of impulsion. Height in passage will only come when the horse is persuaded to shorten the stride behind by lowering the quarters and thrusting upward when the engaging hind leg is in the vertical phase (the opposite of extension when it is in its furthest reach forward – the point of maximum thrust).

Gradually therefore, the rider builds up the feeling of collection in the slower trot and

It has taken some time for Espada to master the elevation required for passage. Work on the circle has helped and so, in particular, has work on hacks when he is agog to show off. He still needs to engage the hind legs more efficiently, but this can only come with time.

starts to bring both legs a little further back whilst sitting taller, so as not to put on the brakes in front. It is at this point that the feeling of stretch through the ribcage, which we talked about in Chapter 1, can be put to real and efficient use. Make yourself full of air – really puff yourself up! By raising your centre of gravity approximately over the horse's centre of gravity – he can scarcely resist the sensation of lift! As you lift, suddenly, he finds that he can lift too.

If this happens – and you will know when it does – don't be greedy! Just savour two or three strides in this way, and then allow your body to relax gently down again and send your horse on in working trot. Reward your horse by rising to the trot and then try the whole thing all over again on the opposite rein.

Alternate Aids

If none of this comes naturally and you wish to be more specific, take the horse onto a circle and ask for rather more lateral bend than normal. In this way we can work on one set of diagonals at a time. The idea will be to increase the engagement of the inside hind and to lighten the opposite shoulder.

To bring more elevation to the outside shoulder and inside hind the rider may start (as with piaffe) to introduce the idea of alternate aids. This involves raising then giving with the outside rein as the rider's inside leg taps against the horse's side and asks for more spring from the inside hind. If just one raised step is offered in this way, pat the horse and go through the same sequence of exercises again. You will be unlikely to get both diagonals 'offering' in sequence at the beginning of work, so capitalise on whichever one is easier for a few more tries, before changing rein and working on the new outside diagonal.

To work with the diagonalisation of the gaits in this way requires a very heightened sense of feel; its effects will not be felt unless

Andorinha, my faithful mare, really enjoys her passage. The feeling through her back is all spring and she has taught many of my pupils how to sit this beautiful movement. (Photograph courtesy of Madeleine McCurley)

the horse is already very attuned to the nuances of hand and leg, and again, only the horse can provide you with that fine sense of timing that will be required.

Working with more bend certainly helps the development of passage in the early stages, but it is the rhythm of the movement we should be looking to achieve long before we concentrate too much on raising the steps. Many riders settle for what is known as a 'soft passage' which can be very beautiful. Once the horse is able to offer a few steps of passage on the circle, the rider can begin to ask from the straight line, but often a feel for shoulder-in at the moment of asking will help. Always be content with a little and rather than prolong the passage, ask the horse to go forward again while he is still enjoying himself.

Building up from collected trot, to soft passage and then into medium trot is something that most horses enjoy; making clear definitions between the gait variants in this way will help both horse and rider to remain focused. While the mechanical effects of the passage are very well explained in Decarpentry's *Academic Equitation*, the best way to learn is to ride a schoolmaster before teaching this to your horse.

Finally, piaffe to passage and back to piaffe can be attempted, but the horse must be very much at ease with himself and his rider to offer this without resistance. Since we have left the uneducated rider far behind us, let us now look at the riding of the piaffe into passage with an educated and sensitive rider.

THE HORSE'S THOUGHTS – PIAFFE TO PASSAGE

- I can feel myself coming more together and 'sitting' a little as we make transitions from the collected walk to halt; then I bring my hind legs right under me as we move into rein-back. I find this very easy now that I am so much stronger in the back.
- My rider is easing the rein for me to move forward again; her legs are around me but there is no tension as she taps encouragingly; I can feel less weight in the back of the saddle.
- This encourages me to round more but also to move forward with lots of hind leg push – but now I feel her seat is deepening towards the front of the saddle, which is rather like a dam coming down to prevent me escaping out the front! What is she up to?
- She is squeezing the rein although it is soft and inviting and I am beginning to recognise all this as an order to think forward but to stay more or less on the spot – I can't really move forward anyway until she opens that dam!
- I diagonalised my steps in the rein-back so it seems natural to keep this diagonal feeling in the forward movement her legs are now demanding. There's too much energy with-

in my body for me to resist her and I find myself dancing on the spot... it's piaffe I'm told.

- Throughout this movement, she feels as though she stretches very tall, so I go up with her through my back and therefore scarcely need the rein – it's a good feeling and we are very much together.
- All at once, the dam has opened – so forward I go again, but she is still so 'up' through her body, I find myself following her. Her seat and thighs feel really deep but soft so although I want to trot on, I can't resist the invitation to fill the space. All at once, I'm light as a feather!
- I am now moving forward, but because her legs are further back than usual, I can't quite go to normal trot. She keeps asking with alternate legs and it's as though she draws each hind leg in sequence more under and through! I can feel my belly move into her legs, first into one, then into the other, so she no longer has to ask – I somehow put myself on the aids.
- The diagonal feeling of this gait gives me the rhythm and energy to produce a lovely, floaty upward trot. Humans call it passage and I must say it feels very good.

Added Benefits

The most noticeable benefit of teaching the horse the higher airs is the increased elevation and lightening of the forehand which will be apparent in all the collected movements. This results from the increased suppleness, rounding and elasticity of the back in addition to the strengthening and mobilising of the joints of the quarters and hind limbs. It is particularly rewarding when a horse with a previously tight and difficult back feels soft, swinging and as though carrying you has become quite effortless and indeed a pleasure.

As for the greater freedom felt through the shoulders, I have always believed that superior

The masters described the passage as a 'gracious, lofty' movement which must be ridden in the same way. The truth is, sitting loftily raises your own centre of gravity, which in turn helps the horse.

extension will blossom once a few steps of piaffe and passage have been introduced. As we have seen in Chapter XIII, the aids to make extended trot truly spectacular are not unlike the aids for passage, insomuch as small releases of the hands and legs are concerned. To develop the extension is such a way that it shows suspension and appears to glide seamlessly and smoothly through from the hind legs into a longer outline, requires far more subtlety than the current fad for 'shortening' the neck and kicking the horse up and into the bridle.

More and more in our quest for a schooled horse, we have found that our aids have relied as much on giving or allowing as on asking. As the horse has grown more receptive, the giving has tended to play the major role.

One could write *ad infinitum* about the subtleties and nuances of the aids, but it is hoped the pictures and photographs in this book will show just how fine these adjustments must now be if they are not to disturb the precious balance of the horse. When we have talked about the aids, the emphasis has always been on less and less, until no one really knows what aids are involved except you and your horse.

Spanish Walk

In this vein, people will ask me to teach them the Spanish Walk and are surprised if sometimes I decline. My reluctance to do so is simply because, correctly taught, this movement requires huge subtlety and should never be isolated on its own. Moreover, it is one I would be wary of teaching until the passage and piaffe are confirmed. Teaching Spanish Walk too early may lead to difficulties with lifting and bending the knee in passage, and incorrectly performed, it can cause the horse to drop his back. However, whatever some critics say, it is in fact a natural movement as can be seen by the photograph opposite and aficionados agree it has particular value in teaching the horse to mobilise the shoulder.

The first thing to recognise is that Spanish Walk should have four beats as in the normal walk. The key to success is to have a very collected horse, who bends easily through the poll and jaw. Together with a light and judicious touch of the rein, we then use the weight aids of legs and seat to displace the balance of the horse rather more onto the opposite foreleg which, grounded together with the corresponding hind leg, allows the chosen foreleg to stretch and extend.

In Spanish Walk, the elbow of the advancing foreleg is freed away from the horse's body; straightening the leg is done with panache and expression and in the words of Oliveira as though the horse 'were trying to seize an object out of reach'. Thus, while the hocks are clearly required to bend to walk forward in their normal way, almost every vestige of knee action is removed from the advancing foreleg, which is expected to achieve height as well as

Spanish walk is, in fact, a natural movement and its practice can really help free the shoulders for other advanced movements, such as the half-pass. (Photograph courtesy of Katya Schumann, USA)

cadence in its straightening. In a really good Spanish Walk the knee is extended almost to the height of the elbow.

Many people start the Spanish Walk from the ground, with the light encouragement of the schooling whip applied behind the foreleg which is required to stretch. For my part, I prefer to teach it mounted, for two good reasons. First, while it is relatively easy to teach a horse to thrust out a foreleg by tapping the leg, this can be dangerous. Some horses get carried away with it all and end up striking out at the slightest indication. Second, as with everything to date, I have found that this exercise comes naturally to certain horses, but only when they are ready for it. Our main requirement is their sensitivity to the weight aids, as with the piaffe and passage. In this context, Spanish Walk is very much a feeling thing, which requires very light hands and a subtle use of the pressure from the knee, thigh and seatbones.

The worst thing you can do in Spanish Walk is to concentrate on the front legs alone, which is why I prefer the mounted work. The movement will only be correct if the hind legs are working forward and continue to march under as in normal walk. All this requires correct preparation and aiding and since it is all such a subtle thing it is best learned by watching a *real* expert working within the context of all the movements, or riding a schoolmaster – which is how I learned. No one ever really me taught me except the horses.

Learn and Learn

In your pursuit of the higher skills, therefore, never stop watching, reading, listening – and do emulate! Only copy the very best of riders and remember there are not so many about, but they do exist, if you take enough trouble to find them.

In riding at this level, feel is everything. We have come through prep school and developed our ABC; we have used the bare bones of our language to good effect at secondary school by creating some good essays and introducing many useful exercises in communication, as well as developing our artistic skills. Now we are into university, it is time to refine and hone

(Above) Here, Andorinha, in Portuguese tack, shows off her Spanish walk on a circle. The aid is almost all to do with the pressure of my thighs, which affects the forehand.

Espada, too, really enjoys Spanish walk – my problem is sometimes to get him to stop doing it! As the horse lifts the fore-leg, the knee bends in order to achieve height, before straightening outward. In the downward phase the leg should remain straight, virtually until it touches the ground.

our work and concentrate on our arts degree. It is not so much a case of throwing the mechanics of riding into the wind; it's simply a question of knowing them so well, using them so unconsciously, that we no longer really have to think about them – at least not all the time...

Now we are conversant with the tools of communication, the language of our horses, the world has become our oyster. But remember that you have to be around horses all the time, ride them, feel them, learn from them – in order not to lose the art of conversation.

Long and Low, Deep and Round

(Further reading on this work is recommended; please see Chapter 16, The Classical Rider, J. A. Allen 1997.)

It would have been tempting to have placed this section in a chapter all of its own, but the reason it has taken the form of an Appendix is very simple. I was not absolutely sure at which stage to include it, for unlike all the work described to date, long and low work (also known as deep and round work) has no exact place or sequence in the schooling of the horse. It is a very individual thing and the rider should first of all be thoroughly aware of the state of each individual horse's back and his acceptance of the aids before making a decision.

The Concept of Deep Work

In essence, the long and low or deep work (let us now stick to the latter term) reaffirms the *independence* of the horse with regard to the rein. The rein is there to *connect* him to the aids, but he no longer needs it upon which to balance himself. Not only does this apply to work in collection, where the weight is transferred more obviously to the haunches and hocks, but it will also apply to those occasions where we wish to 'open' the frame to a greater extent by lengthening the horse in the extended gaits. Quite simply, we should now be able to ride our horse in any posture, place his head in any position and still feel that he is working from behind, seeking our contact but always remaining in an independent balance achieved through his own superior gymnasticism.

When is it Appropriate?

While some experts believe that deep work should be introduced quite early on to develop *schwung*, others – myself included – feel that it should not be introduced until collection is adequately established. For while this form of suppling should help to confirm and improve the strengthening and development of the topline over the horse's quarters, back and neck, there has to be sufficient muscle and flexibility there in the first place to keep everything 'connected'!

To introduce deep work to very young, elderly or relatively unmuscled horses would to my mind be harsh and irresponsible. Even the most balanced horse will shift more weight to the forehand and that is the very last thing we need to encourage with a horse already on the forehand. As for the aged horse, the forelegs need to be carefully preserved and in my own yard I work only the middle-aged horses 'deep and round'; never my veteran schoolmasters who have only lasted so long because they are ridden fairly collected at *all* times, including hacking, on a relatively short but light rein.

What is Involved?

Unlike the free walk on the long rein, which should still be used at all times to relax the horse and give him a breather, deepening exercises are generally ridden in trot and later developed into canter. The idea is to open the horse out and positively stretch the supporting muscles of the topline and the undercarriage in just the same way as you or I do when we stretch our own bodies to unstiffen or to release tension. In this way all the muscle fibres unlock and 'learn' to become more yielding and elastic when pushed to their limit, for remember – in the horse's case we are combining this stretch-open and support feeling with forward impulsion.

Warning!

It is for this reason that when we first enter the school, we should refrain from introducing the deep work in trot and canter until the horse has first relaxed in walk on a long rein, and then started to *round* and lift the back with some collected exercises. Quarter pirouettes in walk and some walk shoulder-in and other lateral movements, even a few steps of piaffe (if at that level) should be quite adequate for this. The whole point of these exercises at the start is to ensure that the hind legs are stepping sufficiently under to *lift* the back as opposed to merely propelling it along – which would merely drop the horse when we go to start the deep work.

This, in fact, happens in many training scenarios with dire results. We see the horse stretching down to seek the rein, but because the rider has failed to engage the hind legs at the outset, the horse drops his back, and falls onto the forehand. The rider then tries to rectify the situation by using more hand and more leg, which simply pushes the horse more 'downhill'. In some cases, an over-strong contact is applied to lower the head artificially. This may cause the horse to lean on the reins and to bring his head behind the vertical. All the time he is becoming heavier and heavier in the shoulders and the whole point of the exercise is lost.

To avoid making mistakes, deep work should never be attempted by novices. Even competent riders generally prefer to have a pair of expert eyes on the ground when they start, since so much harm can be done unless one has a very good feel for the subject.

Benefits

Despite all the warnings, however, deep work can bring about enormous benefits. As with most matters equestrian, advancing the horse's schooling to this level will definitely enhance the work achieved hitherto. Here are some of the improvements we would hope to see:

- The normal working gaits will assume a new purpose and buoyancy about them.
- Any tension which may have been present in the collected gaits should now fully disperse as the steps become more lively and elastic.
- The medium work, which may sometimes have verged towards the forehand, should emerge much more 'uphill' and balanced.
- The canter work should show a greater depth of engagement, which will better prepare the horse for half-pass, changes, pirouettes, etc.
- Overall balance should be so much improved that the rider will feel the horse's outline is determined wholly from behind, no matter where the head is placed.
- To sum up, the rein seems almost irrelevant!

The deep work will particularly help to develop the horse's confidence and ability (without assistance from the hand) to move from a collected, to a medium, to an extended gait and back again, whether in trot or canter. By raising and filling the back – the horse should resemble a sprung bow in this work – the musculature of the topline will become elastic enough to allow these changes to take place easily and instantaneously. Thus, in the extensions, the horse should now be able to lengthen and stretch his entire frame more impressively forward than ever before without losing balance, tempo or rhythm. As I have constantly pointed out, muscles can only build and develop with flexion and stretch, and the deep work is the ultimate so far as the stretch is concerned, the piaffe being the ultimate for *flexion*. So, just as earlier we discovered 'throughness', now we will begin to have the sensation of the horse working through and 'over the back'.

Where to Start and Pointers

We have already prepared the horse mentally and physically for the basic stretch exercises with our early work on a long rein; so it should not be too difficult to take this a stage further, now that he is so much more educated to the aids.

The idea must always be that, wherever we place our hand, the horse will seek it. From a normal rein contact therefore, the work is best started on a 20 m circle and, to help the horse, our trot work should be ridden rising. (There is no point in going to canter until the horse has accepted the deep work in trot, which may take some weeks or months to perfect). Everyone has a slightly different way of approaching these matters, but here is a rough pattern of events which can be used for both the trot and canter.

- Look for a steady but expressive working gait with your horse thinking forward and bending nicely on the circle.
- Once into a rhythm, place the hands considerably lower than you would normally. Don't drop the rein suddenly; gently lower and widen your hand position until your fists are closer to the horse's shoulders than the withers.
- You may need to lean forward a little unless you have long arms or a very supple back! It is quite acceptable to lose verticality of posture, provided you keep your shoulders squared, loins flattened forward and think *'uphill'* with the diaphragm supported and a feeling of stretch through your tummy.
- Don't think 'downhill', round the back, or fold at the waist which will simply drop your horse onto the forehand – the very last thing we want!
- Now ride on from the leg and allow the horse to *take the rein more forward* in

response. The legs and seat create a feeding-out process and there must no jerking back, the hands merely squeeze and give as normal...

Helping the Horse

The idea is that you are now working the horse into the hand, which yields quietly forward towards his mouth. Remember, if your ground-work has been correct, the horse should always want to follow your hand so long as you make it inviting for him.

Do not draw your hands up and forward to follow the neckline; just allow your horse to fill the rein from your lowered hand position as he stretches his neck forward and down and ultimately opens the entire frame. Remember your legs, seat and upper body posture continue to support and keep him over the crest of the wave. Sit light, taking your weight down into the stirrups and as you rise, urge the horse to fill the vacuum you have made for his back. The feeling is very much one of projecting his energy forward and over his back.

Visualise what you want to see your horse doing! Just as collection could be likened to coiling a spring, now is the time to think of uncoiling that spring to allow all the kinks and curls to be ironed or smoothed out. The most important thing in all this is to remember that the horse is still working from behind into your hand. Think of the flow of energy like a never-ending stream, bubbling up from his quarters, pulsating along his back, which expands upwards to meet you, and then allow it all to be taken forward, extending, rounding and arching low to find your asking, opening fingers. It may then all be rechannelled, flowing and still bubbling back to its source.

What You Should Feel

As the horse stretches, and lifts his back, you should really feel the hind legs swing through more. There should be a greater sense of suspension and overtrack and the feeling is very much that the hind feet may now connect into

(Right) Whether in the double bridle or snaffle the horse should always reach actively forward with his neck to accept the contact, and this, as already discussed, includes the work on the long rein.

(Below) When you commence the deeper work, it is helpful to open the hands so that they remain quite wide apart. This has an 'opening' effect on the horse which is the opposite of 'hands together, horse together'.

(Right) It is very important that you retain a good upper body position when you ask the horse to deepen into the widened contact. If you collapse forward, the horse will do the same, so stretch up tall with toned tummy muscles.

(Above) Once the horse becomes confident in the contact, a good working trot should evolve, with the horse really stretching through his loins, over his back and neck. The head may be just a little behind the vertical for the deep work, but there must be no sense of leaning on the rein. However, with less contact we risk losing the connection from hind legs to forehand. Here, Espada shows really good engagement behind in his trot.

(Left) Progress with care to canter, and deepen your weight into your thighs and stirrups to avoid pressing down on the back of the saddle. Again, as with trot, we can see good engagement in this canter on the circle.

(Right) Many people ride like this all the time, particularly in competition, and are not marked down for doing so. For me, this is the intermediate stage between the long and low work and the normal work and should only be pursued for a few moments. Note, my hands are still held low, but now that Espada is accepting the shorter rein, I will gradually resume my normal position, and ride with the neck carried correctly so that the poll is again at the highest point.

the flowing circular pattern which the horse's energy is creating.

Now the jargon that is too often used by people inappropriately makes sense. The term 'over the back' takes on real meaning. The energy really does travel up and over, but since it must be retained we must continually guard against dropping it.

Neither must we block the flow by pulling back. A correct workout will only be achieved when the horse is able to remain with his nose just in front of the vertical. The poll can no longer be the highest point because of the shape of the exercise, but we must be very careful not to create a break in the flow by 'breaking' the horse through the neck.

Improving Step by Step

If everything is set up correctly, the horse will really enjoy this work and will get the idea very quickly. You can then start to develop his suppleness, whilst creating stretch at the same time by spiralling in on your circle and moving out again.

Initially, don't do too much deep work at one time, but return to a normal posture and normal hand position in between. Don't forget either, the walk on the long rein as a reward and never let this be neglected in favour of the deep work. Each exercise has its place.

Many will know the expression: 'Hands together brings the horse together!' which was a favourite saying of the late Reiner Klimke. Arthur Kottas, Chief Rider of the Spanish Riding School, with whom I have been fortunate to work, asks his students to open or widen the hands so the horse can move *through* them, long and low.

Since most learning processes are reinforced by contrasts, the classic one being – ask and give – it does not take long for the horse to recognise that the lowered hand means deep work. Since this work encourages greater freedom, the horse will soon show his enthusiasm, particularly if our own riding is free of constraint.

Everyone will have their own idea about when or for how long to ride the deep work exercises. Normally about five to ten minutes towards the beginning of a schooling session should be about right. As much as possible, let the horse be the judge of when to do things after that.

If you feel your horse a little tense, or having difficulty with a particular exercise, then work him deep again for a few circuits, then relax him. It can work like magic, but as with everything, deep work is not a cure for all. There are no shortcuts to good performance; everything is linked to the whole and deep work comprises only one tiny segment of that whole.

Remember, nothing you do in the training of the horse should be in conflict or appear to undo or go against anything you have done previously. Schooling and training is about building with blocks and this building block is not the foundation stone; it's merely one which will enhance the overall structure.

Finally, remember there are a lot of bad riders out there. Some may even be seen to be successful but the state of the horse behind the scenes, away from the glare of the public arena, usually holds the key to the methods of training. Contented, happy horses are not only physically in good shape, they will be interested, alert and always pleased to see you.

Do not copy harmful practices and do not be deceived by glossy adverts which promote shortcut training aids for outline which bypass the old and practised methods. If you miss out on your horse's ABC and skip the stages we have explored so individually and painstakingly in this book, you will end up with a horse who may speak part of your language, but who will never be able to communicate with you on full and equal terms.

Be patient – listen to him; he knows the language and the challenge is for you to learn it too. Then you can both enjoy the opportunities which this language opens up for you – a wonderful world awaits.

Let the Horses Speak for Themselves

The living proof of correct training methods is very easy for all to see. It has little to do with how many cups or rosettes are displayed in a rider's tackroom. While some trophies and ribbons may be well deserved, others are less so; in particular where someone else has schooled the horse. They can be very motivating for those who have the time and opportunity to pursue them, but occasionally they can get in the way of real scholarship. Since there are as many fine riders who do not compete as those who do, this cannot be taken as a complete yardstick.

As regards tangible results in dressage, investment nowadays plays an important part. Genetically planned progeny, raised from conception to adulthood under ideal conditions, will tend to look and move better, long before one ever gets on their back.

Once in the arena, a certain amount of luck and personal taste will always affect the final marks when it comes to judging one skilled rider against another. Although dressage judging has to be objective, who can blame a judge when a degree of subjectivity enters the equation? Often this has as much to do with the standards and perceptions of the judge as those of the rider. As Nuno Oliveira once pointed out 'How can art be a competition?' It would certainly be hard to know to whom to give the prize if you lined up the work of the greatest artists from the Renaissance to the present day – the different styles, the different talents, the different visions of genius would be quite impossible to equate.

So, in the end, with what standard are we left? We are left with something very solid and so obvious that it is often overlooked – the horse himself. Here is our ephemeral but living canvas and here with one knowledgeable glance we can observe all his training, most of his history and a good deal of his secrets without even moving him out of the stable. Whatever his breeding, the state of his quarters, back and neck will tell much, as will the look in his eye and the way in which he comes to the stable door, setting aside stallionish tendencies. If he doesn't come to say 'Hi!' but remains in a corner, something is very wrong. These are just some of the tell-tale signs of good or bad training.

Once he is outside and under saddle, things become even more obvious. General Josipovich (1869-1945) wrote 'The aim of dressage training is to eradicate from the horse stiffness in the joints, to develop in them flexibility, ease in moving in a well balanced attitude in which they can continue a long time, much longer than an untrained horse, and with less expenditure of strength...' and this is so true. But just as important, everything should look natural and unforced, with the horse retaining his sense of pride, the *glory of movement* in which *'he delights'* as Xenophon reminds us.

I am often asked why I keep such elderly horses. The truth is I did not ask them to last this long, but something to do with their schooling and lifestyle has, thanks be to God, protected them and allowed them to flourish in this way. However, they were not always like

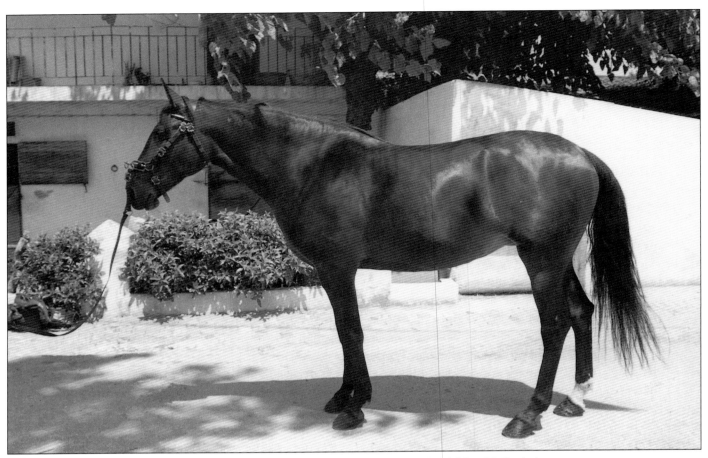

Andorinha outside her box in Lisbon (aged eight). (Photograph courtesy Madeleine McCurley)

I was struck by the 'turned off' look in her eye, but despite this, there was an immediate rapport when my friends and I went to talk to her. (Photograph courtesy of Madeleine McCurley)

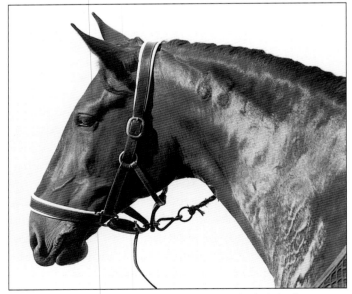

Andorinha, in her prime, aged eighteen. The look in her eye has completely changed and most people don't believe the two pictures show the same horse. Fortunately the stud brand on her neck shows she really is!

that, and here for the record are my horses with *before* and *after* photographs and histories to show just what can be achieved with correct and patient schooling. The competition side is only mentioned to show it can be done, but because I've been lucky enough to write, there's never been time for it to take huge precedence in my life.

The following horse profiles are given in the order of how they came to be in my yard. After the death of my late husband in 1982, I was forced to close down our big East Anglian dressage school the following year and rehome all the horses. I am glad to say this was very successful, so with a clear conscience I then decided to retire from teaching. After twenty-two years of helping others, the time had surely come to concentrate more on my own riding and I had my young daughter to look after. By now remarried and much encouraged and advised by my lawyer husband, I started to write. The plan was a complete change of lifestyle and from now on, only keeping one horse. Well, that was the plan...

Andorinha (meaning 'Swift' or 'Swallow'; registered stud name Vipaca) pure-bred Lusitano Alter Real mare born in Portugal 1979; 15.3 hh

Before:
I went out to Portugal, intending to buy a young stallion, and ended up buying an eight-year-old mare! She was just out of the old Royal Stud at Alter (now state-owned) and had recently been backed.

Virtually the opposite of what I originally wanted, Andorinha's breeding was, however, impeccable and there were no Alter Reals in Britain at that time. So far as riding was concerned, there were some obvious drawbacks. As with many brood mares, she had a long, rather straight back, slightly capped hocks from the hard ground at night and a rather disinterested temperament. However, after riding her – I felt

there was something about her – the result was I bought her! Later, I learned she had had two foals and was probably sold because she had failed to produce any more. Not for the first time I wondered how on earth I would school a horse – who been roughed off at grass all those years – up to the levels I had in mind. After all, eight is quite an age to introduce dressage from scratch!

After:
At the time of writing, Andorinha is twenty-one years of age and was UK champion Lusitano mare on five separate occasions. One year, the Portuguese state judge placed her above all the stallions to become Champion of Show at Stoneleigh. Between 1992 and 1997, we gave dressage demonstrations all over the country, including the Royal Mews in London. With *Dressage Magazine*, we travelled as far south as Ardingly and as far north as Gleneagles. I only competed her in affiliated dressage for two seasons (in between books!) with any real consistency. She won two Elementary qualifiers and although she was doing good piaffe and passage at home, the highest level at which we participated was Advanced Medium, since tempi changes and pirouettes were beyond her. Even in the straight changes however, the judges did not like her high, rounded action, which I could understand, but when I was repeatedly told that such a 'little horse' demeaned me, I decided just to enjoy her at home apart from some clinics with Arthur Kottas and a moment of pride when he worked her in-hand at the TTT Gala Day in 1997.

Today, I still demonstrate work in-hand with her, which she much enjoys, and she is probably my best piaffe and passage horse for teaching students the feel of these movements. A natural video star, lunge horse, and lovely safe, kind hack, she is a consummate flirt with her 'eyelined' doe-like gaze and long, fluttering eyelashes.

Palomo Linares in a hot, dusty 'paddock' near Sintra (retired at fourteen). Because of lack of muscle over his topline, he looks more of a pony than 16hh stallion.

The only real muscle displayed by Palomo was where I did not want it!

Over the years, Palomo has gained the affection and respect of so many pupils all over the world. Here he is at home, aged twenty-seven, with one of his favourites, dear Lesley.

Palomo Linares (named after a famous Spanish matador) Lusitano X Arab stallion – born in Portugal, 1973; 16 hh

Before:

Whilst visiting my mare near Lisbon, I went to a drinks party as she waited for clearance to the UK (prior to EU membership, Portuguese export licences were subject to long bureaucratic delays). Suddenly, I was thrown into a situation where I made an totally unexpected, emotional decision.

Palomo was a retired bullfighter and stud horse, and the lady who had bought him as a potential schoolmaster from his bullfighter breeder now wanted to sell him. She also had a 'proper' horse, a 17 hh dressage gelding with whom she attended clinics with Harry Boldt in Germany, and the idea was that Palomo would teach her the higher movements to help her teach him. Unfortunately however, Palomo was so busy doing airs above the ground, she felt very unsafe. He also 'blew up' at the sight of other horses and she was worried about his melanomas which she thought would be responsible for an early demise.

I felt very sad to see this aged stallion – he was fourteen but looked older – in a small paddock under the hot Iberian sun. He shuffled around picking at his hay – there is no grass at this time of year – with a look of futility. Having attended many Portuguese bullfights, where the man fights from the back of a highly schooled stallion and the horse is never touched, I could imagine just how he must miss the attention, the music, the lights, the crowds and so on. His present owner hadn't ridden him for over a year.

I asked to ride him, and his owner was shocked, however I insisted I could not realistically help her rehome him, if not. Reluctantly a saddle was found, but I was only to be allowed a 'sit for five minutes at the most' in the paddock – which was actually more of a pen (about 15 metres square... poor Mr P).

The moment I was on board however, the elderly ears pricked up, Palomo's poor, unmuscled back tried to lift and he gave me thirty-odd seconds of the most floaty collected trot I had felt for a long time. It was love at first sight so, needless to say, a second horse came back to England with Andorinha and I realised that, in order to keep the unexpected visitor, I would have to start teaching again! (Oddly enough, his former owner died suddenly just months after he left, which made it seem that everything was meant and it brought us even closer together.)

After:

Palomo competed extremely successfully in advanced dressage to music at Stoneleigh at both the Lusitano and Andalusian National Shows, winning numerous championships year after year. At twenty however, we decided he'd done enough, although he did continue with demonstration appearances until his twenty-third birthday. Four years on, he is still used as a schoolmaster here at home in Scotland with wonderful smooth flying changes being his particular speciality. He too, has proved an invaluable video star but most of all he is a constant source of inspiration to us all with his amazing, wise and noble temperament and incredible movement.

Fabuloso (meaning 'Fabulous'; registered stud name Folar) pure-bred Lusitano stallion, born in Portugal 1987, 16.1 hh

Before:

I bought this horse from the Countess of Cadaval's stud as an unbacked three year old, and it seemed we had the perfect dressage horse in conformation, breeding and temperament. Disaster struck just as we were about to export him from Lisbon; African Horse Sickness closed the Iberian Peninsula for the export of horses to the rest of Europe. Tragically for him and for me, Fabuloso's arrival in England was delayed by well over a year. This was a great setback since, somewhere along the line, mistakes were made and I heard of real difficulties with his character at the training yard where I had left him. Thus, instead of the raw, unspoiled character I had hoped to develop, a horse described as 'frankly dangerous' arrived at my yard in Suffolk in 1994. The kind gentleman in whom his latter care had been entrusted, begged me not to ride him – but I was determined. However, it took two years to reschool him starting again from scratch and we never totally won back his confidence and goodwill.

I was able to compete a little, but then as months of overseas teaching and judging loomed in the diary, I decided it was unfair on my household to leave this sensitive character at home. Despite now being a safe ride with really stunning potential, I sold him to a caring home when he was working at roughly Elementary/Medium level with some nice piaffe and changes showing promise for the future. It was clear that he should go to a person less busy than I and preferably someone who had good professional help at hand. This was accomplished, but sadly circumstances changed and before we knew it, we lost touch with the new owner.

After:

Today, after several changes of home and sorry

Fabuloso (aged four) waiting for permission to export, at Vilafranca, near Lisbon. He had a very distrustful look in his eye and I was severely warned against him.

(Above) Mounting and dismounting required two people to hold him during the first month. No wonder I look relieved as I slip off his back!

(Right) By the time he was seven years old, one could do anything on top without him batting an eyelid.

sagas, Fabuloso enjoys a wonderful and understanding lifestyle with Classical Riding Club member, Rhoda Belchamber. Restored to equilibrium, they have resumed work where we left off. A beautiful horse, it still saddens me that I had to let him go, but the end of the story is happy and it is a pleasure to be able to show some of those early pictures of his very novice progress in these pages.

Espada (meaning ' Sword') Lusitano X Thoroughbred, born in Portugal, date unknown. 16.1 hh

Before:

I first saw this tall, leggy, handsome black horse at the Lisbon show, being ridden by an old bullfighting friend, Manuel Sabino Duarte. On a visit to his stable I was greeted by a vision of two black ears flattened against a turned-away head and a hind leg poised to strike. He really was sharp as a sword. I was, however, assured that his bark was worse than his bite, or something to that effect in Portuguese. Thus, having mentally dismissed him, I had to change my thinking very quickly the moment I sat on him. The trouble was, despite a very high head carriage and unyielding back, I liked him. Oh – how we women allow our hearts to rule our heads!

After:

Today, Espada is very much my horse. He is not suitable as a schoolmaster and it has taken me four years to persuade him not to put his tongue over the bit which he may still do when excited or in a strange place (unfortunately he was first ridden in a big Spanish curb). Finally I have made myself make time for a few competitions each summer in order to satisfy those who claim you shouldn't teach if you can't do. Espada has been placed on virtually every outing, so the odd red and blue ribbon hangs in the tackroom, which is pleasing. However, it's not the points or the ribbons that really count, it's how the horse went for *you* that really matters.

I would like to get Espada to Grand Prix, but I have found out he was backed much too young and he has always told me he does not have a strong back. Nevertheless with careful saddling and riding in lightness we are now working towards Advanced – but only time will tell.

(Below) Espada was very leggy and coltish when he arrived in the UK. His papers said five years old; the vets all thought him much younger.

(Right) In the year 2000, I believe that at last, Espada is beginning to grow up!

Vaidoso (meaning 'Vain') Pure-bred Lusitano stallion, born in Portugal at the National Stud in 1979; 15.1 hh

Before:

Vaidoso was another horse I never meant to buy. I did not look for him, did not have a stable for him, neither did I have the budget. I firmly resisted the offer to take him. Then I capitulated.

At the age of seventeen, Vaidoso had suffered some sort of viral disease in Portugal and was apparently about to be put down on humane grounds when a visiting Australian lady fell in love with him, telephoned me (the only connection – she had read my books...!) bought him and shipped him at considerable cost to England. Mentally and physically he was not in good shape and I expressed doubts about rehoming, since who would want such a horse? In the meantime I had to farm him out locally – not the best start in a new country, but once I got to know him, I knew he had to stay.

So again, a purchase, transport costs and the acquisition of another cast-off elderly, grey stallion.

After:

Vaidoso has turned around in every way possible. Today he is muscled, straight in his work – he used to be so crooked – flexible and wonderfully sensitive and forward-going to ride. Someone had obviously schooled him very well once upon a time, although he had got into terrible habits along the way, but these have now almost gone although, occasionally, he still has the odd panic attack in canter. He has turned into a much-loved schoolmaster and is a clear favourite with all my pupils. A proud, noble, beautiful horse; I feel privileged that he came my way.

Sadly, I have no early pictures of Vaidoso, but the photograph right (courtesy of Barbara Torney) shows him at eighteen shortly after our move to Scotland. However, even in the last couple of years, I think the photo of Vaidoso below (now aged twenty-one, shows he has improved his muscle tone.

There are also the guest horses:

Thomas

Ridden in the photos by Jodie Crisp, Thomas was a six-year-old gelding who was taken on by the Crisp family as a potential dressage horse for junior championships.

I worked with Jodie and her sister Nikki over a period of two years, teaching at their manège in Essex on a regular basis of twice a week and sometimes more during school holidays. I also taught Sally, their younger sister, as she was starting out on her 12hh pony.

Unfortunately, Thomas proved a little too hotheaded for Jodie's liking and was later replaced by Winki (Forty Winks) who went on to represent the UK in Junior dressage both at home and abroad. Sadly, I have no pictures of him since most of our photographic work was done during the early days with Thomas. However, I feel these pictures are a testament to Jodie's dedication to her horses and riding and I am sure that Thomas taught her most of what she needed to know before we went on to work together with Forty Winks.

(Above) Milo was most resentful about making the transition from hunting to school work. Here he is shortly after his arrival (aged seven) treating the manège with due contempt.

(Right) Today, at nine, he adores his owner and seems much happier about life in general. Only time will tell if he ever becomes a dressage star...

Millennium (Milo)

Milo belongs to my daughter Allegra and appears here as a guest horse since, for a greater part of the year, he is stabled at school with her in East Yorkshire. Milo is essentially a hunter, and his real forte is cross-country and participating at indoor showjumping events. He has, however, kindly lent himself to have some photographs taken with various students and Allegra, as a special favour. As one can see, dressage has helped him to develop some topline, which was lacking when he first came to us, hunting fit from Cheshire. In those days, he had a very pronounced gullet muscle which I'm glad to say he has begun to relinquish with surprising good grace. Thank you Milo! And to all the horses and riders who appear in this book.

Conclusion

There is no doubt that to be a sensitive and knowledgeable rider, competitor or teacher, you have to ride, ride, ride. Only the horse himself can build up our sense of feeling so that the fine balancing acts required by our bodies can become disciplined and second nature. For those of us who instruct or train, we have to try to impart that knowledge and make that feeling 'happen' for our students.

Thankfully, every horse is different, so nothing should be boring, nothing taken for granted and nothing pre-ordained. At the end of the day, we should never stop learning and every horse, whatever his age, size, type or breed should make a difference by leaving an imprint on our skills. Each and every one has something to offer; the older ones in particular, harbour great wisdom. If for no other reason, this fact alone should continue to inspire all horsemen and horsewomen, whatever their ultimate goals.

In return, we owe it to every horse to allow our increased sensitivity and awareness to benefit him. He gives to us, we give back. Nothing should stand still, everything should move on, no man and no horse is an island. In the end it will be our love of horses that makes all this possible. Dressage in lightness has to be our aim; no one wants to struggle in the dark, especially your horse, and he will never cease to thank and reward you when you find the light way forward. Thank you for reading and may the spirit of love and lightness go with you in all that you do.

There are many titles, ancient and modern which have inspired me over the decades in which I have been involved in classical riding. Since these are too numerous to mention and are often very hard to obtain, I have instead selected some obtainable modern titles which are in accord with and reinforce most of the ideas and precepts contained in this book. Occasionally, there may be points of difference – such is life – but under the suggested subject matter (shown as headings) further reading should help enlarge and develop the reader's specific understanding. Please note that occasionally some subjects will overlap but for simplicity, books are only listed once.

The Seat & General Position

Albrecht, Brigadier Kurt *Principles of Dressage* J.A. Allen 1993

Frederiksen, A.K. *The Finer Points of Riding* J.A. Allen 1969

Licart, Commandant Jean *Basic Equitation* J.A. Allen 1968

Loch, Sylvia *The Classical Seat* D.J. Murphy Ltd 1988

Stevens, Michael *Practical Schooling* Kenilworth Press l995 / Half Halt Press (USA)

von Dietze, Susanne *Balance In Movement* J.A. Allen 1999 / Trafalgar Square (USA)

General Schooling Techniques

Becher, Rolfe *Schooling by the Natural Method* J.A. Allen 1963

Bürger, Udo *The Way to Perfect Horsemanship* J.A. Allen 1986 / Trafalgar Square (USA)

Decarpentry, General *Academic Equitation* J.A. Allen 1971 / Trafalgar Square (USA)

Herbermann, Erik F. *Dressage Formula* J.A. Allen 1980

Jousseaume, Col André *Progressive Dressage* J.A. Allen 1978

Klimke, Dr Reiner *Basic Training of the Young Horse* J.A. Allen 1985

Loch, Sylvia *Classical Riding – Being at one with your Horse* J.A. Allen 1997 / Trafalgar Square (USA)

Oliveira, Nuno *Reflections on Equestrian Art* J.A. Allen 1976

Podhajsky, Colonel Alois *The Complete Training of Horse & Rider* Harrap 1967 / Wilishire (USA)

Sivewright, Molly *Thinking Riding* J.A. Allen 1979

Stevens, Michael J. *A Classical Riding Notebook* Kenilworth Press 1994 / Half Halt Press (USA)

von Blixen-Finecke, Hans *The Art of Riding* J.A. Allen 1977 / Half Halt Press (USA)

Wynmalen, Henry *Dressage, A Study of the Finer Points of Riding* Museum Press 1953

Competition Technique

de Kunffy, Charles *The Athletic Development of the Dressage Horse* Howell Book House 1992

Gahwyler, Max *The Competitive Edge* Half Halt Press 1989

Hester, Carl *Down to Earth Dressage* D.J. Murphy Ltd l999

Podhajsky, Colonel Alois *The Art of Dressage* Harrap 1976

Philosophy

Albrecht, Brigadier Kurt *A Dressage Judge's Handbook* J.A. Allen 1988

Belasik, Paul *Riding Towards the Light* J.A. Allen 1990

de Kunffy, Charles *The Ethics & Passions of Dressage* Half Halt Press 1993

Loch, Sylvia *Dressage – The Art of Classical Riding* Sportsman's Press 1990 / Trafalgar Square (USA)

Podhajsky, Colonel Alois *My Horses, My Teachers* Harrap 1969 / Trafalgar Square (USA)

Paillard, Col. Jean Saint-Fort *Understanding Equitation* Doubleday & Co 1974

Equine Biomechanics & Instinctive Behaviour

Giniaux, Dominique *What the Horses Have Told Me* Xenophon Press 1996

Gray, Smythe, Goody *Horse Structure and Movement* J.A. Allen 1993

McBane, Susan *How Your Horse Works* David & Charles 1999

Racinet, Jean-Claude *Total Horsemanship* Xenophon Press 1999

Rees, Lucy *The Horse's Mind* Stanley Paul 1984

Skipper, Lesley *Inside Your Horse's Mind* J.A. Allen 1999

Winnett, John *Dressage As Art In Competition* J.A. Allen 1993

Wyche, Sara *Understanding The Horse's Back* Crowood Press 1998 / Trafalgar Square (USA)

Bitting

Etherington, Alixe *A Bit of Magic* Your Horse Magazine & John Dewsbury 1998

Index